Barefoot Heart

Stories of a Migrant Child

Bilingual Press/Editorial Bilingüe

General Editor
Gary D. Keller

Managing Editor
Karen S. Van Hooft

Associate Editors
Karen M. Akins
Barbara H. Firoozye

Assistant Editor
Linda St. George Thurston

Editorial Board
Juan Goytisolo
Francisco Jiménez
Eduardo Rivera
Mario Vargas Llosa

Address:
Bilingual Press
Hispanic Research Center
Arizona State University
P.O. Box 872702
Tempe, Arizona 85287-2702
(480) 965-3867

Barefoot Heart

Stories of a Migrant Child

Elva Treviño Hart

Bilingual Press/Editorial Bilingüe
TEMPE, ARIZONA

ISBN 0-927534-81-9 (alk. paper)

Library of Congress Cataloging-in-Publication Data

Hart, Elva Treviño.
   Barefoot heart / Elva Treviño Hart.
      p.   cm.
   ISBN 0-927534-81-9 (alk. paper)
    1. Hart, Elva Treviño. 2. Mexican American women—Biography.
3. Mexican Americans—Biography. 4. Mexican Americans—Social life
and customs. 5. Migrant agricultural laborers—United States—
Biography. 6. Migrant agricultural laborers—United States—Social
life and customs. I. Title.
E184.M5H365   1999
973'.046872'0092—dc21
[B]   99-11731
                                   CIP

PRINTED IN THE UNITED STATES OF AMERICA

Sixth printing, February 2006

Cover design, interior by John Wincek, Aerocraft Charter Art Service

Acknowledgments

Partial funding provided by the Arizona Commission on the Arts through appropriations from the Arizona State Legislature and grants from the National Endowment for the Arts.

Prologue

I am nobody. And my story is the same as a million others. Poor Mexican American. Female child. We all look alike: dirty feet, brown skin, downcast eyes.

You have seen us if you have driven through south Texas on the way to Mexico. We are there—walking barefoot by the side of the road. During harvest time there are fewer of us—we are with our families in the fields.

Some of us grow up and move to cities. We work downtown and speak perfect English. Others of us stay. I don't know which is better.

Sometimes we move to places where people don't know that underneath the wool crepe suit is a brown, barefoot little girl like me. Behind the university-speak is a whole magic world in Spanish. We play the game well and it looks as if we are happy. Sure, we're happy.

But then, when we're flipping through radio stations on the way to the office, we get to the Mexican station, and they're playing our favorite corrido. It makes us long for mamacita, for tortillas, for the comadres and the tías, for dancing rancheras in the hot, sweaty night under the stars at the fiesta.

Then the nine-to-five life seems dry as a stone and without a soul.

"How did I get here?" we ask.

I'll tell you.

PART ONE

Migrant Workers

*Aunque seas muy grande y rico, necesitas
del pobre y chico.*

Though you may be wealthy and tall, you
will still need the poor and the small.

(Mexican dicho)

Chapter One

Al que madruga, Dios lo ayuda.

God helps the early riser.

(One of Apá's favorite dichos)

My whole childhood, I never had a bed. In the one-bedroom rancho where I was born, my apá suspended a wooden box from the exposed rafters in the ceiling. My amá made a blanket nest for me in the box. It hung free in the air over my parents' bed, within reach of both. If I cried, they would swing the box.

We moved to Tío Alfredo's house in town two years later when Apá left his job as a sharecropper on the McKinley farm. Tío invited us to come and live with him right after he built the house on my grandmother's property. So my parents, my five older siblings, and I settled into the two-bedroom house with my uncle. My brother Rudy and I shared a room with my parents. I slept on a little pallet on the floor, sort of in the hall that connected the two bedrooms, but still close to my parents' bed. They had a double bed and Rudy had a cot. My three sisters, Delia, Delmira, and Diamantina, slept in the other bedroom. Tío Alfredo and my brother Luis had beds in what would one day be the living room.

When the lights got turned off at night, it was such a small house that we could all hear each other saying good night.

"Hasta mañana, Apá."

"If God wills it, mija."

"Hasta mañana, Amá."

"Si Dios quiere."

We went around this way until we connected and were reassured our family was all right. Close and sweet and loving. Lucky me on my small pallet on the floor.

There was a bathroom in the house, but it had no plumbing or fixtures, so we used it as a closet. The outhouse was behind the dirt floor shack in the back yard that used to be my grandmother's house when she was still alive. My mother still scrupulously swept the dirt floor to leave it hard packed and neat in memory of her mother, who used to cook, iron, and sleep in that room.

In the back yard a huge mulberry tree dropped purple stains on the dirt below. In the front a Chinese loquat made juicy yellow plums. These were our growing-up fruits along with the red pomegranate jewels that grew in my Tía Nina's yard. Occasionally, a round cactus that Tía Nina had in her front yard sprouted pichilinges, tiny red fruits the size of a raisin. The taste was so distinctive and the fruit so rare that my siblings and I fought over who got the next one.

Tío Alfredo's house was situated directly between two cantinas. Excitement on either side of us: the click of the billiard balls, the throaty, smoke-filled laugh of the cantineras, and the occasional drunken brawl. Amá made me come in the house when a fight started. The music of my nursery days started just before the coming of night like an invocation. I sang "Gabino Barrera," "El Gavilán Pollero," and "Volver, Volver, Volver" along with the borrachos and the jukebox. Amalia Mendoza filled our back yard with Spanish, the trumpets and violins in the background.

In the spring of 1953 Apá interrupted our family life at Tío Alfredo's to take us to work in the beet fields of Minnesota. Since we had no car, we went in a troca encamisada with another family. The back of this huge truck was covered with dark red canvas. It looked like a tent sitting on the flatbed, except the sides were reinforced with wood. The man who owned the truck was nicknamed "El Indio" because his skin, like that of an Indian, was the same color as the canvas, a dark, strong red. I thought he must be very rich to own a huge truck like that. We, on the other hand, owned no car, no house, almost nothing.

He was rich in strong, hefty children, too. Three of them looked like him, with dark red skin and big, stocky bodies. The other two looked like their mother, "La Güera," with light, cream-colored skin, but still big and strong. One girl was my age and all the rest were older.

It was still dark when the truck arrived and parked under the light of the street lamp. El Indio didn't have to honk because my father had been pacing by the fence next to the street, waiting and calling out orders to everyone else.

"Hurry up! I don't want to keep him waiting . . . Put it all in a pile, right here . . . No! You can't take that! There's no room . . . Mujer! What are you doing? Get out here!"

My mother went to the outhouse one more time, wanting to put off as long as possible the embarrassment of peeing in the basin in the back of the truck.

Some of El Indio's kids peered out of the flap in the back and others got out. His wife graciously got out and went in the house to ask my mother if she could help. My mother was frantic. She was going to the other end of the world with six children and no way to get back for four or five months. She was leaving her brother's house where we had been living. It stood on her mother's property. She had to leave her brother, her sisters, and the grocer who would give her food on credit if she needed it. The last time she had been on the migrant circuit was when Delia and Delmira were toddlers. Now they were in high school and there were four more children, of which I was the youngest. The farthest she had ever been was Arizona to pick cotton. Minnesota was thirteen hundred miles away, and it would take days to get there in the big, lumbering truck. People told her to bring coats and warm clothes for the children. We didn't have any. That's why my father had put us in El Indio's hands, because we had nothing. Apá wanted a better life for us.

We piled our few bundles in a corner of the truck that they had left empty for us. Then my mother spread my grandmother's quilts on the floor for us to sit on. We said good-bye to my uncle under the light of the street lamp, the dirt under our feet smelling of damp and of last night's beer from the cantinas on either side of Tío Alfredo's house. My mother cried when she said good-bye to him. He represented the life she had always known. She was leaving that now. Taking her children and herself to a place she knew nothing about.

My father, confident and full of hope and life, climbed into the front seat along with El Indio's oldest son, who also got to sit in front, of course. El Indio would drive until daylight and then his two oldest sons would help. I looked at my father through the tiny window that connected the cab to the back of the truck. His face was full and happy; he knew this would turn out well. My mother settled herself on the floor of the truck. She sat on a blanket with her back to the piles of clothes. She dried her tears and sighed a big sigh and tried to make conversation with El Indio's wife. I sat as close to my mother as I could, to feel her warmth. My brothers and sisters were all talking and laughing nervously with El Indio's kids. A lot of them were roughly the same age and knew each other at school. They hadn't really been friends there, but now they would be forced to be.

The truck lumbered off down the street. The engine roared and we had to get used to it because the deafening sound would be with us for days. The roar of the truck was awful, the close quarters weren't very nice, and everyone got tired of the hard floor and the bumpy ride, but the worst part of the trip was peeing. My teenage sisters died every time they just couldn't hold it any more and had to use the basin, which was up front, close to the cab of the truck, wedged in so it wouldn't spill. Everyone looked away and pretended not to hear when it was used.

We had no control over when the truck stopped. You could bang on the little window all you wanted, but if the truck was going full speed they would never hear. And they didn't want to stop just for going to the bathroom, anyway. El Indio was in a hurry to get there. Any stopping now would mean time lost, work not done, money not made. So our family was forbidden by my father even to attempt to knock on the window for a stop. "Either hold it or go in the basin." Those were our orders. They were doing us a big favor by taking us.

My sisters hated the peeing and my brother Luis hated the confinement. He sat as close as he could to the flap and always hit the ground first any time we stopped. His muscles, aching to be used, made him run around the gas station. Once he was almost asleep when the truck stopped for a stop sign. He leaped off the floor and out of the truck. We all had to bang on the little window furiously and scream for the truck to stop. Luis ran up sheepishly and waited for the ladder to be lowered to get back in. My father was furious, but that was just the way Luis was.

I loved everything. The doll house, secret cavelike quality of the back of the truck. Everyone lying about on blankets and bundles. I could lay my head on my mother's lap any time I wanted and she never sent me away. In fact, she would draw me closer to her; there was nothing for her to do but cuddle me and talk to La Güera.

I sat next to Luis and looked out the flap. In the morning, the mist still hugged the ground like filmy cotton. It was cool outside, but I was safe and warm covered with a blanket sitting next to my big brother. Everything going by outside was new, and I was seeing it all from the safety of this canvas-covered cocoon that had all my family in it. And they had nowhere to go and nothing to do but be with me.

We ate the tacos my mother had brought, of flour tortillas with scrambled eggs and potatoes. She had made hard-boiled eggs, too. When we ran out, we had to buy bologna and white bread at the store. What a treat! The Rainbo white bread was a luxury my mother would never have thought of at home.

The third day was the longest. The bumps really hurt our sore bottoms and everything was tiresome. Rudy and Luis shouted at each other and almost came to blows. Luis even left his station at the flap to get away from him. The truck left the highway and started making lots of turns, working its way through the Minnesota countryside. We were getting close and now everyone wanted to be looking out the flap.

The sun was low on the horizon when we got there. The truck stopped at the edge of the migrant camp and El Indio told us to unload our belongings while he and my father went to see what was what. We used only one eye to unload; the other eye wanted to see where we would be for the next two or three months. We all tried to drink it in all at once. My mother only sighed.

The migrant camp was a group of five buildings. One small, two-story structure, one long row house, two tiny houses, and one medium-sized house shaped like a stop sign. These buildings formed an L. Across the dirt road from the migrant camp was a huge barn, open at one end, and a small toolshed next to that. Behind where we had parked was the farmer's meticulously landscaped house, with a huge lawn bordered with evergreens. We tried not to look at that; it was not for us. Our home would be one of the five buildings.

My father and El Indio came back with another man. He introduced himself as the mayordomo, the Mexican in charge. He told us that El Gringo would be back shortly and that, until then, we had to wait.

El Indio had brought us to work at this farm, but his family was to work at another farm. He was in a hurry to get there and get settled. So we said our good-byes and they left us. The mayordomo left us also to go tell the gringo that we were here. He was apparently out in the fields somewhere.

When our family was alone, we huddled closer to each other next to our bundles. It was early May. There was a light sprinkling of snow on the ground from a late snowfall. We stood there shivering. My father picked me up. It was the first time he had ever done this. "This will be our home for a while, mija." His voice was low and quiet. Gone was the confident bravado. Even he sounded afraid, there with our bundles in the dirt, thirteen hundred miles from anything familiar, with no car, and only the very little money he had borrowed from his brother.

I felt his fear seep into me from his unaccustomed closeness. I wanted to change the subject and I wanted an excuse to get down. I pointed to the barn and asked, "Do you think that's a store where they have candy?" Everybody laughed and the tension broke. "No, mija, there are no stores here for miles." I insisted that I wanted to see for myself. So he put me down and we walked over there with Rudy, Luis, and Diamantina.

It was almost totally dark when the mayordomo came back with the gringo. He welcomed us and told us that our house would be the one-room, stop-sign-shaped building. We had a place to be.

The stop-sign-shaped house had only one door, and windows all around. We walked in the door with bugged-out eyes. It was all one room, fairly large. The large wood stove in the middle dominated the room. My father went outside to get wood for it from the pile we had passed. There were two metal double beds and two canvas cots. I immediately figured out who would sleep where and knew that, as usual, I would sleep on the floor. I was used to it. Besides the beds, there was a small kitchen table and two chairs.

There was nothing else, not one other thing, in the room. This would be our home for the next two or three months. At my Tío Alfredo's house we had an icebox that took a block of ice in the bottom. Here there was no icebox, no bathroom, no chairs for us kids, nothing. My father didn't seem to notice. Beds, a stove, and a kitchen table were all he thought necessary for living. Without looking, we knew there would be an outhouse in the back. We sat on the bare mattresses, reluctant to unpack, as that would be acknowledging that we were staying. Amá sent Delia next door to borrow a broom. She couldn't proceed until she had swept.

By the time Apá had the fire going, it was completely dark outside. The windows were bare and the naked light bulb hanging in the middle of the room from a brown cord did little to dispel the gloom and scariness of the new place.

When my father had the fire crackling and putting out heat, he said "Ya, start unpacking." We looked around, thinking we had missed something. There were no dressers to unpack anything into. Later we would get wooden crates from the grocery store for this and for use as kitchen cabinets.

We said nothing, just did the best we could. We made the beds and cots and, for me, a pallet on the floor. On top of the mattresses, we first put what my mother called lonas. These were single layer patchwork quilts made out of old jeans and khaki pants. We hoped these would be an effective barrier between us and whatever was in those mattresses that sagged in the middle. I wanted to be between the two double beds, between my parents and my sisters, where I felt safe. My brothers were to sleep on the two cots. We put the clothes under the beds. We covered up the windows as best we could with sheets, shirts, and towels. The pots and pans went on the floor in a corner.

And then we went to bed. Exhausted, disoriented, and apprehensive of tomorrow as we were, we couldn't go to sleep. We went through our "hasta mañana" family ritual, just as we used to do every night in Texas, but that night, you could hear the fear and nervousness in everyone's voice. Maybe God had made a mistake bringing us here.

That night, even Apá, who usually started snoring immediately, stared at the ceiling for a while. The beds were unfamiliar, as was the room and the Minnesota countryside noises. The wood stove made the room warm, but we could hear the wind howling outside. We shivered in the blankets as it whistled through the poorly sealed windows.

Delmira tossed and turned. I knew she continued to worry silently. "What will I tell my friends when I get back to school?" she had said earlier as the shame washed over her again like cold water. "That I went to visit my uncle? A long vacation? Or only Apá worked in the fields; for us it was great! They'll know it's a lie. The truth? Ay, but how?"

We heard another carload of migrants arrive. We felt glad that we were already settled. With something to be glad about, we went to sleep.

In the new morning light, I heard Apá putting more wood in the stove. The coldness of the floor and the excitement of our new life made me jump out of my little makeshift bed on the floor. I went over to the stove to warm my hands, but while my front got warm, my back got cold, so I had to keep turning around and around. The wood stove was the heart of the room. We all gravitated to it first thing in the morning, making a circle around it. It was our place of solace, warmth, and family closeness.

I put on more clothes and went to the front door to see what the camp looked like in the new day. Apá woke Rudy up and told him to go to the well and get some water for washing up and for coffee. Apá had already been walking around and had found the well.

I asked if I could go and followed Rudy outside. We walked out of the bend in the L shape of the buildings. We walked through some tall weeds on a narrow, well-worn path. Rudy worked the well while I practiced making little warm clouds with my breath in the chilly air. He filled our bucket from the well bucket. It looked clear and wonderful to me. On the way back to the house, we passed two other kids going to the well with a bucket. All of us kept our eyes down and walked way into the weeds to avoid brushing each other on the narrow path. We didn't trust anything here yet.

Amá had brought coffee from Texas. She boiled the grounds in a saucepan and poured a cup for my father. He had to wait for the grounds to settle to the bottom before he could drink it. We ate the leftover bread from the trip; there was nothing else.

After the coffee, my father went out to arrange for a trip to the grocery store. Close by, in Sabin, was the "company store." It was a small convenience store, and the gringo had arranged for the migrants to buy groceries there on credit. It was the only store in town. The bill would be settled at the end of the season. The migrants got paid only once, at the end of the season.

Amá and Apá went with a neighbor to get groceries at Sabin. They took Delia in case they needed an interpreter. We sat around the house trying to get used to the place.

While they were gone, the farmer's wife brought us two frozen chickens. She told my sisters that she always cleaned out her freezer and gave the food to the migrants when they arrived, then she stocked it with fresh food.

Delmira's face went hot with shame and anger when she heard this, but she bit her lip to keep from saying what she wanted to say. She didn't want to offend anyone on our first day there, so she just said, "Thank you," and cursed her in Spanish after she closed the door. She banged the chickens on the table and said she was going to pitch them before my parents got home, but we didn't let her.

While the adults were gone, the boys brought round, thick pieces of tree trunk from the woodpile to use as chairs. Diamantina and I made the beds.

They came home with the staples: coffee, sugar, twenty-five pounds of white flour in a patterned cloth sack, lard, baking powder, eggs, potatoes, dried pinto beans, vermicelli, onions, cumin, garlic, salt, and packages of Kool-Aid for the kids to drink. The extras were a piece of bacon to flavor the beans and three quarts of milk. What we didn't drink that day would go on the window sill that the wind seemed to hit first, to keep it cool. There was never enough milk, so all my brothers and sisters had tiny teeth. My mother brought a small piece of candy for each of us kids and a black rope of licorice for herself.

We showed Amá and Apá the frozen chickens. Apá smiled from ear to ear and was now convinced that this was a good gringo that we were staying with. He felt welcomed and taken care of. We looked at Delmira, but she kept her eyes down and said nothing.

We ate our candy while Amá made lunch. A lady from the house next door came over to talk to my mother. She had been there many years, she said, and told us about the routine. We were starting to feel that we had arrived. We didn't know it then, but that stop-sign-shaped house would be our summer home in Minnesota for the next six years.

When my father had told us we were going to Minnesota with El Indio to work in the beet fields, all the kids had different responses—all silent and internal—we never said anything. He was taking a bunch of children to Minnesota, but he didn't see it that way. My father knew nothing about children. He treated us all like adults, expecting adult responses from us. We were a team going to work.

Delia was in her first year of high school. It was the first of May. She would have to leave the new boy who smiled at her in a secret way in the hall. Her friend Chayo liked him, too. Would the new boy remember Delia when she came back in September or would Chayo have prevailed?

Delmira looked around her eighth-grade class, full of adolescent juices. She would miss her eighth-grade graduation. She didn't know how she could ever tell them that she was being taken out of school to go in the back of a canvas-covered truck to work in the fields. She knew their responses would be cruel. She decided to face the problem at the end of the summer. So she told no one— just walked out of school at the end of the day with a fake smile and said, "See you tomorrow!" and didn't return until September.

Luis, in the sixth grade and a boy, was not so mortified. So he bragged to his friends that he would be doing a man's job that summer. But in his heart of hearts he was afraid. He had worked in the peanut fields for years, but he suspected the beet fields would be much crueler and Apá a harder taskmaster.

Diamantina, in the fifth grade, was terrified. She worried about everything anyway, and she wanted to do well. Would they make her work all day? Would they make her go to a new school? Would there be gringos there? Or would it be a Mexican school for the migrants? She hoped so. She didn't like the gringos—they made her feel ashamed to wear her hand-me-down clothes. She bit her nails until they bled, and then she bit the inside of her lip. At night, she couldn't go to sleep for the pain at the ends of her fingers.

Rudy, in the fourth grade, didn't care about anything. He didn't care to tell anyone, but he didn't consider it an ugly secret either—he would just do what was needed. He was the one who responded best to my father's need to have all of us be adults, albeit short ones.

The gringo who owned the farm and the mayordomo came to see Apá the day after we got there to talk about the kids' schooling. All the school-age children at the migrant camp had to attend school until the end of the school year or the gringo would get in trouble.

This was a new development my father hadn't expected. But actually, he was glad. His dream was for all of us to finish high school and to have better lives than he had. So he told my mother to get everyone ready for school.

Amá, already overwhelmed with all the new challenges, exploded. "I didn't know they would have to go to school! You told me to pack light! We brought mostly work clothes! The girls only brought a couple of dresses to wear in case there was an occasional day off! How can you expect me to dress five children for a month in a gringo school when we didn't bring anything! I'll have to wash clothes daily after being in the fields all day! ¡Esto es el colmo!"

My father looked distressed as he always did when my mother yelled at him with a legitimate point. He mumbled something about having to make do and went outside to sharpen the hoes.

When he left, my mother started to cry. We watched, helpless. Delia said, "Amá, Delmira and I will wash the clothes when we get home from school—for everyone. It's only for a month. We can do it, Amá. You won't have to wash clothes at all."

Amá blew her nose into the handkerchief that she always carried in her pocket. "I don't know how that viejo could have brought us so far so unprepared."

The next morning, while Apá and Amá prepared to go to work, everyone except me prepared to go to school.

Since it was the first day of school, the parents watched from the doorways and waited until the bus came before they went to the fields. We went to the bus stop all bunched up, juntitos. In Texas we fought constantly, but here the fear and the morning cold made us loving manitos again. I went to the bus stop to wait with them.

Delia, Delmira, Luis, Diamantina, and Rudy stood there bunched up and nervous. They would be showing up at a strange school unannounced. They would have to register themselves, of course. My parents knew no English and nothing about papers.

The Minnesota farmland is as flat as a table—you can see for miles—all the way to the horizon. We went to the bus stop much too early. It was a freezing cold early May morning. The wind blew directly at us with nothing to stop it.

They weren't dressed for the weather. They were dressed for a warm Texas school day, the way they had always been. The cold air blew through Luis's shirt that had been washed a hundred times. The fear and dread of the unknown about the bus and the school made them even colder. Would they have to sit at the back of the bus because they were Mexican? Would they have to sit next to gringos in class? What would they say about our clothes? Vicious things probably.

Diamantina was the smallest and Rudy was the youngest. She was the first one to break. She was wearing little nylon socks with ancient patent leather shoes that had belonged to Delmira and they were still a little too big for her. The cold wind blew across the little hairs on her legs and made her get goose bumps all over. It would blow through her cotton dress like netting, lifting the hem. It blew all the way to the back of her heart, where the tears were waiting. And they came out. The others rushed to comfort her, but they felt like crying too.

Rudy was the first one to see the bus, a yellow speck on the featureless horizon. They composed themselves. Delmira wiped Diamantina's cheeks with the underside hem of her dress. They swallowed their fear like a big, ugly pill. They had to be brave no matter what came next.

I stood there watching the bus drive away. My brothers and sisters would do what they had to; they always did. I felt forlorn and abandoned. We had been together, all of us, for days. When I turned around to go back to my parents, I saw a black Ford pull up next to the migrant camp. Three nuns in black habits got out. They were walking toward the stop-sign-shaped house, where my father was sharpening hoes on the front step. I ran to get there first.

I burst through the door and told my mother we had company. When she came out, they asked her how the children would be cared for while the parents worked in the fields. It was the first time my mother had been on the migrant circuit with six children. She said she didn't know.

They offered to take the littlest ones with them for the summer. It would cost only what they could pay—a dollar a week, they said. It was a charity the church offered for the migrants.

My mother felt she had no choice but to send me there. Leaving me at the edge of the field while they worked was dangerous, since the rows of beets were half a mile long and I was only three. My eleven-year-old sister, Diamantina, was too young to work. The child labor laws said you had to be twelve to work in the fields. So Diamantina would go with me and be schooled there. Rudy was also too young to work, but because he was Rudy and a male child, he didn't have to go to the nuns.

They took the two of us on Sunday. Apá borrowed a car and everyone went. Amá cried quietly and sighed despairingly all the way. Everyone else was silent. Apá drove faster than usual, wanting it to be over.

When we got there, he gave us each a quarter. He said they would come to visit us the next time it rained and the fields were unworkable, if he could borrow a car.

The school was huge, with an asphalt playground and a tall, wrought-iron fence surrounding everything. When it was time, Diamantina and I clutched the bars and pushed our faces through to say good-bye to my mother and father and to all the others. We were overwhelmed with abandonment and sadness. And it was still daytime.

When nighttime came, then I really knew what it was to feel abandoned. They took us to a really big room, a gymnasium, with long rows of cots. They looked like the long rows of sugar beets that we had just left. This was where all the children lay down together. Thanks to God, they gave me a cot next to my sister. I covered myself with the sheet while the tears leaked out. I didn't want to cry. I wanted to be strong, as my father liked for me to be, but the tears wouldn't obey me . . . and they kept wetting the small pillow.

"Diamantina," I said to my sister very quietly, "would you hold my hand? I'm afraid and I feel very sad. I want my mother . . . I don't want to be here."

"Shhh, be quiet. Don't be afraid. Give me your hand. I'll take care of you. Don't be afraid."

The nuns walked up and down the rows of cots. I didn't want them to see me cry. I didn't want them even to see me. I closed my eyes very hard to keep the tears in and to make my heart hard. But the lump in my throat wouldn't go away and I felt more alone and sad.

I squeezed my sister's hand tightly . . . it was my only link to the life that I had known up until that time. She squeezed it back. Then I felt less alone. And the lump in my throat got smaller. The tears dried on my cheeks and I dreamt.

I dreamt that it was a beautiful day with a blue sky and small cottony clouds. We were in a park and I was dressed in a beautiful yellow dress and patent leather shoes. My amá had me by the hand. She was laughing, her face full and happy. Close to us were my brothers and sisters with my father. Someone had said something funny and everyone was laughing, especially my apá. I felt so lucky to be at the center of this family, loved and comfortable.

We started to play on the playground equipment. I got on the slide. It was very tall. When I got to the top of it, I stopped.

Everyone looked small below me and I got scared. I didn't want to be a coward and go back down the ladder. And besides, there was a little boy behind me. I had to go. I went with all my fear and with my wild hair blowing behind me. When I got to the bottom, my sister Delmira caught me in her arms. Again I felt lucky and happy to have so many people who loved me.

The next morning, the nuns made us bow our heads and pray to thank God for breakfast. I prayed for rain.

During recess a vendor sold popsicles through the bars of the fence. They were five cents each. My sister took our quarters out of her sock and bought us each one. They were yellow and deliciously cool in the summer heat of the asphalt playground. The next day we only got one and shared, to conserve our money.

"Do you think they're coming back to get us?" I asked Diamantina as we took turns with the popsicle.

"Of course they are, silly!" she said. But then her eyes got a sad, faraway look.

I imagined them hoeing the beets and wondered if they were thinking about us as they hoed. Maybe Apá wished he had given us more quarters in case it didn't rain for awhile. Maybe Amá missed my laying my head on her lap after dinner when all the work was done. I missed it too. Her apron was soft from being washed a thousand times. It smelled like tortillas and dinner and soap. She rubbed my head with her fingers.

Maybe Amá felt like crying as she hoed, as I did at the school.

When Amá wrote a letter, I made Diamantina read it over and over. Especially the part that said "Your amá, who loves and appreciates you." She let me sleep with it under my pillow. I put it in my sock during the day. The sweat of the playground made it get wet and the letters blurred, but it didn't matter. I couldn't read, anyway.

One night, a clap of thunder woke me from a dead sleep. My eyes were round by the next flash of lightning.

I looked over and Diamantina was awake too. The thunder had awakened some of the little ones and they were crying. I had never been afraid of weather, even though my mother was. I loved the wildness of thunder, lightning, and driving rain. My wild nature reveled in it.

"Do you think they'll be here tomorrow?" I asked her.

"It may not be raining where they are. It might only be raining here," she answered.

That was a disappointing possibility.

When it continued to rain all night and into the morning, we started to feel hopeful. The rain stopped around mid-morning. We waited all day with our hearts in our throats. Every car that drove by took our full attention.

After dinner, neither of us spoke. Words wouldn't help, anyway. Our heads were swimming with disappointment. We were becoming older too fast. A part of our childhood was dying.

In bed, I stared at the high gymnasium ceiling. My eyes would fill and empty as the sad thoughts came in waves. Diamantina was crying too.

The next morning, I was in the play room, feeling terribly lonely. The three-story doll house, taller than I was, and the blocks didn't interest me at all. I looked at the nuns and ran out of the room, down the hall, out of the building, and across the asphalt school yard, the nuns screaming and chasing me.

I was determined and hell-bent to be with my sister since I couldn't be with my family. I struggled with the big church door and ran down the aisle, headlong into Diamantina, who was practicing for her first communion. I wrapped myself around her legs, sobbing now, and screaming. They came up to us out of breath. "She ran out. Not supposed to be here," they gasped. They tried to take my hand, but it just dug deeper into my sister's leg. Embarrassed, she tried to talk sense into me. Senseless, I couldn't listen, I just screamed louder. My little soul feeling as if it were going to fly apart. Pandemonium in front of the altar now, the priest coming out of the sacristy to see.

I couldn't tell them what was going on inside of me. How could I? Maybe if I screamed louder they would know. My wild screams would tell them. Diamantina could see. She saw into my eyes and knew.

And the conflict started for her. All these adults wanting us to make nice. And my screams and imploring eyes that I couldn't take off her, begging her to help me. She couldn't do it. She was too small and only eleven and my father had taught her too well to mind.

"What happened?" she asked. I just screamed and shook my head wildly. I couldn't say the words, not here, in front of all these people.

She hugged me and cried too, but quietly, despairingly.

"Shhh, ya. You have to go back with them," she said quietly.

"NOOOO! NOOOO!" I begged, but I knew I couldn't fight this crowd. They would do what they wanted to with me.

They peeled me off her, still screaming, but only hopeless screams now, knowing that there was no help for me.

She watched them carry me off, but I forgave her. She couldn't do more, I knew that.

Later, we found out that my father hadn't been able to borrow a car. Naturally, on the first rainy day off, all the migrants wanted to use their cars to go to town—to grocery shop, to buy supplies they had forgotten to bring with them, like work gloves and metal files to sharpen the hoes.

The whole family had wanted to visit us, but he couldn't make it work. His powerless feeling had made my father crazy. So he had talked to the mayordomo about helping him get a used car. It had become obvious to the mayordomo and to the gringo that our family was hard working and reliable. Together, Apá and the mayordomo went to the gringo and he agreed to advance my father the money for a used car if he promised to come back to this farm next year. Half the amount would be due this year and half the next. The money would be taken out of his paycheck at the end of the season.

The next time it rained, they arrived bright and early in a gray and white Chevy. It felt like Christmas. I could love the rain again even though it had disappointed me so badly last time. My brothers and sisters were glad to see us, thrilled to have a holiday, and ecstatic about our car. My father proudly drove us around town.

We stopped at a grocery store and got snacks for a picnic. We ate at a picnic table in the park with the grass glistening all around in the sunlight after the rain. I had never been happier.

When they left us later in the afternoon, it was not so sad. We would miss them. But now we knew they had missed us too. We had a car, whereas before we had nothing. Things were looking up.

The next day, at recess, I realized Apá had forgotten to give us quarters for popsicles. Diamantina said she had remembered, but was afraid to ask him. We looked longingly at the other kids with popsicles.

When Diamantina opened the next letter from Amá, a dollar fell out. It said:

Diamantina and Elva, my daughters,

I think about you every day. My hope is that God will reunite us soon.

We forgot to give you money for the popsicles. On our way back, your father kept saying, "How could I have forgotten to give them money?"

Here everything is the same. The fields were very wet at first, but now they are almost dry.

My daughters, take care, each of the other.

Su mamá, que las quiere y las aprecia.

Olivia P. Treviño

Delmira had put two red ribbons for my braids in the envelope. I wore them every day, feeling beautiful and loved.

After leaving us with the nuns for three months, the whole family came to get us at the end of July. The beet thinning and weeding season was over. Beet topping and harvest season wouldn't start until mid-September. All the migrants packed up and went elsewhere to work for a month and a half. Apá said we would follow El Indio's truck to Wisconsin.

"We made a place up here for you," Delmira told me, indicating the ledge behind the back seat. They had put a sheet and a pillow up there. The ledge was the perfect size for me, the exact length of my body and a lot wider.

"Amá, do they have nuns in Wisconsin?" I asked when I was settled.

"Pos, quién sabe." She had never been to Wisconsin, just as she had never been to Minnesota, so how could I expect her to know?

"Yes, they do," Rudy said, looking up at me from the back seat. "We're going to leave you there. But don't worry, we'll pick you up next year when we come back."

I rapped him on the head with my knuckles as hard as I could, but he didn't care, since he had made everyone laugh.

"Apá, do I have to stay with the nuns in Wisconsin?"

"No sé hija, pronto veremos," he said. He wasn't really paying attention to me, since he was concentrating on staying on El Indio's tail. He didn't want to get lost on the way.

We were heading to the farm where El Indio's family had gone the previous year. He had warned us that Wisconsin was not like Minnesota in that nothing was certain there. If the fields were ready, then there would be work. If there were no fields ready to be picked, then either you went on to the next farm or you went to the lake and fished. Also, in Wisconsin, the season was short and there were no contracts with the migrants, so people went to different farms every year.

The farm we went to that first year had plenty of work, but no place for us to stay right away. The house where we could stay was rented and the occupants wouldn't be out for several days. The farmer really wanted his fields picked, though, so he said we could stay in the barn until the house became vacant.

The barn? Everyone looked at Apá, alarmed. The barn was for pigs and cows.

"Sí, bueno," he said. The barn was fine with him as long as there was work. The accommodations didn't matter; we were there to work and make money. No one could argue. But everyone, even Rudy this time, seemed upset and ashamed.

The barn was no longer used to house animals, but it was full of rusty old equipment. There were several old buggies, once drawn by horses, that we had to move out of the way before we had room to live there for a few days.

The work in Wisconsin was to pick green beans, cucumbers, and occasionally tomatoes. The cucumber fields were picked several times during a season. A machine sorted them by size, with the smallest ones paying the most. The rows were short, so our car was nearby. I kept watching for nuns, but none came. In Wisconsin, even Diamantina worked, as it didn't require much skill, just to get the fruit off the plant. All the kids were used to this kind of work. They had picked peanuts for years in Apá's sharecropper plot when we used to live at the McKinley farm. Being used to it didn't mean they liked it, though. In fact, they hated it more than the beet fields. In Minnesota, they worked standing up, touching only the hoe. Except for the days after a rain, they could stay fairly clean. Not so in Wisconsin. To pick the green beans and cucumbers, you had to put your hands right into the plant, soaked with dew early in the morning. In half an hour, your work gloves and shirt were soaked up to the elbow. After they dried in the sun, the prickles from the plants started to make your skin itch. At first, people couldn't decide whether it was better to work bent over at the waist, and have the lower back hurt, or to squat down, and have the knees hurt. Most people started bent over at the waist, but after the first day or two they would go for knee pain instead. At least knee pain stayed localized. The back pain made you feel bad all over. My job was to bring the water bucket and dipper whenever Apá declared a break.

As promised, we stayed in the barn only for a few days. The house we moved into was a two-story farm house, probably at one time occupied by the owner. It was surrounded by fields and stood high on a knoll. On one side, the ground was fairly level. On the other side the ground fell away steeply. At the bottom of the hill was a golden, ripe wheat field. On the other side of the wheat field was a creek reputed to have lots of fish. Rudy was dying to fish it, but it wouldn't be for a while. El Indio's family got the upstairs and we moved into the ground floor. I was fascinated by the stairs, never having been in a two-story house. But Apá forbade me to go up there, as he wanted to ensure their family's privacy. So I would sneak halfway up and run down if I heard anyone coming. Rudy and I got bunk beds. He made me take the lower one, of course.

Even though the nuns never came, I still felt lonely and cut off from the family. Even Diamantina was part of them now. I spent long hours alone by the car.

That year the crops were plentiful and work was continuous, seven days a week for several weeks. Time passed quickly and by early September, we could feel a chill in the air and smell the coming of winter. The sycamores were already dropping their leaves. There came a day, finally, when there were no fields that were ready to be picked. The farmer wanted to wait two more days, and then do the final picking of the season.

Apá went into town to buy meat for a barbecue. He asked Luis to rake the leaves while he was gone. Rudy was finally to go fishing at the creek on the other side of the wheat field. He promised to be back by noon. I watched him walk down the hill, since he had refused to take me. By the time he was at the far end of the field, he looked like a tiny black speck in the gold of the wheat. Amá and my sisters did the laundry early. By noon the sheets were flapping in the breeze over the green grass.

Delmira turned the radio on at the same time that Apá started the fire for the barbecue. Everyone happy, they congregated in the back yard. Apá, thrilled with our success and our prospects for the future, was the happiest I had ever seen him. Generosity and celebration were the order of the day. Meat on the grill, the radio playing, and no work for two days. All of them talking happily.

I went to the front porch alone. From there I could still hear them laughing together in the back yard. There, as with the nuns and later at the Wisconsin fields, I felt cut off from everyone. They were talking among themselves and I was alone, as usual.

Seeing the pile of leaves Luis had raked, I threw myself in the middle. Soft and crunchy at the same time. Light blue sky above me. Over the top of the house, I could see the smoke from the barbecue. This gave me an idea. I went into the kitchen where Amá had some matches for the gas stove. I was going to light just one leaf and have my own little fire . . . all mine, as they had theirs.

But I burned my fingers and let go of the leaf, still burning. It fell into the pile of leaves. Before I could move or think, I had a bonfire. Terrified for my life at the hands of my father, I ran inside and crawled into my bunk bed, crying with fear.

Pretty quickly, they saw the smoke and came running. With lots of shouts, they put it out. I thought my life would be over soon.

I could hear and feel them coming in the house, especially Apá. He didn't say anything for a minute, but I could feel him there by the bed, with the rest of the family standing behind him. I wouldn't open my eyes. "Did you light the leaves on fire?" he asked.

"Sí." The word was barely audible, even to me. I kept my eyes shut tightly.

"You shouldn't have done that." The tenderness in his voice surprised me so much that I almost opened my eyes. He had been feeling grand, and his generosity extended even to me. "You could have burned down the house, and we could have gotten hurt. Do you understand?"

"Sí." He patted me awkwardly with his hand and left. The storm I had expected had passed, and the sun had come out. I opened one eye. Rudy was looking at me, angry and reproachful. I closed it quickly and turned to the wall.

Four days later we left for Texas. Many of the migrants, including El Indio's family, went back to Minnesota to work on "el tapeo," the beet topping and harvest. The Minnesota farmer wanted us to come back, but Apá insisted on getting his children back into their regular school. His dream was for all of us to graduate from high school. The kids wouldn't quite make the beginning of the school year, but they wouldn't miss by much. So he decided to forego the money that he could have made by staying another month.

Chapter Two

*Más enseña la adversidad que diez años
de universidad.*

Adversity teaches more than ten years
of university.
(Mexican dicho)

"Chaataaa . . . ¿Ya volvieron?" asked Rosendo, the vegetable vendor, even though he wouldn't have turned into our yard unless he already knew we were back. It was our first day back in Pearsall, but Rosendo had already found out we were in town from someone else on his route. White stubble covered his face as usual. Two huge baskets were suspended on a wooden yoke that went across his shoulders. When we came to the door, he bent over until the baskets were on the porch and then he rested the yoke on them.

"How did it go up there in Minnesota?" he asked.

"Pos como la pura fregada. But we made it back, thank God," Amá answered, already starting to sort through the tomatoes. She turned each one over to look at all sides.

"Did you hear that Celia's daughter had twins?" Rosendo gossiped like a woman. It was part of his job, since he talked to housewives all day.

"Of course not; how could I hear if we just got back?"

"Sí . . . they came out still in the sack. The midwife had to cut it open and take them out. But they came out fine. Now the girl has one on each breast."

"So is that girl married?"

"No. The father is from Mexico. When he found out she was gorda, he disappeared and no one has heard from him."

Amá chose tomatoes, onions, and chiles from Rosendo's baskets. She paid him and he bent down to put the yoke on his neck again. I knew that now everyone would know we were back. He was still smiling when he straightened. The enormous weight didn't seem to bother him at all.

"Do you want me to swing by on Friday? Or wait until next week?

"Come by Friday. These kids of mine eat a lot."

I waited to see if he would give me a pilón. A small sprig of grapes maybe. If he did, I would give it to my mother after he left, as grapes were her favorite but she considered them too much of a luxury to buy. A pilón was something hoped for only from Mexican vendors—the gringos never gave a pilón. But the Mexican tendajos and vendors frequently did. If your mother bought meat at the butcher's, and the piece weighed one ounce over a pound, maybe the butcher would give her the extra ounce free as a pilón, to sweeten the purchase. Or maybe the grocer's wife would give a child a penny candy as a pilón when the mother bought groceries there.

But no, Rosendo was too poor to give a pilón. "Bueno, adiós. Que Dios los bendiga," he said as he went out the front gate and down the street.

I was alone in the house with Amá. My brothers and sisters had all gone to school. Tío Alfredo left at dawn for his job as foreman at the McKinley farm. Amá packed plenty of hot tortilla tacos for him, something he had missed very much while we were gone. Apá left early also, in his new used car, to see about finding work now that he was back in town.

Amá went inside to start lunch. She had packed lunches for the younger kids, but Delia and Delmira were ashamed to take tortilla tacos for lunch. They were afraid the gringos would laugh and say nasty things. We still tried to hide our Mexicanness, not believing yet that it was impossible. So they walked a mile home for lunch. They had to walk fast, eat fast and walk back fast in order to make it before the bell.

I sorted through the pinto beans for Amá, taking out all the little pebbles and broken beans. Then she sent me to the tendajo, a little store three houses away to get a piece of salt pork for flavoring the beans. When I came back, Amá was making tortillas.

White flour tortillas. Fresh stacks of them three times a day. Amá was always busy, always moving, in her typical take-charge way. She threw the flour in the bowl, mixed in the manteca quickly, and then sprinkled it with scalding hot water. The dough, clean and creamy white, looked like the smooth, almost transparently clean skin of her face.

Quickly she transformed the bowl of white ingredients into a bowl of soft tistalles, the biscuit-sized mounds of tortilla dough.

Then she began to get the comal ready. When the cast-iron griddle glowed red hot, she wet a washcloth and wiped the griddle to clean it. It made a sizzling-hot clean sound. Ready.

She took the palote and began to roll the first tortilla. One, two, three rolls with half turns in between and it was ready. She swirled the tortilla onto the comal. As the tortilla absorbed the heat, it bubbled just slightly. By the time one side had cooked and it was ready to turn, she had rolled out another one. The aroma of the cooking tortillas on the hot comal overshadowed the smell of the wet dough.

She swirled the second one onto the second place on the comal, turned the first one, pressed out the bubbles with a slight pressure of her hand, and then started to roll out the next one. Her hands were in the wet, lardy dough and over the intense heat of the comal three times a day. This kept them soft, smooth, and pliant.

Overwhelmed, as always, by the aroma of the fresh brown and white tortillas, I went to find the butter. I had my plate ready and the paper pulled back on the butter stick so I could use it to smear butter on the first tortilla. I asked for it and she swirled it onto my plate, not breaking her stride.

I bit into my childhood. It tasted sweet and salty and hot and clean. It tasted of my mother. Of her hands and her love for me. It tasted pure and clean and good.

By the time I finished it, she had a stack of tortillas done. I watched her in the steps of her dance. Swirl, roll, turn . . . then press, turn, roll. She never missed a beat. A consummate dancer. My heart swelled with contentment and love for her. Mi amacita.

When Delia and Delmira came home for lunch, Apá was there also.

"Apá, my friend told me that there's a gringa who would like help cleaning her house. I could make some money to buy some green corduroy I need for a pep squad skirt," Delmira said.

"No hija, con gringas no. I don't want you to do that kind of work. We don't clean gringo bathrooms. Working in the fields with the vegetables is honest, clean work. Being a maid is not for us. You tell your mother how much you need and I'll give her some money to take you shopping for material to make school clothes." Over the years, all of us would ask the same question as Delmira, but the answer was always no. They never let their daughters be waitresses, either. We never went to restaurants, ever since they had told my father that Mexicans had to use the kitchen door—only gringos got to go in the front door. The closest my father had ever gotten to a waitress was the barmaids at the cantinas. Everyone knew what they did after work. No, we couldn't be waitresses either; it was better to have your daughters next to you in the fields, covered with pants, a work shirt, and a hat, where you could protect them.

After school we saw Delmira's friend go by, barely tall enough to be visible sitting in the back seat of a big car, with the gringa driving, her hair having been freshly piled high at the beauty shop.

"Amá, can I go to Margarita's?" I asked later.

"Sí, but put on your shoes."

Reluctantly I put them on. I preferred my feet bare, even though they got very dirty. If my feet were bare, the dry, sandy dirt felt soft and comfortable. Socks were only for dress-up. So in my shoes, my feet got sweaty and sticky. But Amá was afraid I'd step on a nail. So to go out of our yard, I had to do what she asked.

Margarita's house was at the end of the alley and across the street. But as I passed Sulema's house on the other side of the movie theater, I saw that Margarita was there, along with five or six other kids. She saw me and waved me over. I went reluctantly. Sulema was older and she never seemed to like me. They were playing la vieja Inez and I joined them. Sulema was the oldest and the ring leader of the play group. She was playing the part of la vieja Inez. The rest of us were colored ribbons.

Tan Tan.

¿Quién es?

La vieja Inez.

¿Qué quería?

Un listón.

¿De qué color?

Verde.

She seemed annoyed that she picked green and the green ribbon was me. As I walked over to her side, I focused on the pigeons where they were cooing in their nests above the movie theater. It seemed there were hundreds of them. Their gray necks had shimmery pink highlights.

We were playing in the bare dirt. There was no grass at all anywhere in the yard—all hard-packed dirt. I squirmed in my shoes and wondered if I dared be disobedient. Sulema's mother came to the screen door and told her to bring in the wash from the clothesline. The game broke up.

"Wanna go to my house?" I asked Margarita.

"I have to ask my mother," she said. I went with her to ask permission. Her mother was visiting a lady across the street. I hated to go in that house. The lady had a disease that made her legs and arms huge as tree trunks. The rest of her was normal size. The only way she had to support herself was to take in ironing from the gringos. She was standing there on those huge legs pushing the iron with her giant arms and sweating. It seemed she was in agony. I went outside to wait for Margarita.

As we walked down the alley toward my house, I asked her, "Did you go to the movies last week?"

"Yes."

"Every five minutes they were kissing each other."

"Yes."

"Have you ever kissed anybody?"

"No. Mencho wanted to kiss me but I didn't let him because he's too ugly. Have you?"

"Me either. But it looks like fun on the screen."

So we decided to try it in the outhouse. It tasted like spit. I didn't like the way her mouth smelled. I noticed for the first time that spittle accumulated at the corners of her mouth. I decided the movie stars were wrong.

On the other side of the cantina to the left of our house was El Teatro Ideal, the Mexican movie theater. The popcorn smell filled the theater and the sidewalk out front. The charge to get in was ten cents for children and twenty-five cents for adults. But the owners let me in for free because I was so small and they knew my parents. Besides, the ticket-taker only collected tickets early in the evening, anyway. Then she fell asleep in her chair with her head back and her mouth open. My brother and his friends crumpled empty Juicy Fruit gum wrappers and tried to make the paper wads land in her mouth. When they succeeded, she choked violently. They ran fast, in case she decided to tell their parents.

The older kids had to pay admission, so my brother Luis swept the theater on Saturday morning in trade for a movie ticket.

One night the movie featured Tongolele dancing. She danced in very few clothes which, even in a black and white movie, seemed to take on colors. She wore big baskets of fruit on her head, too. Her big, dark lips never stopped smiling as she whirled around, the fruit tipping but never falling. She stamped her bare feet and sang with a delicious throaty voice. The marimba music made it hard for me to stay still in my seat. I walked home feeling like twirling and swinging to the music in my head.

The next morning everyone went to work in the peanut fields. Delia stayed home to baby-sit me and clean the house. She was washing dishes with the radio on when the same song came on that Tongolele had danced to the night before. I got out of bed still only in my panties and started stamping my feet and whirling as I had seen Tongolele do, carefully so my fruit basket wouldn't tip. I pushed out my big red lips and smiled at the customers. I belted out the song, trying to make my voice throaty and flowery like Tongolele, but only managed to get a high-pitched wail.

Delia came around the corner with dish suds on her hands.

"What are you doing?"

"I'm dancing like Tongolele."

She convulsed with laughter, leaning against the door frame.

My usual shyness overcame me. I hurried to put on my little dress over my chones, begging her to promise not to tell anyone. She promised.

But of course she had lied. When the family came home, she told them all. They all laughed and wanted to hear the story over and over. I wanted to die. I promised myself I would never dance outrageously like Tongolele again.

My favorite movies were the Pedro Infante and Luis Aguilar ones—where they wore big charro hats and rode white, dancing horses and sang to the ladies at the fiesta. The beautiful lady in her silk rebozo rebuffed the hero at first but finally gave in when he came to her window with the mariachis for a serenade.

Afterwards, on my small pallet on the floor, I went to sleep to the sounds of the music from the cantinas. And the black and white dreams started. In my dreams, I danced in my own rebozo, with a fragrant, white gardenia in my hair, under the moon and the stars. And I smiled happily.

Chapter Three

El sol es la cobija del pobre.

The sun is the blanket of the poor.

(Mexican dicho)

"To get ahead, hijos. That's why we go a los trabajos. When I first came from Mexico, I got paid dos reales al día. I worked at building the railroad, digging holes for bridge supports, clearing land . . . all over this county. The only thing I would never do is strap on the contraption to burn brush with liquid fuel. Too dangerous. Men burned and died working with those things. No, not that, but everything else. So work hard, do your homework, finish high school, and then you'll be set. You'll never have to work as hard as I did, or for as little money."

I fingered the nickels in the pocket of my sun dress and tried to imagine Apá working for fifty cents a day. And I felt I understood why we had to go to Minnesota. Our family could make more money in the migrant fields than anywhere else that was available to us. Enough to live on and some to save. With an eye toward all of us graduating from high school, Apá waited until the morning after the last day of school to leave Pearsall. A family where everyone in a family graduated from high school was a rarity on the Mexican side of Pearsall. Apá's life had been, and continued to be, hard because he couldn't speak English and had not gone to school. He wanted better things for us.

By now, all our friends knew where we were going, and the family of Delmira's best friend, Carmela, was going also. The shame everyone had felt the first year was mitigated by acceptance.

The night before we left for Minnesota, after the car was packed, Apá sat down with Rudy and Luis to plan the trip. He had bought a map of the United States. The route to Minnesota was fairly clear, Highway 81, the Pan-American Highway, almost all the way. Highway 81 ran right through Pearsall. He had Luis mark it off with a pencil. "Cut our road out of the map," Apá said to Luis. "Leave an inch on either side of our route all the way from Pearsall to Minnesota." The rest of the map would be thrown away. As we passed landmark cities, the used part of the map would be torn off and thrown away also. This was the kind of common sense creativity we had come to expect from my father. The route planned, everyone except my mother lay down for awhile with the alarm set for three in the morning.

Amá continued wandering around the house, packing more small things that we might need in the three or four months that we would be gone. I watched her take her embroidered handker-chiefs out of a drawer and carefully put them in her purse. Amá never wore makeup, but her dainty embroidered handkerchiefs were very important to her. You never knew when you might need to cry at a velorio or a funeral.

"Go to bed, mujer," Apá said. Whenever he went to bed early, he thought everyone else should do the same.

"Go to bed! How can I go to bed? I'm worried we'll forget something. I have to make sure we're prepared for all that time away. You never worry about anything. I do all the worrying." As I lay on my mat on the floor, I could feel the vibrations of Amá's reassuring footfalls as she padded around the house, worrying. In the way that was typical for many nights of our growing-up years, Apá started snoring immediately and we lay there, anxious about the future along with Amá. It was true that Apá didn't worry. He had absolute confidence in himself and in the future. Apá, the family optimist, went to sleep as soon as his head hit the pillow, with his conscience clear, trusting in Divine Providence.

It helped us some, seeing his confidence, but not much. We had our own little worlds to worry about that he didn't concern himself with. I was worried about the nuns. Would I have to go there again? Would they make me go there alone and make Diamantina work this year?

Finally Amá went to bed. She sighed a big, shuddering sigh and with a soft "Ay, Diosito mío," she let go of her cares for the day. I closed my eyes and relaxed into my last night in the familiarity of home.

The car seemed huge inside. My father always drove. One kid sat in the front between Amá and Apá. The other four sat in the back seat and I roamed around. They made a blanket bed for me on the floorboards of the back seat. My favorite place to lie was on the rear window shelf behind the back seat.

The ride was uneventful until we got to Dallas. We got lost going through Dallas and ended up on Mockingbird Lane. Luis craned his neck looking for a Highway 81 sign.

"¡Chingao! All that school and you can't read a map!" It annoyed my father tremendously that his children, educated in the gringo schools and able to read perfect English, could not navigate him through Dallas. So, as my father swore and yelled, the educated kids sat there stumped and mute in their embarrassment. All the road signs were in English, of course. On the way out of town, Luis tore Dallas off the strip map and wrapped his gum in it.

No one was in a hurry to get there except my father. But he tried to keep the troops happy, so he let us stop at Buffalo Ranch in Oklahoma for a couple of hours. Buffalo Ranch had real buffaloes, a souvenir shop, and Native Americans dressed up in beads and leather who danced for the audience. That stop was the highlight of our exhausting trip. As we drove away, Luis threw part of Oklahoma out the window.

That night, my father asked us to look for a motel—"not too luxurious!"—But to us, they all looked luxurious. We looked out the window eagerly, as if shopping for candy.

The food Amá had spent so much time packing did not last long. With six growing kids, the tacos disappeared fast. The next day we stopped at a grocery store for supplies to make bologna sandwiches on white bread with mayonnaise. These were supplemented with Fritos and Coke. We feasted on the unusual food sitting on a blanket under a tree at the side of the road.

The next milestone was the billboard that said "You are now halfway between the equator and the north pole." All the kids hated that sign, especially Delia, because it somehow meant that there was no turning back. Pearsall, Buffalo Ranch, and all the good stuff were behind us. Only the long, dirty work days were ahead.

Everyone got quiet after that. It seemed the only thing to look forward to was the ride back. And there would be many hard days between now and then.

The gringo had saved the stop-sign-shaped house for us. Small as it was, we were glad to see something familiar. The school year had been completed in Pearsall, so no one had to go to school in Minnesota. My mother felt more comfortable with my staying at the edge of the field since I was a year older. Thank God, Diamantina and I wouldn't have to stay with the nuns. Small blessings, but we were glad of them.

My mother brought a two-burner gas stove to supplement the wood stove in the center of the house. It would take less time to get it started up after working all day. That night when Amá wanted to use it, Apá gave Luis the instructions for the stove, printed in English, to read. Luis cleared his throat loudly and, as if he was the town crier, said loudly "Deeeereeections!"

"Give me that paper!" Apá said, annoyed, and threw it in the trash. You just didn't do that kind of thing in front of Apá, but Luis always forgot. Apá put in the liquid fuel and started it up. It spurted flaming droplets everywhere and there were little fires all over the room. It took all of us to stomp them out.

The alarm of the wind-up clock woke me the next morning. The clock that, when we went to bed, wouldn't let us sleep with its tic toc tic toc tic toc. Amá and Apá got up in the dark. I felt happy that I could stay in the warm, soft quilts a bit more. I wiggled deeper into the softness, with my eyes closed but hearing everything that happened.

Apá got up full of things to do, happy in his world, full of life. He put on his shirt, pants, and shoes and went outside to bring in wood. He came in loaded and leaned down to open the door of the wood stove that sat in the middle of the room. I got up and went to watch him. He stirred the ashes until they glowed red, then put in the logs. They thumped against each other and caught fire easily. The stove was like a heart, glowing red in the middle of the room, giving out warmth and drawing us to it.

"Get up, mujer," Apá said quietly to my mother. Amá, with long, deep sighs for her seemingly too-hard life, got up, dressed, and started to make the masa for the tortillas under the light of a bare bulb. This was the start of her work that wouldn't be over for many hours—better not to think about it. By the time the fire was hot, she had a mountain of tistales ready to roll out into tortillas.

When the first tortilla went onto the comal on the stove, Apá said, "Ya, get up, hijos, Delmira, Delia . . . ya."

They had all been awake since the alarm went off. But Apá let them stay in bed until they could get up to the smell of cooking tortillas. That tempered, somewhat, the pain of knowing that they would spend yet another long day in the fields.

Sad and resigned, they got up, eyes sandy with sleep. Having left some dirt on the sheets, we felt cleaner than last night. Baths were an occasional luxury.

Apá looked outside. "It's starting to get light. Hurry up! The day is dawning!"

His yelling always made everyone move faster. Dressing quickly and grabbing a potato and egg flour tortilla taco, hot from my mother's hands.

While they ate, Delia and Delmira wrapped potato and egg tacos in waxed paper for lunch. Rudy and Luis gathered the hoes and drew water from the well for the day. There was one well for the camp and it was fifty yards from our house.

A glass of milk to wash the taco down and vámonos!

The first few days, everyone rode to the fields in the back of a big truck. My father always rode in the front of the truck. He was one of the señores of the camp, referred to deferentially as "Don Luis." He was full of life and vigorous enough for all of us. If he hadn't been so strong, we wouldn't have been so strong either. The sun was not yet up when we all piled into the truck, but the morning was already full of blue light. The birds, chirping and singing to make the sun come up for one more day, were the only ones who were happy.

"Good morning."

"How are you this morning?"

"Pretty well ruined."

"Everything hurts."

"This damn knee!"

Apá got down from the truck first to hammer in wooden stakes with "LUIS V. TREVIÑO" written on them. Claim lots of rows to do today. We can do it! There are seven of us. Yes!

Delia looked at the field and said, "Ay, Luis, the rows look even longer here! And it hasn't dried! The mud on our canvas shoes will be awful!" The girls complained to Luis because he was sympathetic. Rudy was disdainful of all complaints. It was all just work to him.

Resignedly, they picked up their hoes and started. My mother, with her sighs, didn't say anything. She just tied on her garsolé, a hat of cloth and cardboard that all the women made for themselves, and started hoeing.

There were no good days here. If it rained and the air was cool, then the clay mud attached itself to the bottoms of the feet and made them heavy and cumbersome. You had continually to take it off with the blade of the hoe. And the clay stuck to the hoe too, when you dug into the dirt to thin the beets. This you had to remove frequently, or the hoe would get heavy and useless. If it hadn't rained, the sun would start to burn your skin very early in the morning, making it feel prickly. And it wouldn't get better until late in the afternoon. But by then, all would be sweat and dirt.

I was the only one still considered too young to work in the beet fields, even with the short hoe. "Stay on this side of the truck so I can see you," Amá said to me. "Or underneath it if the sun gets too hot." Other kids my age got to stay at the migrant camp, maybe to baby-sit younger brothers and sisters.

But Apá brought me so I could do my part. "Your job," Apá said to me, "is to bring us a bucket of water and a dipper when we get thirsty. Fill the bucket from the big barrel on Goyo's truck. Look for me to tie my handkerchief to the top of my hoe. That will be your signal to bring the water. ¡Águila!" Then they started hoeing and left me.

The days went by. One much like the other. Apá started driving our car to the fields instead of going in the truck. He parked in a shady spot under trees at the edge of the field and moved it

two or three times a day to keep it in the shade for me. I got used
to being alone at the edge of the field.

From my shady bed on the hood of our '52 Chevy, I lazily
watched the aqua-blue, green, and yellow dragonflies flit around.
A blue one stopped on the windshield wiper in the middle of a
patch of sunlight. The iridescent blue of the straw-thin body shimmered in the sun. It flew up and I watched it go into the clouds.
A cloud shaped like a puffy jack rabbit moved slowly across the
blue sky. I fixed a point next to a tree branch so that I could be
sure the cloud was moving. I was all alone, so I said these things
aloud to myself. I liked that. I sang loud corridos and made faces
like movie stars. No one laughed at me and I didn't need to
explain anything to anybody.

Even though they were only specks in the distance, I could
always see my family through the blurred heat waves, so I felt
safe. The rows were half a mile long and the land flat as a board,
not a rise or a hill anywhere. If I didn't want them to see me, I
went behind the car, or into the small stand of woods at the edge
of the field.

I checked to make sure they were out of earshot and far
enough away so they couldn't pay attention to me. Then I screwed
up my face and talked nonsense and chewed on my tongue. The
dragonflies didn't care. I enjoyed being surrounded by silence. I
was in a clear cocoon of aloneness. Totally myself. I didn't have
to be responsible, proper, or smart. I was silly and stupid and I
still liked myself. I thought about sticking out my tongue, just
a little bit, at my father for yelling at me that morning when I
hadn't seen the handkerchief tied to his hoe right away. But even
this bit of rebellion was scary to me. Apá was so big and powerful and could crush me with one hand. He just kept on working
and moving through the waves of heat.

Then my father stopped and mopped his brow. Oh, oh. He
was looking at me to see if I was looking his way. He waved his
white handkerchief before tying it to the top of his hoe. Time to
be sober and responsible. I filled the water bucket, put the dipper
in it, and began to walk toward them. I kept changing hands as the
handle of the full bucket dug into the crook of my small fingers.

It sloshed around and spilled on my chocolate brown leg. The water felt cool on my leg as the sun beat down on my hair, bleached red by full days in the sun. I started to hear the sound of their hoes slicing into the dirt. My brothers and sisters looked glad that they could have a break. They stopped and let themselves feel their thirst. They took the cool water from the wet dipper. I waited patiently until they all took their fill. My father started to hoe again, the signal that the break was over. My brothers and sisters reluctantly started also. I walked back with the empty bucket. Soon they would get to the end of the row and, for a few minutes, share my space.

When I heard them coming closer to the edge of the field the picture changed. I heard my sisters talking to each other. But they were still far enough away so that I couldn't hear what they were saying. Then Rudy said something funny and all of them burst out laughing. Jealousy made my belly burn. They had each other all day, while I had no one. So I asked my father if I could walk with them for the next one-mile turn. He looked annoyed, since if I walked with them, there would be no one to bring water. But he said yes and told everyone to get a drink before they started the next row.

I was wearing a sundress that my mother had made out of the twenty-five pound flour sacks that we bought. She tried to find the same cloth pattern the next time we went to the store. This was rarely possible, but she always tried. I wore no shoes when I was alone at the edge of the field, but to walk with them for a turn, I had to get my shoes out of the car or my feet would burn on the hot dirt. I wore chanclitas, shoes that at one time were dress shoes, but were now old and down at the heel.

Apá always worked two rows of beets at once, walking between them and slicing three times to the left, three times to the right, like a dance. He was a popular dancer at the Mexican dances in his younger days. In the beet field, he didn't hurry and he never slowed down, his pace was even and continuous. My mother usually talked very little, unless she happened to take the last row of our set of rows and there was another lady in the next group of migrants. Amá, a great listener, could really get the other lady to talk a lot—to dump all the gossip she knew in one length of row. My mother just said "uh-huh" and "no me digas!" and gave her lots of attention and amazed looks. Delia and Diamantina talked together. Rudy and Delmira worked fast, faster than everyone else. Luis chattered on.

By the time we got back to the edge of the field where the car was, I was ready to be alone again.

I found things in the dirt to be interested in. No toys; no one even thought of toys. An adult looking at the scene would have seen a child with not one thing to occupy her mind. But I found a thousand things to interest me. The dragonflies, the red-winged blackbirds with their shiny black bodies, brilliant red wings, and hopeful songs. No two leaves were the same on the trees at the edge of the field. The wind sighed like my mother as it blew through the leaves. The clouds endlessly changed and moved. The sky changed colors all day: baby blue just before dawn, then orange and yellow at dawn, light blue at mid-morning, almost washed white at noon, and pink, purple, and orange as it got close to sunset. From far away, the dirt looked like just dirt. But up close as I was, it was full of life and smells. There were ants busy doing their work, worms having lunch, and beetles playing. The dirt was heavy black clay that had trouble absorbing water. Then when it rained, the dirt held the water for a long time. As the dirt was baked and cracked by the sun, the surface looked like millions of broken pottery shards, no two alike. I loved the way the dirt smelled, earthy and somehow clean. I tried to pick up the shards intact and build things out of them: houses, cities, bowls, and dishes, all the while keeping an eye out for my father's handkerchief.

My older brothers and sisters had to work mercilessly hard, while I had time to dream and create out of nothing, just because I was the youngest. I felt it wasn't fair to be so lucky.

Soon I was totally alone with my thoughts again. Making solitary memories. Stamped with aloneness.

The sun had gone behind the trees that separated one field from the next. My family was almost to the edge of the field where I waited for them, so I walked out to be with them for awhile. The skinny legs and arms of all the kids were full of pain and felt heavy, even though they weighed nothing. The hour had come when the hoe got very heavy. "Ya Apá, say it's time to go home," Delmira whispered so Apá wouldn't hear. It sounded like a prayer. But Apá just continued hoeing as if it was nine o'clock in the morning.

I had heard stories from Apá's nephews about the time he used to pick cotton. He had a reputation for being the best and the strongest. Apá had a competitive streak and a need to win—and physical strength to match. Maybe he was a bit of an exhibitionist too. He would start picking before daylight, using the headlights of the car to see. When they weighed in their sixteen-foot long sacks, 500 pounds was the milestone that they all strove for. Only the best pickers made it, and only rarely. Apá regularly weighed his sack in at six or seven hundred pounds of pure, clean cotton. One of Apá's nephews said 1000 pounds. I'm sure he was exaggerating. But from the awe and respect in his eyes, it was clear they saw Apá as some sort of Hercules.

No one spoke. All you could hear was the sound of the hoes slicing into the dirt. Diamantina, rebellious because she was tired, thinned out the large, strong plants and left runty ones. I noticed and she looked at me sullenly as if to say "What do I care?"

When we were very close to the edge, we noticed that other people had started to put their hoes into the trucks and cars and wait for the drivers. But we had our own car. We could stay as late as Apá decided.

I could see they were all scared inside. This is what their faces said:

"And what if Apá says one more row? I'll either faint or cry, I don't know which."

"Please God, make him tell us to go home."

"The rows are so long! I can't finish another one."

Apá finished his row first. Late in the day he worked faster than anyone else, not because he hurried, but because everyone else slowed down. He took out his handkerchief and wiped his face to be able to see better how much sunlight was left. The others finished their rows and leaned on their hoes awaiting Apá's decision. But the sun had already gone down. Dusk had come.

"Bueno, hijos, for today, let's go home."

"Gracias a Dios," my mother said with her voice and we with our thoughts.

"The only thing I know is that I wouldn't have been able to finish another row," Delmira said as she put her hoe into the trunk of the car.

No one else said anything when we got in the car. Everyone was torpid except for Apá—as always he was full of life and energy. He looked out at the field as he drove away and said, "Here the dirt is soft but not wet; the hoe goes in well. In the morning we will stake out more rows than we did today. If we hurry just a little, we can do more."

Delia closed her eyes and looked as if she wanted to die.

When we got home, Delia and Delmira threw themselves on the bed like dead people. Luis looked at them and quickly ran out the front door and around to the back of the house so he could cry alone. I ran after him. The tears came out fast and hot and he gritted his teeth tightly so he wouldn't scream. "He shouldn't, he shouldn't! Apá shouldn't make the girls work so hard! Me and Rudy yes, we're men. But they're girls and they shouldn't be used like this!"

He wouldn't look at me as he talked, but scanned the sky desperately, as if he might find an answer written there. The rage in his eyes melted into despair. He went to hide in the outhouse to finish crying.

Apá sat on the front steps to file the blades of the hoes so that they would go in more easily the next day.

For Amá, there was still a lot to do that day. She washed her hands and face and went to see what there was for dinner. Fried potatoes and frijoles guisados . . . the same as always. She looked at Delia and Delmira. Then she looked at me and said, "The girls look so tired. What can I make for them special today? Gravy . . . I haven't made gravy for awhile." And she measured out white flour to make tortillas for eight.

Delia dragged herself up off the bed when she heard Amá getting flour out of the canister. "Amá, what can I help you with?" Her voice was soft and her eyes looked old, even though she was still a teenager.

"Nothing, mija—I'm not tired—lie down for a while."

The next day dawned cloudy and ominous. We could smell the rain coming. Apá worked fast and urged everyone else to work faster also. He wanted to get as many rows done as possible before the rain came. It came in the afternoon, along with a strong, cold wind. They didn't make it back to the car before getting drenched. We went home and sat looking at the rain through the open door for awhile. Then it got too cold, so we closed it.

Nothing to do. Rain, rain, and more rain. The wood stove wouldn't take away our shivers and goose bumps. One lay down here, another sat over there. All bored but contented that for once there was no work. But if it stopped, the next day would be worse. It didn't matter when it stopped; the next day would be worse.

We watched through the window as the trucks got stuck in the black clay. The men put boards and rocks underneath the tires to get them out.

There was only a tiny slice of the day when my mother ever had time for me—at the end, after dinner was eaten and dishes were washed. It was pitch dark and we would be in bed soon. But for a few moments, everyone just sat and talked.

By the light of the one bare bulb, Rudy taught us cats' cradles, which he had learned from other migrant kids. Luis told adivinanzas and we tried to figure them out. Apá told us misty-eyed, wistful stories of his childhood in Mexico.

My mother started to relax in her chair by the warm pot-bellied stove. I went to her, sat on the floor, and held her hand. The ends of her fingers were soft and sensitive even though she had four hard, calloused nubs on each of her palms from the hoe. I ran my fingers over the calluses. All the women wore cloth work gloves, which allowed them to develop calluses instead of blisters that popped and ran.

She let me lay my head on her lap. I asked her to feel my scalp to see if I had any piojos. I guess this was really another job for her, but I told myself that she didn't mind. We liked to think that we could find all the head lice and eradicate them. I thought maybe I was the only one that had them because I was the smallest.

I felt her apron against my cheek. The apron was old, soft, and always clean. She always wore an apron to cook, but she was so fastidious that it seemed she never got it dirty. She made conversation with everyone else while she ran her fingers over my scalp, searching. When Rudy said something funny, I felt her belly laugh through her body. I loved this time with her. My mother massaging my scalp. Holding my head with one hand while she ran her fingers through my scalp with the other. I was glad when she thought she found something, because that meant that she would continue for yet a while longer. We tried to be clean.

When she was ready to go to bed, she told me she couldn't find anything else and sent me to bed also. I got ready for bed with the feel of her fingers on my head and the smell of her apron in my nostrils.

"Ya, everybody go to bed," Apá said. Tomorrow we will get up very early to see if there is a field that is well drained and not too wet."

Without sleepiness, but obedient, everyone went to bed.

"Hasta mañana, Apá."

"If God wills it, mijita."

"Hasta mañana, Amá."

"If God wills it," and Amá sighed deeply.

Delmira said something to Delia that made her giggle. Apá scolded them, "¡Ya!" And everything was quiet again, except for my mother's occasional sigh and quiet "Ay mamacita."

Soon my father's loud snoring started. "Now we'll never get to sleep," whispered Diamantina.

The morning arrived very quickly, cold and clear. As Delmira put on her socks, she knew that within half an hour they would be soaked and black and oozy with mud. She wanted to cry, but she fought the tears back inside. "I will *not* follow in my mother's footsteps. I swear that I will *not* marry a man who has dirt under his fingernails, and who drags me from field to field. No, señor, not me! I will get *out* of here, one way or another." She spit the words out since Apá had gone outside and couldn't hear. And she finished putting on her canvas sneakers, no longer sad, but mad. She ripped the waxed paper for the lunch tacos with a vengeance, *swearing* that she would get out of there.

She didn't say anything else. For today, she would go where Apá said. But soon . . . no.

We all got in the car without talking. This family never talked. Hard work, sadness, and silence.

When we got to the first field, the first thirty feet were a lake. "Vamos a hacerle la lucha. Nos vamos al pasito. We'll start on the other side," Apá said. Of the lake he meant. My father is stubborn and determined. "By this afternoon or tomorrow, it will dry and we can do this piece," he continued. We looked at the lake doubtfully.

But we didn't say anything. Like sleepwalkers we marched around the lake, but there was nowhere to step that wasn't muddy. The feet sunk in. And when you pulled them out, they came out covered with heavy clay. After two or three steps, each foot was heavy with several pounds of mud. And it wouldn't come off, no matter how hard you shook the foot, it stuck like a gigantic piece of black chewing gum. We walked as if we had heavy black boots. Gangly birds with heavy, ungainly feet.

"Look at me! I'm wearing high heels!" Delia said as she lifted one shoe and then the other to show us the clumps under her heels.

The first bite of the hoe into the clay had the same result. The hoe came out heavy with a sticky mud mass.

Don Panchito had the rows next to ours and he asked: "What do you think, Compadre? It looks to me like it's still too wet."

Apá, not wanting to stop, but seeing it was useless, said: "Yes, it looks like . . . Yes, let's go to another field to see if it's better. Let's go!"

And again around the lake to the car. Delmira looked down at her black, soaked feet and swore to herself again.

There was another family putting their hoes into the truck. Apá said he remembered the man from last year. He had said, "Yo ya no vuelvo aquí, ni de rey!" (I am never coming back here, not even if they make me king!)

"So, did they make you king?" Apá yelled over at him. The man grinned sheepishly and waved at Apá without saying anything.

When we got back to the car everyone tried to get the mud off their shoes with the blade of the hoe. But of course only the largest pieces came off. All day we went around with ruined shoes and black, wrinkled toes inside. In Pearsall we would be ashamed, but here everyone was in the same condition.

We got to the next field. Delmira, not being able to help herself, said, "¡Ay, Luis! It's the same!" My father said nothing, just opened the trunk and started taking out hoes. We knew then that we'd stay there, no matter what the conditions.

That afternoon the rains came back with a vengeance. We were forced to go home again. Two days later, the sun finally shone down from a cloudless blue sky on a lovely summer day, with lots of fresh, cool breezes. It had rained so much that for the next day or two there could be no work until the fields dried somewhat. Apá packed some supplies and took Rudy to fish at the Red River. The rest of us spent the day doing laundry, resting, and being with friends.

When it started to be dusk, my mother said, "Ay, why doesn't that old man come home!" And she put on her worried face. We kids, we didn't say anything. She started to make tortillas.

While she washed dishes after dinner, her worry infected all of us. Delmira rinsed and Delia dried. Conversation ceased. No one wanted to talk or hear talking; all we wanted to hear was the sound of the car coming and my father's voice. But there was only silence.

She kept cleaning, cleaning, cleaning. We were stiff, waiting. And what if they're drowned? Maybe the current was too strong after the heavy rains and it took them. They crashed while passing someone on the two-lane highway and they're lying bloody in the hospital.

A crack of thunder made us jump. Lightning flashed through the windows. Yet another summer storm. When we heard the first big raindrops, Amá started to cry. The storm gathered fury and started to blow rain sideways into the door. Luis rushed to close it. Our fear switched from concern for Apá and Rudy to Amá. Our noses quivered and we started shaking because we could smell the anxiety and knew what was coming.

Trastornada. That was the word for Amá's malady. And it would strike fear in all our hearts. It would fell us like the swing of the machete. My mother was the only person in my short life that I had seen trastornada. What an awful, terrifying word. I thought she was going to die, and full of fear, I wanted to die too.

The first signal was that she wet a washcloth and draped it on the back of her neck. Then she got out the bottle of rubbing alcohol and smelled it . . . inhaled it as if the fumes could save her from what was coming. And then she got the way we had all been terrified she'd get. The screams from the bottom of her soul started. "¡Ay! . . . ¡Ay! . . . ¡Ay mamá! . . . ¡Ay mamacita!" Each scream took a piece out of each of us. She fell backwards on the bed where she had been sitting, giving up her sanity. We all ran to the bed, wanting to save her from the abyss she was falling into.

Horrified, we watched the familiar process. Her left side got hard, hard, with her arm and her leg extended. Then she started to scream crazy things: "CALL YOUR FATHER! . . . WHERE IS ALFREDO? WHY DOESN'T HE COME! TELL ALL THESE PEOPLE TO GO AWAY!!!"

Well, there weren't any people there besides us, but there soon would be. Her screams would call the entire migrant camp, as they had drawn the neighborhood in Pearsall.

We, crazy too by now, rushed to assure her that my father would come soon, that her brother, Alfredo, was in Texas, not here, and that yes, we would get rid of all these people.

Her moans continued: "Ay . . . ay . . . AIEEE!!! My arm hurts A LOT!!!"

My sister, fighting with her tears, massaged Amá's stiff arm and her tight fist that she could not open.

And then the people started arriving. The comadres and the neighbors. The screams called them, even through the thunder, the lightning, and the rain. "What is happening to you?" they asked with their foreheads and eyebrows all knotted up.

"Pues, Amá . . . está trastornada. Apá went fishing and he hasn't returned." So the comadres started to make manzanilla tea to calm her. We let them, even though we knew that they would never be able to pry her jaws open.

Others prayed softly at a respectful distance from the bed. But Amá didn't know about anything. She had loosened her hold on the world and was in her own private hell. No one could reach her. She continued with her deep sighs and moans. My sisters and I were crying, especially me. I made myself into a little ball on one of the other beds and cried into my knees. They tried to comfort me, but how could they? My father lost and my mother dying across the room.

It seemed to continue like this for hours. Outside, the men made a big fire when the rain stopped. They wanted to be close to the house, where their women were keeping watch. Outside they could smoke their cigarettes.

By the time my father and brother finally got home, my mother seemed no longer connected with this world. Even though she was still breathing, she seemed dead to us. She didn't move or speak or respond in any way. My father was embarrassed with so many people in his house and his wife so sick . . . all because of him. He went directly to my mother, through the people. We were hardly moving, but following him with our eyes. Ours was a wait-and-see kind of family, not the kind that rushed to embrace each other. "¿Pos qué tienes, mujer? I'm here. There's nothing wrong with me. Come on, get up." And my mother was like a dead person.

My tears dried and I started to hate him. How could he come so late, so full of life and beer—and my mother in so much pain? It was all his fault, and my brother's too, with all his fish on the line.

Amá didn't wake up, but pretty soon her arm and her leg became normal again. She opened the hand that had been frozen in a fist for hours. Then we knew that she had gone to sleep and was resting.

The people started to take their leave. Sunrise would come very soon. The men doused the fire outside and we finally closed the door with only our family inside. Everyone started to go to bed. When the last light went out, all the fear came back. What if she died in the night, alone, without us knowing? All I wanted to hear was her soft breath, in and out, in and out. I strained to hear it among all the rustling noises everyone made while they were getting settled for bed. When my father started his heavy beer breath snoring, I hated him again. If she died, it would be he who had killed her.

In the morning, my mother got up before everyone else and started making tortilla dough and lighting the stove, as always. I heard her from my bed in the new light of the morning telling my sister Delia that her left arm, hand, and leg were very sore, but she didn't know why. My sister told her she had been muy trastornada. "Pos, I don't remember," she said. "Good," I said softly to myself smiling. God had given me my mother back.

Chapter Four

*De músico, poeta y loco todos tenemos
un poco.*

Of musician, poet, and madman, we each
have a little.
(Mexican dicho)

We survived a second summer in Minnesota and Wisconsin. The smell of eggs frying in bacon grease woke me at Tío Alfredo's. When I opened my eyes just a little, I was met by the unpainted floorboards in the pre-dawn light. I was home.

The pre-dawn morning was the coolest part of the day in the September heat of Texas. My body felt cool in a damp sort of way. I lay on my side with my eyes open and listened. Tío Alfredo told Apá that they still needed help for the harvests. He could start that day. Amá said nothing, but I knew she was there with them because I could hear her rolling tortillas. One of my sisters padded down the hall in her bare feet and stepped over my pallet on the floor on her way to the outhouse. Rudy got up and went to wash his face at the backyard faucet. I got up and peered into the kitchen.

"Wash your face and get dressed," Apá said when he saw me. It annoyed him particularly for people to go around in their night-clothes with unwashed faces. I obeyed.

My uncle and aunt came to visit us that same night. Tía Nina and Tío Nides lived only three blocks from Tío Alfredo's house where we continued to live. The two families visited each other almost daily. Nina was my mother's youngest sister and Nides was my father's youngest brother. They married several years before my parents did. Some things about Nina weren't talked about when she was around. My mother wasn't much for telling stories, but she had a shoe box full of old pictures inherited from her mother, and some of them had long stories behind them.

There was the picture of Tío Leonardo's general store in Uvalde. Nina eloped from there when she was nineteen to get away from the ironing, the washing, and the control. They were visiting Leonardo and Sofía in Uvalde and she never came back when Doña María sent her to get sugar and coffee. She had arranged to meet Lionides "Nides" Treviño there. When my grandmother, Doña María, found out what Nina had done, she declared she had one less daughter and went back to the dress she was working on for Sofía.

As soon as Doña María went back to Pearsall, Don Manuel, as the patriarch of the Treviño family, came to call on her. He politely begged her to accept Nina and Lionides as her married children. Although she had received him as politely as he had come, she stood up and said she didn't know what he was talking about and went in the back yard to weed her zinnias. He left quietly.

Several years later, Lionides and Nina were allowed back in Doña María's home as if nothing had happened. It was never spoken of again, except as a joke, and never in Doña María's presence.

Another picture showed Nina attempting to look glamorous as she reclined on a large rock at the edge of the ocean. Nina and Lionides had wanted a child very badly. But for ten years, none came. The tenth year, God gave them prosperity instead. Lionides harvested a bumper crop in the peanut fields. They made so much money that they decided to go to Mexico City to fulfill a promesa and then to Acapulco for a month.

Nina had made a bargain with La Virgen de Guadalupe, whose picture was pasted on a holy candle. Nina promised to go to the Basílica de La Virgen de Guadalupe in Mexico City and go thirty yards on her knees, from the entrance gate all the way to the door of the church, in return for the Virgen making her pregnant. This was after years of spells, teas, curanderos, and little powders that she sprinkled under her bed and around her house to no avail.

The promesa had been made and sealed and both sides kept their part of the covenant. Nina went to the basílica (she had the scarred knees to prove it) and then to Acapulco to reward herself. The baby was conceived there.

My mother got pregnant at the same time.

Nine months later, the labor pains came fast and strong for Nina. The baby was very large and didn't make it through the birth canal. A cesarean was performed and they practically tore her body apart to dislodge the dead baby. Nina almost died. A few days later, my mother delivered Rudy, her fifth and healthiest, lustiest child to date.

I've seen pictures of the tiny grave, with Lionides standing over it alone, his hat lowered over his eyes. The whole time I knew him, he always did what Nina said. His soul was buried with that baby.

Nina never got pregnant again. She would beg my mother to let her adopt one of us. Amá would waver, feeling sorry for her. She almost let her have Rudy, and then almost let her have me. But then she changed her mind, twice, at the last moment. She had even let Nina name me, at the hospital, in anticipation of the adoption. My mother had wanted to name me Diana, so that all four of her daughters would have names starting with the same letter: Delia, Delmira, Diamantina, and Diana. But after Nina named me, my mother wouldn't let me go.

Nina was lonely, so Amá let her take me home with her often. She had a collection of dolls I was allowed to play with. One hot summer day, she took my clothes off and filled a tub with water for me to play in. She and Lionides put it on top of an old rusty metal cot that they had in the backyard. Then she started hanging the laundry on the clothesline. I dropped one of the tin cans that I had been using to pour water over the side. Rather than call, I decided to fetch it myself. But my wet feet slipped on the way out. The rusty corner of the metal cot made a long, bloody gash between my legs as I fell to the dirt below. I screamed as the blood ran down my legs. Nina wrapped me in her apron and Nides drove us to Dr. O'Connor's clinic. After that I wouldn't stay with her anymore.

After Guadalupe failed her, she made promesas to the Virgen de los Lagos in the Texas valley. She had saints and candles all over the house. Her favorite was San Martín de Porras, the black-skinned saint. She called him "Martincito" familiarly, as if he was her saint alone.

The bane of her existence was her neighbor, who she was sure would send her curses and malice through the runners in the St. Augustine grass that connected the two yards. Nina was forced to pull up the grass and have a bare dirt yard to protect herself.

There were several kinds of curanderos in Pearsall, some of whom my mother trusted implicitly, much more than a doctor, and others whom she trusted not at all. The word curandero means healer, but some associated the word with magic, not all of it white. There was El Cieguito, who saw with his fingers. He could be trusted with any ailment of the bones or muscles. He could massage dislocations and strains away, or else tell you when he couldn't. Then there was Doña Tacha, who worked with prayer and herbs. She could be trusted. Then there was Manuelito in the next town over. People lined up outside his house to see him. To get to the consultation room, you had to go through a bedroom. People dropped their money in the center of the chenille bedspread. It was always piled high with coins and bills. He never charged. You paid according to what kind of cure or magic you expected. He doled out powders to sprinkle on your perpetrator's lawn at midnight. This would return the evil he had sent you back to him and make him sick.

Then there was the kind of curandero that worked with owl feathers and wild rabbit livers in the light of the new moon. Amá would never go near this kind of curandero. But Nina did.

We wouldn't go but Nina brought the curandero's magic to us. My mother submitted me, doubting every minute that it would work, to Nina's ministrations for the mal de ojo. The symptoms of evil eye disease were fever, chills, and vomiting. She started by lighting holy candles to San Martincito. Then she prayed Padre Nuestros and Ave Marías while she passed a white chicken egg in her warm hand all over my body. I felt the warmth of her hand as she glided the egg over my shivering body. She seemed perfectly comfortable mixing the magic of the egg ritual with Catholic church prayers. I wondered what the Catholic priest would say about the egg ritual.

And yet I wanted it. I wanted her hands gliding over me and her soft voice intoning the familiar prayers. I didn't want it to be over. I felt healing happen through the attention.

When the prayers were finished, she broke the egg into a cup and threw away the shell. Then she broke one straw from the broom standing in the corner and made a simple stick cross. This she gently laid directly on top of the egg in the cup. Then she put the whole thing under the couch where I was lying.

By then I was drowsy under warm blankets. The healing had already started. It worked every time. The women retired to the other room to gossip and hope for the best. The cup holding the egg remained on the floor overnight, under the couch where I slept.

The next morning she greeted everyone at the door with lots of good news about how the patient was all better. She pulled the cup out with her eyes shining. Through the egg under the cross, the spirits had sent a message. The shape of the egg designs and the amount of congealment told her the extent of the disease and the possibility of cure. Everyone gasped at the egg congealed into a grotesque form that looked like an evil eye. This was a sure sign of a very bad mal de ojo and also of a profound cure. She interpreted the contours and colors. The patient was rosy-cheeked and fully recovered. Everyone left the room in awe of the healing and the mysteries of life.

Nina's wounds made her the family healer. The rest of us lived close to the earth, but fought the closeness, striving to keep it at arm's length. Tía Nina embraced it. When storm clouds gathered in the sky, she went in the back yard and cut the clouds with a butcher knife, to disperse them into the four directions while she prayed.

Nina fed us teas out of an herbarium in her kitchen cupboard. Manzanilla for stomach ailments, yerba buena for debilidad, anís for something else. We never learned her herbology, we just did what she said. She got her teas from the curanderos and from her friends. We drank whatever teas Nina said we should, not wanting to take any chances. She had kind of a reluctant confidence about the healing arts. A "somebody has to do it" determination.

In spite of all her tragedies, Nina was an uproarious laugher and an inveterate gossip. She had a habit of smoothing her hair over her ears as she listened to a particularly juicy piece of chisme. Family observers joked that this habit was to remove even the tiniest obstruction to hearing and remembering every detail of a piece of gossip.

Nine years after Nina's baby died, an out-of-town family friend came to visit her.

"I know a young woman who is in trouble," the friend said. "She is pregnant and cannot support a child. The child will need a mother and father." Nina said yes immediately, she would take the child. When the child was born, Nina went to the hospital and took the baby home, hours old.

I was three years old then. Tío Nides was my father's brother and Nina was my mother's sister. So Hilda, which I pronounced "ilda" in Spanish, became my double cousin. Everyone was crazy about this baby, especially the new parents. Soon, she had a wardrobe bigger than my whole family's. Her first Halloween, Nina spent days making Hilda an orange and black crepe paper dress, with crunchy ruffles everywhere, and a hat to match. Her disposable Halloween paper dress was more magnificent than any I had ever had. She was the adopted one, but I was the one who felt like an orphan.

Everyone felt sorry for Hilda as she was the only adopted child in our family. I wasn't allowed to fight with her the way normal cousins and siblings fight. "Pobrecita, she's adopted," was the excuse always given to protect her. She was possessive with her new toys. "Déjala, está chiquita." When she cried or acted out, her mother said "Está cansada, mijita," and the bratty behavior was excused by everyone present. Soon I began to refuse to play with her, watching her from a distance instead. She couldn't understand.

I got chicken pox. They propped me up in the bed in the living room and brought me ice cream. Princess for a day. Nina, Nides, and Hilda came to see me in Nides's prize Model T car. Everyone sat in a semicircle around the bed. I was the center of attention and Hilda the outsider for once. Amá, feeling prosperous since we had started going north every summer, had started collecting porcelain animal figurines, one to three inches high. She had them arranged on a starched white doily in the living room. Without warning, Hilda took a porcelain elephant and threw it at me. Incredibly, it struck the bridge of my nose, right between my eyes, and broke off a chip of bone. Everyone screamed while the blood streamed down my face. They bundled me into Nides's Model T Ford and took me straight to Dr. O'Connor's house. He patched me up and they brought me back and propped me up in the living room again. I decided never to forgive her.

She knew from the beginning that she was adopted, and that she would never have brothers or sisters. It was a wound that wouldn't heal for her. I had a big, noisy family, with lots of brothers and sisters and their friends. Amá was the first one visited when uncles and distant relatives came from out of town, maybe because we lived in the place where my grandmother had lived. Hilda loved the noisy camaraderie that went on at our house and hated her empty, cold one. So she was always making Nina spend as much time as possible at our house. I couldn't see her loneliness at being an only adopted child.

Later, I started telling myself that this was all temporary, and that in fact, I *was* adopted. Soon my real parents, who were rich and had missed me terribly, would come back to get me.

I thought I remembered what they were actually like. My real mother was very beautiful and elegant and always wore drop jewel earrings that glittered in the sun. My real father wore a dark suit at all hours of the day and a black hat, perched on his head at a rakish angle.

The details of their life grew and multiplied in my mind. They lived not in a two-story house like the ones I had always coveted, but in a three-story mansion with acres of rooms. I started looking for their car, which I was sure was a black and white Buick with white leather upholstery.

They only had one sorrow in their lives and that was that they had given me away. There was one detail of the story that my mind skirted around and wouldn't go very near to. And that was the reason they had given me away. Was it because I was too plain when they had hoped for a beautiful child like themselves? Maybe it was because they hadn't had time for me in their glamorous, world-traveling life.

No matter, whatever the original reason had been, they would come for me soon.

The Christmas after our second trip to Minnesota was the first one marked in any way by our family. Before this, Christmas had only been an occasion for my mother and sisters to go to La Misa de Gallo at the church. I heard stories about Santa Claus. He gave gifts at Christmas and he came down the chimney. I was very concerned that we had no chimney. We had no colored lights at our house and no Christmas tree—nothing to indicate to Santa Claus that we were important and he should stop here. They reassured me that we would leave the porch light on and that he would stop.

Because I was the youngest by seven years, and because we had been north and had a little money, I got presents. On Christmas Eve, they distracted me in the kitchen while my brother took a couple of things out of hiding and put them on the porch. Then everyone acted as if they heard noises and sleigh bells on the porch. They asked me to go out and look to see if it was Santa. I ran out and found a cardboard painted stove and a tin tea set. I felt bad to be the only one in the family who received presents that year.

The only time my birthday was celebrated in any way was when I was six. It was the last year we were at Tío Alfredo's house. I guess my mother felt sorry for me. We invited five friends and the four poor pachuco kids from across the street. She bought me a gray jumper with a pink poodle appliquéd on it. It was the first store-bought dress I had ever owned. Nina, who was famous for her skill at making wedding cakes, made the cake and we even had a piñata. The boy from across the street gave me a plastic pearl necklace and bracelet set. I was ashamed and embarrassed that they had spent that much money on me when they were so poor that they rarely wore shoes.

In the spring, Goyo Vargas, the mayordomo from the farm in Minnesota came to ask Apá if we would sign up to go north again. Of course we would go. As he had every other year, the mayordomo asked again if Apá would be willing to go in early May and stay till October. Apá answered as he did every other year after the first. We would go the day after school ended and we would return the day before school started. Apá told Goyo again how important it was to him that his children finish high school. Goyo smiled, shook his head at Apá's stubborn dreams, and agreed.

Chapter Five

La conversación es el pasto del alma.

Conversation is food for the soul.

(Mexican dicho)

We continued going to Minnesota and Wisconsin for several more years. In Minnesota, every day was the same. There were no Sundays, no holidays, no days off. Every day, sunup to sundown, was the same. Work all day, eat what you can, crash for the night. Do it again the next day.

Only rainy days or grocery days relieved the grinding work. My family never talked much; they just worked silently, doggedly. It seemed there wasn't much to talk about. The only subject we could all connect with was "remember when." The best was when Apá and Rudy went fishing after a rain because then we could tell stories about Apá, which we would never do in his presence. We told ourselves it was out of respect, but it was really out of fear.

"Remember when we lived at the Rancho and Apá punished us by making us kneel in the gravelly pebbles?" someone would ask. My ears would perk up. I loved to hear the stories and I would always pretend I had never heard them before. Luis supplied the facts—he could always remember facts—and he left the story line to the women.

"What's the worst thing that ever happened to you, Delmira?" I would prompt.

"The worst thing was when Apá tied my hands behind my back." Every time Delmira told this story, Delia looked as if she was going to cry, as if just the telling hurt her deeply.

I turned to Delia. "How about you, Delia, what's the worst for you?"

Amá jumped in. "The worst thing for me was living with my mother-in-law!" And we'd be off into the story.

Apá was a born storyteller, as his father was before him. Don Manuelito ("Welito Melito," as his grandchildren called him) would gather his many grandchildren around him to tell stories of his life in Mexico.

We had no TV and no radio. The only thing to do, and the only entertainment, was stories after dinner. My brothers, sisters, Amá, and Apá forgot the cares of the day on the evenings when we played "Remember when . . ." Their eyes would get bright and animated and the tiredness seemed to leave their muscles. The love and closeness in the room was like a warm sea in which we swam.

The bare bulb hanging from the brown cord was turned off. The firelight from the open door of the wood stove danced on the faces of the people I loved. It softened, somewhat, the pain that crossed their faces when they remembered something painful. I never wanted the evenings to end.

These are the stories as I remember them.

Apá was born on the sixth day of the twentieth century outside Villaldama in the Mexican state of Nuevo León. His family had lived there for generations. The records in the Villaldama church go back to 1780. He had five brothers and one sister. His parents were prosperous ranchers. They owned thousands of goats and hundreds of cattle. They had a string of horses that were all named, and each of the six sons had a favorite mount. Two of his older brothers, Tiburcio and Eulalio, wore holsters with guns at their hips.

My father went to school in Sabinas for only three years. He boarded in town with a childless couple. After that his parents let him come home to the ranch, where he could ride horses freely and spend the night on the mountainside with the goat shepherds.

Those years in Mexico were burned into his memory. He would tell us about riding from Villaldama to Sabinas with his father on their two favorite horses. It was after a rain and the river was swollen. He took off all his clothes and swam across, holding his horse by the reins. This was his favorite story, and so we let him tell it over and over.

His supply of stories was endless.

Los melones. There was a flood and the cantaloupe field washed into the swollen river. My father and his friends were diving for melons. Apá dove and grabbed what he thought were two melon vines. He surfaced with a snake in each hand. Adding insult to injury, his mother beat him for endangering himself that way.

El arroz. The parents had gone to Lampasos to buy more horses. Apá and Tío Manuel planned to surprise them by having dinner ready. They started up the fire outside, as their mother always did. They filled a pot with rice and put it on to boil. As it absorbed the water, it overflowed the pan, so they divided it into two pans. Then four pans. By the time the parents came home, all the pans were full of half-cooked rice. My father never ate rice again; he claimed it gave him a stomachache.

El clarín. A favorite recess activity at the school was to see who could get to the top of the mountain first. The boy with the trumpet always won. And he would announce his victory by belting out a song from the highest point. His eyes were indigo blue, the same as those of his eleven brothers.

Los chivos. A man came to buy a hundred goats from Apá's father. But this man could only count to ten, so after every ten goats, he would close the gate and add another stone to the counting pile. After the pile had ten stones, he was done with his purchase. Apá's mother kept the proceeds from the sale of livestock in a potato sack under the kitchen table.

They left it all one day in 1911 without even packing. Pancho Villa and his revolutionaries were conscripting young men to fight. The Villistas were sweeping the countryside quickly. My grandfather had three sons of draftable age, and he didn't want to lose them in a war. He left everything to save his sons and ran away to the United States with only his family for baggage. My father was eleven. They never returned.

Apá didn't marry until he was thirty-five. He had plenty of girlfriends, though. My mother would occasionally pull out an envelope of six black-and-white pictures of women. She had taken these out of his wallet when she married him.

There was one whose story I loved to hear. My father kept a "querida." This mistress had tuberculosis and everyone knew she would die soon. In the picture she was beautiful and elegant, dressed like the 1920s flapper that she was. She wore a hat and a long string of pearls. I wondered if my father had loved her—he must have—he stayed with her until she died at twenty-six. I tried to imagine their life together. She, knowing that she was dying and he knowing it, too. It was a racy love affair that the whole town talked about. I wondered if he could forget a love that had died in his arms that way. Perhaps my mother was only a substitute.

But no, he was trying to marry my mother while Petra was still alive. Petra must have been only a "querida," after all. I tried to get my mother to tell me more. But she would put the envelope away and suddenly get very busy doing something else, her face implacable.

Apá was fifty by the time I was born. By then he had become a respected señor and everyone called him Don Luis.

Amá, "La Chata," was born just outside of Pearsall at a farm on Tilden Road named Las Conchas. She was the fourth daughter in a family of nine. Her nickname was "Chata" because of her flat little nose. Her parents, María Vitorina Bazán and José María Pérez, came from Mexico. She came from Agualeguas and he from Mier in Tamaulipas. José María had come from a prosperous family that owned thousands of acres on both sides of the Texas/Mexico border. His father was the Mayor of Mier for many years and was a thirty-third-level Mason, the highest rank achievable. José María had been well educated in Laredo schools and his journal is sprinkled with passionate poetry: "the earth trembled eagerly as she walked over it . . ."

But José María was also a poker player. And the cards were against him more often than they were for him. His gambling losses included acreage, houses and money. By the time my mother came along, they were poor and humble and living as sharecroppers on a gringo's farm outside Pearsall. They had become the poor relations. My mother and her sister, Cidelia (Chela), were sent to school in Laredo for a couple of years. They stayed with their Tía Teresita, José María's sister, in her large, comfortable home. But they were lonely and missed the farm and their mother. They begged to come home. So after two years, they did.

When José María was on his deathbed with colon cancer, his siblings came to his bedside and closed the door. They told him that in life he had used more than his share of the family fortune. Now that he was facing death, the only honorable thing to do was to sign away any rights to the remaining family fortune. By the time they opened the door, he had signed, and he died soon after.

After this, the daughters took in washing and ironing. The sons worked on the farm. My mother and her brother Alfredo remained at home and remained single long after all their siblings were married and gone, well after my grandfather died. My mother cleaned and took in ironing. My grandmother cooked for three. Tío Alfredo worked on the farm and had lots of girlfriends.

My mother didn't marry until she was thirty. And even then she resisted it.

Apá called on my grandmother and said, "Doña María, I love your daughter, Chata, very much. But I don't think she loves me."

"What can I do?" my grandmother answered. After Apá left, my grandmother took my mother aside and said, "While Petra lives, don't marry him."

My mother looked away and sighed. She didn't want to get married. But people were starting to talk about how she was an old maid. "What people say" was very important to my mother.

When Petra died, my mother married him.

The judge came to my grandmother's house. Only my grandmother and two witnesses were present. After the wedding, Apá went home alone. Three days later Amá finally, reluctantly agreed to go with him.

He was still living with his parents in a two-room house. My mother was expected to work with him in the fields. The only work she had ever done for pay was to take in washing and ironing. She longed for the smell of soap and the steam from the clean clothes as she had ironed in her mother's house. The stage was set for the migrant fields.

My father's father, Don Manuelito, was gentle and kind. My mother quickly grew to love him. He would gather his grandchildren to him and tell them stories about Mexico and about fighting the Indians.

His wife, Doña Sarita, was a different story. Her reputation for being autocratic, caustic, and abrasive ranged far and wide. She had a loud voice and an even louder personality. When my mother and father came home from working in the fields, she would place a pan of food on the table and say, "Whoever doesn't like it, she can eat shit!" Well, my mother was the only "she" in the place. But she would bite back her tears and eat—and long for the freedom of her single days doing laundry with her mother.

My father kept none of the money that he and my mother made. He handed it all over to his mother, as a good Mexican son should. She would buy food and give my father an allowance; my mother got nothing. Later, she would complain bitterly to me that if she needed a pair of panties then, she had to ask her mother-in-law for money.

When my mother was to be delivered of my oldest sister, Delia, two years after her marriage, she went home to her mother for the birth. After the baby came, she declared that she would never again live at her mother-in-law's house. She never did. They went to pick cotton in Arizona instead. They continued going there to pick cotton when Delmira came. They took their own goat all the way there. It was a source of fresh milk for the two toddlers.

Then my father got a job as the foreman at the McKinley farm, forever after called "El Rancho" in our family. Apá was the resident sharecropper there. In return for his working on the farm, he was given a piece of land to work as he saw fit and $24 per week, plus Sunday off. This job came with a one-bedroom house on the property. They moved there and this became the house where the rest of us were born and where all our first memories were made.

My brothers and sisters became who they were at "El Rancho."

Delia has dark brown skin. The dark-skinned daughter in a Mexican family was always "La Prieta." The nickname of "the black one" was given in love. And each time they called her that, it was in a voice like a caress.

Delia and Delmira had two dresses each for school. Amá washed and ironed the two that they weren't wearing. Most of their clothes were hand-me-downs from the McKinleys' daughters.

Delia had to walk a long way to the school bus. She went alone until Amá discovered that the coyotes sometimes watched her from a distance. In a few years, all five of my siblings were walking to the bus stop together. The one-bedroom house now held a family of eight. But they were ashamed of the house they lived in. Once they told their friends that the McKinley farmhouse was our house. No way! the kids responded. So, one day they ran off the bus and into the McKinley farmhouse before the bus pulled away to prove their lie. My father punished them by making them kneel in the sharp, gravelly pebbles.

They had a dog named Ranger, who was playful with them and fierce to strangers. They had a pet pig too, but he disappeared suddenly. The kids were suspicious of what had happened to him, but of course Apá could not be questioned about it.

They all learned to swim there in the pila, the holding tank for the windmill, with a rope tied around their middle that my father held as they learned. Except Delia, who never lost her fear of the water, so she never learned to swim.

Tío Alfredo worked on the McKinley farm, too. They had an old radio from somewhere. On the nights when his favorite radio program was on, Tío Alfredo stayed to listen to "La Sombra" on the radio at night. They would turn off all the lights and crowd around the radio in the dark to make it scarier while they listened to "The Shadow."

Luis and Rudy played outside in the rain. We could see them from the screened porch frolicking in the mud and jumping in the puddles, looking joyful and free. I was in Delia's arms watching them, and my other sisters were watching from inside too. I begged to go out and play with them in the rain, but no. It wasn't seemly for girls to play that way.

In the fall, the mesquite trees dropped their brown bean pods streaked with red. All the kids were sent out with bowls and containers to collect them as food for the animals, the cow and the pig. The fat beans were extra sweet, and the kids ate them as they collected more.

To make butter, my mother put the cream in a jar with a lid. One of the kids walked around shaking the jar with both hands until it turned into butter. Amá made soap outside in a huge black cauldron, from lye and fat. It was a simple life.

To my father, Delia was a model Mexican daughter: obedient, gracious, and quiet. She was dependable. She mothered all of us after it all got to be too much for my mother.

Delmira was the free spirit in our family. Tío Alfredo nicknamed her "La Pongui" when she was a toddler because she was always climbing things.

Once when Delmira was three, my mother, father, Tío Leonides, and Tía Nina went to the county tax office, which is next to the fire station, to see about a tax bill. Nina and Amá were talking to Doña Rosa outside while Delia and Delmira ran around the parking lot. Doña Rosa had just walked to Pearsall from Derby, eight miles away, and had news of a deceased friend.

After a while, only Delia was there, quiet. They started calling for Delmira and they heard her faint voice from up above. She had easily climbed the fireman's three-story training platform and was standing on top, waving. My pregnant mother hyperventilated and almost passed out. While Doña Rosa ran in to get my father, Nina sweet-talked Delmira into sitting down on the eight-by-eight-foot platform and not moving. "No te muevas, Chulita, ay quédate, mi amor, no te muevas." She sat down happily, swinging her little legs off the side.

My father ran out and climbed up, trembling. Everyone else talked sweetly to her from the pavement below, begging her not to move. She clung to my father like a monkey as he brought her down.

She did it again back at the farm that same year, climbing up the ladder on the windmill and sitting on the tiny ledge by the turning wheel.

She loved her little athletic body. She moved it constantly, running, jumping, and climbing while she sucked two fingers on her right hand and pushed up her dress with her left to fondle her belly button. She felt connected this way.

My father thought this an embarrassing habit and yelled at her constantly to stop. She began to hide her habit, but wouldn't stop. The summer before she was to start school, my father had had enough.

He tied her hands behind her back with a short length of rope, against my mother's pleadings and tears. Delmira accepted it quietly, but inside she vowed not to let him win.

That night she tried to find a way to sleep, but there was none. On her stomach, on her side, on her back—all these ways hurt. She tried sitting, but then her neck would hurt. After many hours of my father's loud snoring, she finally felt beaten and started to cry, quietly. He had won. She felt my mother's hand on her in the dark, untying the knots. This made her heart break and she started to sob. My mother sat by her and held her until she got quiet. When Amá left, Delmira went to sleep sucking her two fingers and playing with her belly button, her nightdress pushed up.

In the morning Amá woke her as she gently retied the knots, apologizing as she did so with her downcast eyes.

When Apá untied her hands so she could have her breakfast, he noticed that the knots had changed, but he didn't say anything.

During the day, Delmira ran, jumped, and skipped, the same as always, with her newly handicapped body. When she fell, sluglike, Delia and Luis helped her get up. Delia would cry, but Delmira laughed at her own predicament—during the day.

It was only at night that she got desperate, feeling that she couldn't breathe. She would kick off all the covers and sneak out to the tiny screened porch where she would gulp big draughts of freedom air.

For three days, Apá and my mother fought over Delmira's little body. On the third day she was broken. Her fear of confinement overcame her spirit and the love of her body. She begged my father to take off the rope. She would never suck her fingers or play with her belly button again. She never did.

My father had won. She was ready for the first grade.

Luis, "El Prieto," was the first-born son. "El Baroncito," as they say in Mexico. A lot is expected of the oldest son in a Mexican family. He is expected to be everyone's favorite. And he was, until Rudy showed up, that is. Of all the family pictures, the fanciest one is of Luis's fourth birthday party. He is wearing a short-pants suit, complete with a tailored jacket, knee socks and dress shoes. He is standing proudly by his birthday cake with neatly parted hair. Rudy always complained that no such picture existed of him. In fact, no pictures of him existed at all until he got to school. In response to the family's expectations, Luis presented an outer bravado, but inside he was insecure.

Luis would wait up for my father to come home from the cantina, so he could get a pat on the back and say goodnight. One night when Luis was about five or six, my father came home hungry and in a particularly jovial mood. The dinner tortillas were gone, so he got some bologna out of the icebox. He would roll up a slice and eat it with salt. Luis, wanting to be like his father, kept eating rolled-up slices too. Amá got out of bed and yelled at my father for feeding Luis so much bologna so late at night, claiming it was bad for a child.

Sure enough, half an hour after they had gone to bed, Luis came to their bed to say he didn't feel well. When they turned on the light, my mother screamed. Luis's eyes were crossed. The scream woke everyone up, and all gathered around while my father tried to make him focus on things out of the corners of his eyes. His eyes wouldn't uncross.

They didn't wait for morning. They took him to the curandera in the wee hours.

Luis was used to curanderos. My mother had taken him often to an old blind man named "El Cieguito." His son led him around town by the arm. But he could see with his hands. And he knew everything about bones. Luis had dislocated his elbow, twice before, and "El Cieguito" had fixed it. He would feel the arm, gently all up and down, and then flex it all the way, popping it back into place and then massage it to take away the pain.

They got Doña Tacha out of bed apologetically. She was very old, and the creases in her brown face were so deep they looked like cuts. She looked at Luis and put more wood in her stove. Then she started heating two blankets over it. When they were almost too hot to touch, she spread them on a bed and told him to lie in the middle, quickly. She wrapped one side around him and under him, tightly. And then the other, until he looked like a tightly-wrapped tamal. "It's too hot!" he complained. "Do you want crossed eyes forever?" she countered. "Close your eyes!" she ordered. Then she started to pray over him. He wriggled uncomfortably and soon started to sweat profusely. She kept praying and pretty soon he began to relax. When the blankets were merely warm, their tightness started to feel like security. Doña Tacha's voice was soft and comforting. He went to sleep. She said a final prayer and gently guided my parents into her kitchen.

While she put on coffee, she let Amá and Apá talk about how all this had happened. They needed some healing too. She assured them that Luis would be fine. When they awoke him in an hour, he was.

Routine medical care, check-ups, and exams were not part of our growing up. A tooth with a too-large cavity was extracted, rather than filled, as this was cheaper. My mother had no concept of nutrition: we were totally free to eat or not eat whatever we wanted. Luis and Delmira played a game to see who could stare directly at the sun the longest. Luis always won.

When my father was a sharecropper at the McKinley farm, we had a cow. This was where all the milk and butter for the family came from. It was never enough. The cow was kept in a fenced-in pasture. All the kids took turns going to get it in the late afternoon to be milked. All the others would wait for it to be brought in and then follow my father, like chicks after the hen, to the barn. Each of the kids had a cup. Apá let them have the warm foam from the top of the milk bucket. It was all air and bubbles, but to them it was a daily treat.

All of this worked fine until it was Luis's turn to get the cow. His eyesight was failing badly and he was ashamed for anyone to know it. No one in our family wore glasses. At school he had to sit in the front row, even though his friends called him "lambiache!" Even then he had trouble focusing on the teacher's writing. For tests, the teachers wrote the questions on the board. He could kind of make out what they said. After he wrote an answer, he would reread the question. Looking up from his paper, his eyes focused differently and it would seem to say something else. Hurriedly he erased and rewrote. His papers were incomplete and had many erasures. Luis was quietly desperate.

So Luis had trouble finding the cow. His strategy was to walk the perimeter of the pasture quietly, hoping he would hear her. His ears became sharper and he would hear birds, insects, and the dirt crunching under his feet. But sometimes the cow would be maddeningly quiet. Sometimes he walked all the way around the perimeter, only to discover that she was right by the entrance gate. He would curse his blindness and his luck, wondering how long he could keep it a secret.

By the time Luis got his coke-bottle glasses, he had an undeserved reputation for being an awkward bungler. Rudy became the favorite son.

Diamantina was the little, pretty one. "La Bebé" was her nickname even after Rudy and I came along and she was no longer the baby. Her other nickname was "La Muñeca" because of her doll-like beauty. She was small and nervous.

She drank gasoline when she was old enough to know better and had to have her stomach pumped. She stuffed her nasal cavities with bits of tissues and my mother had a hard time getting them out. She always bit her nails below the growth line, making them bleed, and then she bit the inside of her lip.

She had elf ears to go with her small babyishness. They didn't curve at the top like normal human ears; they had flat, thin edges that made her look like a flower pixie fairy. She was ashamed of them, so she let her hair grow and was constantly reaching up into her hair, bending the edges of her ears, hoping they would develop a normal curve like ours. Only one did. The other is still a pixie elfin ear.

True to her elfin ears, she was a magical artist. She would take tiny multicolored lantana flowers that grew wild in our backyard and make necklaces and bracelets. I have never had jewelry that was more beautiful than those flower creations that she seemed to make so easily. When I tried to make them, they looked clumsy and crushed and wouldn't stay together. She had such a light touch that hers would look freshly picked even when she put them around my neck, finished.

She made rag dolls and rag doll clothes for me out of Amá's cloth-scrap box. She learned sewing from our maternal grandmother. Her perfectly straight seams had millions of tiny, exactly even stitches. And she was fast—she would go from an idea to a finished piece the same day. The clothes looked like real people's clothes instead of doll clothes. And the dolls' expressions that she sewed on seemed to have life in them.

She had a tea set made out of opaque glass. Each piece was a different color. There were pieces missing, but it was a treasure. The farmer's wife, Mrs. McKinley, had given it to her when her daughters no longer wanted it.

We would go behind the house and sit where the dirt was really sandy and soft. She would make perfectly round mud tortillas and serve them to me on a tiny red plate along with mud scrambled eggs. Then she would hand me a tiny coffee cup on a saucer with water and a little bit of mud (for coffee color) swirled in it. We would take tiny pretend bites and sips as we played "comadritas" and talked about the health of our babies. I loved being a guest at her tea parties.

Rudy's real name is Rudolfo, but no one ever called him that. Rudy was the "valiente" in the family, the Emiliano Zapata type of macho guy, even at six years old.

The Mexican kids had to sit at the back of the bus on the way to school. Delia, Delmira, Luis, and Diamantina had all accepted that this was the way it was. They were the first ones on the bus route. Every day, obediently, they sat in the back. One day, while all five of them were waiting at the bus stop, Rudy asked, "Why do we always have to sit at the back of the bus and the gringos get to sit at the front?" They looked at each other. That's just the way it was.

"I'm going to sit at the front," declared Rudy.

"If you're going to, then I am too," Delmira chimed in.

"You better not!" said Delia, the obedient one.

But as the bus was coming in sight, they convinced her that it had to be a team effort. The bus driver couldn't fight all of them.

Rudy was the first one in and he planted himself firmly in the first seat. The others, suddenly tentative, settled themselves around him. The bus driver saw what was happening. He put on the emergency brake and stood up. "What the hell are you doing here? Mexicans in the back! You know that!"

Rudy, with fire in his heart and in his eyes, said calmly but firmly, "If you want me to sit in the back, you'll have to pick me up and move me."

To the bus driver, and to all the others sitting tense and quiet, Rudy looked like a fierce dog poised to bite. Silence. Then, "Goddamn it! They don't pay me enough for this!" the bus driver yelled as he swung back in his seat and lurched the bus forward.

After that, they sat in the front every day. And no one said anything.

But Rudy had a soft spot. His parents.

My father had a few philandering episodes. My mother left him once before I was born and took all five children home to their grandmother. Rudy cried constantly, piteously, for his father. My mother claims that's the only reason she went back to my father—for Rudy.

After I was born, my mother got very sick several times. It looked to all of us as if she was going to die for sure. Then the three-year-old child that Rudy kept hidden inside himself would come out. And my big macho brother, who could physically handle whatever the world dished out, would cry like an inconsolable baby.

As for me, my mother was embarrassed when I was born. I was living proof that she still let my father part her legs, and she was ashamed. She had wanted the world to think that she was done with babies and with sex. Rudy was already seven years old. My mother was forty-five and my father was fifty when I was conceived.

My mother hoped fervently that her lack of periods was due to menopause. But it wasn't. It was me. She didn't tell anyone. She hid me under floppy house-dresses, sweaters, aprons, and continual plumpness. Amá is a good liar. When she brought me home from the hospital, my five siblings were shocked.

Amá was tired of babies at her breast. Instead, she turned me over, with baby bottles, to my sisters during the day. They played house with me and combed my hair like a doll. For a while. Then they got tired. My mother was already tired, doing the wash and cooking for eight. My sisters tell me that before I came, she used to sing while she was doing the wash. Her favorite song to sing was the corrido named "Santa Amalia" by Los Relámpagos del Norte. By the time I came, she no longer sang. She just did her work doggedly and sighed a lot.

My sisters fought for years as to whose turn it was to comb out my hair. "It's your turn; I did it last time!" My hair was long, curly, and full of tangles, hence my nickname "Greñas" (wild, matted hair). They would sometimes braid it into two braids. If they were feeling good, they would make Shirley Temple curls all around my head.

I grew up with a vague feeling of being unwanted and wondering if anyone could love a child like me. I spent much time feeling as though I bothered everyone; the only time I was all right was when I was alone. And I was alone a lot.

Chapter Six

Como me la toquen bailo.

I will dance to whatever music is played.

(Mexican dicho)

Miss Esther had been the first-grade teacher for my five siblings before me, and she was mine also. The first-grade teachers at the Westside School had quite a challenge, as almost all of the entering students spoke only Spanish. Bilingual education had not come to Pearsall.

We were segregated until I was in the fifth grade. Mexican children attended the Westside School and white children attended the Eastside School. Once a week or so, my family drove by the Eastside Elementary School when we went out to a farm that sold eggs. There was a green, grassy lawn all around the Eastside School. The playground of the Westside was bare red dirt and weeds. Down the street from my friend Margie's house, there used to be a one-room black school, but it was closed before we started school. There were only two or three elementary-school-age black children in town. They went to the Eastside School along with the white kids. In Pearsall, Mexicans came last.

The night before my first day in the first grade, Delmira warned me not to speak any Spanish. Since I spoke only three or four words of English, this meant I would mostly be silent. She told me that there was a pen on the playground labeled "pigs." She said this was the word for marranos in English. This was where they put the kids who spoke Spanish in school. I was normally a quiet child, anyway, so I knew I could handle this.

Miss Esther held up pictures cut out from magazines and picture books and we were to repeat what she said. "Cow." "Cat." "Bird." We repeated. Helen Keller's first word was "water." My first word in the class was "armadillo," as the pronunciations in English and Spanish are very much the same. We were communicating.

Gilbert sat next to me in his starched shirt and creased pants. He didn't speak English, either. He didn't make it to the chocolate milk break. He just sat there quietly in his slicked-down parted hair and then started sobbing when the yellow puddle spread from his chair to the floor. He was led away and I'm not sure what they did with him after that. Miss Esther came back to the room and took us on our first field trip to the bathrooms. With lots of hand motions she let us know that we were to raise our hands.

The Westside School sat by itself on a red, dusty city block. It was surrounded by red, dusty streets and a few mesquite trees. Only half of the playground was usable, as the other half was weedy and full of cardillos, burrs that stuck to your socks and made your fingers bleed when you pulled them out. So we stayed away from the weeds and played on the bare dirt part of the playground.

Our favorite game was "Ring." To play ring, you draw a big circle in the dirt with a rock, a circle big enough to hold half of the players. The other half of the players stand outside the ring. The object is for an "inside the ring" kid to run outside the ring, around the playground, and back into the ring without being touched by an "outside the ring" kid. As soon as you run out, however, they run after you. If they touch you, you have to freeze until a teammate also runs out and touches you. Then you are "unfrozen" and can run back inside the ring to safety.

This was a great game because it required no equipment—which we didn't have, anyway. We also played red rover and hopscotch, as these required no equipment, either. We drew the hopscotch rectangles on the bare dirt with a rock. The girls preferred to play la vieja Inez, but we could only play this out of earshot of the teachers, as we only knew how to play that game in Spanish.

At the end of first grade, our class was to participate in the May Fair at the high school. The boys were to be elves, the girls fairies, and we were to dance in a circle around the maypole while another group wound the ribbons. Miss Esther arranged us from the tallest to the smallest. As long as I can remember, I have always been the tallest in my peer group. She said I had to lead the dancers onto the field because I was the tallest. I didn't want to be the leader; I have never wanted to be the leader. She said I had to because I was the tallest.

Now that we were back in town from Minnesota, the back and forth visiting with the relatives started. My mother had eight siblings and my father had six. They were all married except for Tío Alfredo. Seven plus six is thirteen, and that doubled is twenty-six. So I had twenty-seven aunts and uncles that we visited or who visited us—to say nothing of the cousins—many of whom were much older than I and had children my age or older.

Tío Blas was the oldest of all. We visited him first since he was in a wheelchair. He was my father's oldest brother and he was already married with a child when they left Mexico in 1911. When I met him, he was a tiny, wizened old man with very black skin. He sat in his wheelchair in the middle of his grocery store and supervised all the goings-on and greeted the customers. He was Delmira's first employer, aside from the migrant fields. She worked in the meat market slicing bologna and grinding hamburger. Once, when she nicked her finger, Tío Blas paid her extra.

The first weekend we were back in town, we went to San Antonio to buy school things for my brothers and sisters. After shopping, we stayed with one of our city relatives, Tía Chela. She and Tío Emilio rented a house in San Antonio. They paid the rent for fifty years until they died and the house was torn down to make room for a freeway. I don't know what Tío Emilio did for a living. He was retired by the time I knew him. He mopped the porch with the blackest, dirtiest water I ever saw. His skin was dark too, almost black, not brown like ours. He had diabetes and eventually his toes turned black—really black, from lack of circulation. He died soon after.

Tía Chela was the whitest member of our family. Her skin was almost chalk-white. My mother, ever a prankster, replaced her face powder with White Wings tortilla flour and then watched while Tía Chela rubbed it carefully on her face with a powder puff after her bath. "Ay, why is this powder so thick?" Tía Chela started saying as Amá dissolved into gales of laughter.

Along with Tía Nina, Tía Chela was a big believer in curanderas. She was always convinced that people were trying to do her in with evil spells. If she found powder sprinkled somewhere it wasn't supposed to be, she became convinced that it had been sprinkled by an evil person along with a harmful spell.

That night, Delmira got up in the middle of the night to go to the bathroom. When she opened the door she saw a huge red chile on the floor, stuck all over with straight pins, surrounded by burning candles. She stifled a scream, went back to bed, and held it all night. In the morning, everybody was acting normal. So she went back to the bathroom to check. No chiles or candles, but a few drops of candle wax from when the candles had been blown out, so she knew she hadn't been dreaming.

My sisters tell me that Amá used to sing. But she had stopped by the time I was born. I only heard her sing once, at Tía Chela's house in San Antonio. My mother let me sit on her lap even when I was quite big. She didn't really gather me to her, just indulged me. She sat with me on Tía Chela's front porch glider. She let me sit on her ample lap and she sang to me as she worked the glider with her feet, her big arms around me. She sang "Las mañanitas."

As she sang, I felt her love and her warmth and her matter-of-fact caring about me. That's the way my mother's love for me was, matter-of-fact. But it was O.K. It was always there. A secure place that I could depend on. She wouldn't volunteer it, but I could always get it, if I went to her. Her bosom felt close and sweet.

As she continued her song, her thoughts seemed to take her far away. I wondered if she was imagining the life she had dreamed of as a girl. Perhaps of the young man from Uvalde that had given her the ring that she had recently showed me, pulling it out reverently from the bottom of a trunk, where it was wrapped in a soft cotton cloth. He had insisted she keep the ring even though she had turned down his proposal. How different her life might have been.

She unconsciously held me tighter and closer as her thoughts got further and further away. I enjoyed the closeness, the warmth of her, and the singing, even though she was far away, not really there with me. It was so rare that I got her all to myself.

The song ended and she was quiet and still far away. Only the creaking of the glider now. I closed my eyes, wanting to stay in the moment and feel everything. My cheek on my mother's breast, her arms around me, the warmth of her body, and the strains of the song still lingering in the air. I wondered how much time my sisters had gotten with her like that.

She came back to the present moment and seemed surprised at finding me, quiet in her lap. She giggled a little, feeling silly at the singing and the musings, I guess. Both were unusual for her— a rare luxury. I loved my mother giggling and happy, her face open to me.

One day that next spring, Amá sent me to buy shampoo at Danchack's in downtown Pearsall. Washing our hair with real shampoo instead of soap was one of the few luxuries Amá indulged us with.

I walked behind Tío Alfredo's house and crossed the alley. Then I walked through Lenita's yard; she never minded. Across the dirt street from her house was the wide, empty space on the side of the railroad tracks. There was a trail through the tall weeds, mesquite trees and chaparro prieto that grew in this empty lot. The weeds on either side of the trail were so tall that they hid me completely. But the path was well worn. It wound around the trees and bigger bushes.

At the end of the path were the railroad tracks, the dividing line between the Mexican side and the white-owned stores of the gringo downtown. I could see the train coming, but it was far enough away that I could run across safely. I walked one more block parallel to the railroad tracks. At the end of the block, I could see one of the men walking toward me that usually hung out at the Danchack's corner, the only corner in town that had a traffic light. I don't know what this man's name was, but he didn't seem to have all his marbles. He was tall, ungainly, and unkempt, and one of his eyes was always half shut. His hands and face were dirty, so I couldn't tell if he was Mexican or white.

As I got closer, he turned to look at me with his half-shut eye. I didn't like walking by him, but he was directly in the path to where I was going. I approached with downcast eyes. By the time I looked up he was handling and waving his purple, erect penis at me. I froze and tried to scream, but my throat felt as if it was full of molasses. I fell on the sidewalk as I tried to turn around, as my body didn't seem to be working. I got up and ran toward home.

The train was stopped on the tracks. I violated my mother's cardinal rule about going downtown. I scrambled under it to the other side just in time before it lurched forward. Once the train was moving, I knew he couldn't get me and I turned around to look. I could see his pant legs and his old, dusty shoes on the other side, through the turning wheel of the train. As the train picked up speed, I crawled into the weeds away from the path and crouched down to hide myself. Then I let myself cry. No one heard me above the noise of the train.

When I saw the caboose coming, I ran home.

"Where's the shampoo?" Amá asked.

"I didn't go."

"Why not?"

"I saw a rattlesnake in the weeds." Then I started to sob again. Besides not crawling under the train, the other thing I was always to do on the way to downtown through the empty lot was to watch for rattlesnakes.

It was hard to eat my tacos that night. My eyes kept getting big of their own accord when I remembered it. That night I woke up screaming from the purple snakes crawling up my legs in my dreams. They bit me on my chest and face.

Amá decided I had suffered a susto from seeing the snake, so early the next morning she took me to Doña Tacha, the curandera, who knew how to cure people of fright. Amá claimed she didn't believe in curanderas, but for really bad diseases she bypassed doctors and got out the big guns. She went directly to Doña Tacha or to El Cieguito, two well-known healers. They always came through for her. Doña Tacha told Amá to bring me back at sunset. She would have everything ready by then.

She had lit candles in the corner, where she had the statue of the Nuestra Señora de Guadalupe. She asked me to stand there while she swept me with the broom from top to bottom and all around, over and over. While she swept, she chanted to the spirit that had entered my body. "Come, come, don't linger, come."

"Ahí voy," she said I had to respond, in response to each exhortation.

She enchanted it to come out, to depart my body and leave me in peace. Here in the presence of Nuestra Señora de Guadalupe, and being stroked by the broom and chanted to, the spirit departed. After a while, after much sweeping and chanting, I gave a deep, shuddering sigh, and began to relax.

Doña Tacha made a sign of the cross on herself and then on me. She laid the broom aside and continued brushing me, now with her hands only, to help me feel that my body was my own now. She gave my mother a little bag of herbs. This tea was to be cooked for me for the next nine nights and a cup given to me, along with the recitation of a Hail Mary at bedtime.

I felt my usual self again after a couple of days. I didn't want the foul-tasting tea anymore, but my mother made me drink it.

Chapter Seven

El que anda entre miel, algo se le pega.

If you hang around honey, some of it will
stick to you.

(Mexican dicho)

Kit. Corn-blond tight pigtails with pert little hairs sticking out
around her scalp. The smell of a sweaty white child. Her
hands short with stubby fingernails. Skin so foreign to me. I had
never observed a white child up close before. Her blue-green
eyes fascinated me. I felt as if they were drawing me forward
until I had to use my toes to keep from falling into her face. She
had a few freckles—only enough to suggest the blond children in
picture books. And always a rose color blooming through the
translucent skin of her cheeks.

I didn't dare touch her; I was content to smell her, to look at
her, and to listen to the sounds she made. I had never been close
enough to examine a white child's speech before. The sounds she
made were squeaky, not lilting like the Spanish of my playmates.

Strong. Her calves were tight. Her little hands and arms muscular; even her face and neck were clearly defined and muscular.

She would throw herself up on Star, the brown-and-white
pinto pony. Star was short and stocky and reliable. Kit matched
Star, but was lithe and fluid, too.

She invited me to ride with her. When she guided my hands
and put them firmly around her waist, I was shocked at the
nearness. I had never been that close to another child of any
color or race. Her hair brushed my cheeks and her smell filled
my nostrils.

I loved riding bareback behind her on Star. Then I had to touch her.

Kit was the farmer's daughter and when we first came she wasn't allowed to play with the migrant children or to eat the migrant food. But she was fascinated by us and she loved our hot tortilla tacos, so she frequently disobeyed. Besides, she had no one else and she was lonely.

I felt sorry for her sometimes, an only child in that big house. Then sometimes I envied her, an only child in that big house.

She wasn't interested in me the first year. I was her age, but I spoke no English, so she preferred my eleven-year-old sister, who did. I tagged along behind them.

Once she did a really bad thing. She took us into her house when her mother had gone on an errand. This was strictly forbidden. She fed us white bread sandwiches and milk. She spilled the milk on the floor and wiped the floor with the dishcloth. My mother would have been horrified. Our dishcloth never touched the floor. Amazed, I thought she was a dirty child.

We heard her mother's car pull up. She begged us to hide upstairs. She took us through the living room, up the stairs and into her room. It was a picture book little girl's room, with ruffled curtains and dolls everywhere. She made us hide in her bedroom closet. I knew her mother wouldn't hurt us; she would just be mad at Kit. So I enjoyed the perfumy cedar smells in the closet and the feel of her soft clothes and frilly dresses. I liked being in the dark snuggled up to my sister. I could feel that she was scared and maybe annoyed with Kit.

We heard muffled voices and after a little while Kit sneaked us out the side door. Diamantina would never play with her after that.

Delmira baby-sat Kit when her parents went out for the evening. They paid her, even though she would have done it for free, just for the experience of being surrounded by all that clean luxury for the evening. She didn't let herself go to sleep, since she had a job to do. The next morning she was extra tired going to the fields at dawn.

Kit came to our front door riding Star at dinnertime. It seemed Star brought her from another world. She would beg for my mother's food. The smells of cumin, garlic, and hot tortillas filled the space around our stop-sign shaped house.

"Smells good. What is it?" she would ask tentatively.

"Tortillas and papas guisadas, and beans too," Rudy would answer arrogantly.

"Can I have some?"

"I thought you weren't supposed to eat our food."

"I'll hide it and eat it fast. They won't catch me."

"O.K."

She wouldn't stop with the first one; she would beg for more. Usually her dog, Tippy, would get a taste also. It made my parents laugh.

My parents would have beaten me black and blue if I had begged for food anywhere.

After the first year, she would invite me to ride Star with her. We always rode bareback, her dog running behind us. Sometimes with me behind her, hugging her waist, with her braids brushing against my face. Sometimes I would sit in front and grab Star's mane. Then she had the reins with her right hand and would grab my waist with her left. We would trot through the little stand of forest that surrounded the farm on two sides, dodging the low branches. She would whoop and holler and I would smile and laugh a lot. We still had no common language, but we felt comfortable together.

Star was a stocky brown-and-white pony, but I felt as if we were flying. I loved Kit's closeness and her oh-so-unfamiliar smell.

The other migrant children would watch us from a distance. I don't know why she picked me out. But I was glad she had. I guess she was lonely and needed me. I made her feel better.

The first time she invited me to ride, she pulled her pony over to me by the reins. With signs and grunts, she indicated that I should get on. I was not at all afraid of the pony, but I was afraid of her. Where would she take me? Would she be nice to me? Was it all right to touch her?

My father came and boosted me up on the pony. She climbed on in front of me. Her hair brushed against my face as she turned left and right. She urged me to hang on tightly by grabbing my hands with both of hers and placing them firmly around her waist. Then I knew it was all right. She liked me. I wasn't sure I liked her yet, and at this distance it was hard to decide. I let myself get swept along. She was in charge of me as a playmate, as her father was in charge of the migrants.

She trotted the pony. I liked it and giggled and hung on tighter. She giggled too as she leaned forward and urged the pony to go faster. My friend Gloria watched from the door of the migrant shack next to ours. I didn't want to look directly at her, not wanting to see the reproach in her eyes. Out of the corner of my eye, I could see her twirling a black curl from the tangled mass of them on top of her head, nervously, between two fingers and a thumb. If I turned to look at her, she would disappear inside immediately.

I suddenly remembered the hole in the knee of my pants and I became embarrassed. I tried to cover it with my hand, but it was impossible, since I had to use both hands to hang on.

I began to see that I had the advantage. I had lots of migrant children to play with. She was an only child, and there were no other white children her age for miles. She had a pony, but she wanted me. I had nothing to offer but companionship. She bought it with pony rides.

I let myself get comfortable and enjoy the ride. She felt me relax through her body, unavoidably flattened against hers. She giggled again and swung her body sideways, left and right, in a singsong manner. I held my head way back, avoiding her neck, which had little wispy hairs plastered down with sweat.

She turned the pony around and paraded us in front of my family, showing off. They laughed and Gloria disappeared inside her house. I didn't like it anymore. My shyness took over. I wanted to get off, but I didn't know how to tell her. I refused to speak to her in grunts and sign language.

So, mortified, I let her do as she would, turning my face from my family.

Once, after Kit and I had been friends for a while and her parents accepted it, I got invited to another farm. Our farm owner's brother had a farm close by. He had two children, a toddler named Junior and a three-year-old named Twyla. They invited me over there for the day to play with them. My parents reluctantly agreed.

Oh, to be a child named Twyla! Wanted, cherished, petted, who had never known deprivation in her life. Her every wish was granted. My mother had very little time or energy for me. She rose before everyone else and went to bed last. And in between, she worked doggedly with her head down. She spoke little except for little despairing exclamations occasionally that came out with a sigh: "Ay Dios mío." "Ay mamá." "Ay mamacita."

My father always demanded more of his children than seemed fair. He wanted us to keep up with him—strong, muscular, in the prime of his life, and we all skinny, overworked children. We tried; we wanted to be as strong as he wanted us to be.

The only one who succeeded was Rudy. Rudy was a small version of my father. Even at eleven years old, he would never stay behind, and it didn't seem to cost him anything, either. He would even work Diamantina's row backwards, so she could skip a piece and catch up to the rest of the family.

Diamantina was the smallest and the weakest. She would sometimes cry from the cold, the damp, and the exhaustion. Usually my father would help her, but once he yelled at her. "Crying doesn't help; working harder does. If you want to cry, go do it by yourself at the side of the field. We'll do your work." It shamed her into swallowing her tears and she kept up for the rest of the day. But it cost her. I heard her crying quietly that night after everyone else was asleep.

My mother never flagged, never showed her exhaustion. She would just quit talking. The rest of us didn't talk much, either. We all learned to be quiet then.

But that day was a holiday for me. I was to spend the day with Twyla and Junior. They picked me up early in the morning in their big, shiny car. Junior wanted to sit in my lap.

When we got there I tried to make myself useful, the way my father liked me best. The mother was making the beds, so I started making beds. My mother had taught me to strip the bed down to the bottom sheet so I could brush the bed with another sheet to get all the dirt off that people had taken to bed with them. Baths were a sometime luxury for us. The mother saw me doing this and said it was unnecessary, that all I had to do was smooth the bed-clothes down. There was no dirt at all here. I was upset. I had made my first mistake.

The beds were made with snow white sheets and downy, soft blankets. They felt like the two wild baby rabbits that Rudy had caught for me. The pillows were high. I loved making beds walking around on the soft carpet.

She did the dishes next. I cleared the table for her. I arranged the ketchup and the sugar bowl prettily in the middle of the table, on top of a trivet with roses on it. She said no, the table got cleared completely and wiped off. My second mistake.

The kids were pulling on me, so she told us to go play on the screened porch in the back. Twyla had everything. A doll house full of furniture and peopled with dolls and tiny babies in ruffles and lacy hats. We played happily while Junior pushed his tricycle around us. The porch was cool and partly sunny as the sunlight filtered through the surrounding trees.

They took me home late, but they never invited me back. I thought it must have been because of my mistakes. Maybe I had made more than two.

Gloria was another migrant child with a head full of tangled dark brown curls. Every year, her family stayed in the tiny two-room house next door to ours. She was my age, but she had a lot more responsibilities. She was the oldest daughter, and her mother, Cole, was pregnant every summer. That didn't stop Cole from going to the fields every day, and it fell to Gloria to baby-sit and feed all her little brothers and sisters. So she stayed home all day, something which my parents almost never let me do.

Once, when I was seven, they let me spend the day with Gloria and all her little brothers and sisters. They all had masses of curly, unkempt hair like hers. Her three-year-old sister, Yolanda, was a miniature version of Gloria, except that she was so small that she had to pull up a chair to the table to wash the dishes. Our favorite was Armando, the one-year-old baby. We had no dolls, but we had Armando. He was fat, cute, and happy. But when he got yelled at, he would make really pitiful looking pucheros (the sad, mouth-turned-down-at-the-corners look that children get right before they cry). He looked so cute and funny making pucheros that Gloria and I would take turns yelling at him and then hugging him to make him happy again and drying the tears on his long, black eyelashes. Yes, it was cruel, so we would make it up to him by giving him a piece of tortilla and rocking him on the bed. The adults would have been horrified, but there were no adults, just us kids.

Gloria had jobs that took most of the day. Washing the breakfast dishes, making lunch for all the little ones, and starting dinner for her mom and dad and older brother. She accepted it all with a certain cheerfulness. She took little breaks all during the day. And she taught the others how to change diapers and stand on a chair and stir the beans.

Kit was my white child friend, but Gloria had a white child friend in town. The families would occasionally go shopping in Moorhead, usually the day after a big rain, when the fields were impossible to work. The groceries were cheaper there than at the convenience store in Sabin, where the farm owner arranged for all the migrants to buy their food on credit. While grocery shopping, her family would let Gloria go to the tiny restaurant next door. Missy was the daughter of the restaurant owner, and she took a liking to Gloria. I was jealous; I wanted Gloria all to myself. But they became great friends, even though they saw each other rarely. They discovered that they had the same birthday.

One year Missy invited Gloria to have a birthday party together, to be held at the restaurant, of course. She told her to invite her migrant friends, too. To make it special, all the girls would either wear blue jeans or red pants. I crumpled up inside when she told me this. I had no red pants and my only pair of blue jeans had holes in it. I usually wore little dresses remade from my sisters' discards. Maybe if I starched and ironed my blue jeans . . . .

But my mother wouldn't hear of it, even though I cried and begged. She wouldn't have me in town with gringos while wearing pants with holes in them. I watched them drive away, Gloria radiant with happiness. I ran into the woods and cried all day, imagining them having cake and ice cream and laughing.

On a rare occasion we went to Fargo to spend the day. We had been migrants for four years, and we had become somewhat more prosperous. My brothers and sisters went to have a Coke at the restaurant. I stayed with Amá so she wouldn't be alone. We went to the 5&10 store to buy needles and thread.

Inside the store, I looked up to see a jacket displayed flat on the wall. It was a baby-blue color. It somehow represented everything I didn't have. It was frivolous. Anything that color was, of course, frivolous.

I had never begged for toys. But I needed that jacket and I would beg for it.

When I asked Amá, she said no, of course no, and hurried me to the counter to pay for the needles and thread.

"Can't we even look at it and try it on?" I begged.

"No! I said no!" she yelled as she grabbed my hand and pulled me out of the store. Outside, I let out a wail as she dragged me down the sidewalk. I wailed not just for the jacket, but for all the lack in my life. Things seemed so hard, and I was entitled to so little. My wailing that day was not that of a spoiled child— would that I had been spoiled! It was the wail of a broken heart.

My mother stopped and looked at me—straight into my eyes—still holding my hand. And she saw all the way into my heart. Sighing, she shook her head and led me back to the store.

There were no others on the rack. "It's the last one," the saleslady said. She took it down off the wall and I tried it on. The sleeves were just a tiny bit too short. I tried to hide this and pulled my arms in.

"The sleeves are a little short," my mother said.

"No! They're fine!" I said, too loudly, as my eyes filled with tears again. She shook her head again as she took out her slim purse.

She bought it for me and I am grateful to this day. I loved that jacket for years. I wore it until the sleeves barely covered my elbows. Baby blue. When I wore it, I felt rich, frivolous and wanted. Rare feelings indeed for me.

I didn't have any other real friends besides Gloria, even though there were lots of other children at the camp. But I did play with all of them. Kit was never comfortable with any of them but me. Sometimes when I was playing with them, she would beg me to play with her instead. I was really torn. With them, I could play in Spanish. Play our Mexican games like la vieja Inez or bebé leche. But if she resorted to crying along with begging, I would always go with her, feeling like a traitor. I would feel the eyes of all the other children at my back as I walked away.

There was a boy at the migrant camp who wanted to be my boyfriend. I was horrified, embarrassed, and indignant. How could he embarrass me that way! He was always calling to me from across the yard and I would pretend I didn't hear him. He always kept his distance. He would send messages with the other children that they would relay through giggles and laughs:

"Tell her I like her."

"Tell her I love her."

"Ask her if she'll sit with me on the big log."

"Ask her if she'll talk to me at the well."

Oh! If he would only stop!

I don't know whose son he was. I don't remember any other migrants having red hair and freckles. We called him La Mecha because of his unusual flame red hair.

He would watch me walk around the migrant camp. I could feel his eyes on me constantly. He decided he liked me. He decided he loved me. I decided I didn't.

There was a huge piece of corrugated metal tunnel, probably designed to be part of a slough someday. It was a huge thing, the kind they put under small bridges over creeks to let the water flow through. The migrant children liked to sit inside it, all in a row and facing the same way, and talk. It would echo a little, as if we were at the bottom of a well. He was shy, so he would sit at one end. I didn't like him, so I would sit at the other end. The other eight or nine children would sit in between. The game was that he would send a message by whispering it to the child next to him. It would ripple down the row, through the giggling three and four and five year olds. "Tell him I don't like him," "No! I won't sit next to him!" and "No, no, no! He can't kiss me!" would come back my replies. He would look downcast but determined, and he would watch me harder than ever for the rest of the day.

I felt sorry for him because he was different and looked more ragged and unkempt than the rest of us. Why did he have to pick me? Why couldn't he like someone else? But he had, and I had to suffer his love and attention.

I remember most of the children's parents, but he seemed to be kind of an orphan. Tousled, messy hair, and lots of pecas. Part of me felt sorry for him. But I could never let myself express it. He might take it as a gesture of love and press his advantage.

I was constantly aware of him. As soon as I left the front porch step, my inner radar told me where he was. I would look up and, sure enough, there he was waiting for me and looking at me, saying silent entreaties—soundless words and come-hither gestures.

It feels now as if we were older than everyone else. But I know for a fact that this is not true. I think I was wise beyond my years, however, and he was acting with me in ways that I hadn't experienced as a child.

He was lonely. And he never smiled. He was always alone. Always calling out to me. And I never went to him.

The last few years we went to Minnesota were my best years with Kit. We could talk easily, thanks to the Westside Elementary School in Pearsall. Her parents no longer resisted our friendship. Sometimes my father would let me spend the day with her, even though that meant that I wouldn't be available to bring the water bucket to them.

We spent the sun-filled days lying in the weeds, in the woods, talking while chewing sweet sprigs of tall, wild grass in our mouths. Star would be tied up nearby, also chewing the tall, wild grass.

That was the summer she got Jubilee. We had ridden Star together for years. She galloped up to our house. "Do you like her? Her name is Jubilee!" I looked up at Kit, her form a black silhouette against a brilliant white sky. Jubilee was a tall, shiny filly with rippling muscles and a dancing, swishing tail. She stood there tossing her mane and prancing her big hooves.

Yes, I liked her, I loved her, I wanted her. She was a magnificent animal, straight out of my wildest dreams. What I felt for her was the opposite of fear. I wanted to ride with her, to be one with her. Grabbing her mane while we went as fast as she wanted. And I knew she wanted to go fast. FREE!!! The racing gallop and the wind exhilarating us both.

"You ride Star," she said.

"I'll ride Jubilee," she said, as she galloped off down the dirt road, kicking up huge clods of dirt.

I looked at stocky, reliable Star. Plain, safe pony. Kit had turned the corner and I couldn't see her anymore. I wanted to go inside and close the door. I wanted to go eat hot tortillas and eggs and potatoes, my mother's food, to comfort me and drown this feeling of abject disappointment.

Again it was clear to me who was the migrant girl and who was the farmer's daughter. My heart wanted to gallop furiously into the wind. But I was stuck fast to the ground. I would only get to trot.

I promised myself that someday a Jubilee would be mine. He would be black and huge and powerful. And I would let him fly across the land as fast as he wanted. His name would be El Diablo! He would feel me trusting him and he would trust me back. I would feel his enormous muscles between my knees and I would tangle my hand in his mane. And we would fly together. Someday.

But for now I stood on the steps of our shack, Star waiting patiently for me. And I had a choice. I sighed and walked over to Star. I led him by the reins over to the steps so I could get on easily and jumped on. I pulled the reins to the right and trotted down the road after Kit.

I never got to ride Jubilee; I never even asked. And Kit was so thrilled with her that she never offered. We still had a lot of good times, and we invented a lot of new games, now that we both could ride.

There were no books in my childhood. But one magical summer in Minnesota, when I was six, I had the storyteller.

She was a young woman of sixteen or eighteen or maybe twenty-one. She didn't belong at the migrant camp.

I noticed her two weeks after we had gotten there. A new group of migrants had arrived the night before. In the morning, everyone was piling into the back of the truck with early morning groans and sighs and sad, sour faces.

She didn't fit. I was startled when I saw her. She was the only one who looked fully awake and alive even at 5:30 A.M. She had large brown eyes and glossy brown hair. Her skin was a rich, deep brown. She was "La Morenita" of the Mexican corridos in the flesh.

I was already sitting in the back of the truck when she climbed up the ladder. When she took me in with her brown eyes, I woke up suddenly. She came straight to me and laid both her hands on my head in a caress and said, "Preciosa."

I had a sudden, overpowering urge to cry. I felt an all-consuming love for me, and I was undeserving of this love. I felt a great sentimiento.

"My mother and I live upstairs in the two-story building," she said in a voice like little bells being caressed by the wind. "Come to my room after dinner and I'll tell you a story."

She touched the other children similarly. They woke up, too. My beauty's name was Marielena.

Her mother came up the ladder behind her into the truck, complaining and moaning like the other adults. We soon found out that she had no husband, which meant that Marielena had no father. Two women alone—that was hard here, and I felt sorry for them. They had been brought here by the kindness of Don Tiburcio, who worked on another farm.

Marielena's mother was short, ugly, and misshapen. How could that lovely creature who had touched me have come from this gnarled thing who seemed to have no soul? She seemed obsessed with two things: her blanket and her two-foot piece of tree trunk. Other people had blankets and tree trunks that they left in the back of the truck overnight, but she was overly possessive with hers. "Mi tronco, mi tronco, where is my tronco? Mi colcha, mi colcha, where is my colcha? She would fret in the mornings after people had moved her stuff around the night before. They were the two things that gave her comfort on the way to and from the fields. The mornings were frequently cold and dewy wet. The tree trunk meant she wouldn't have to sit on the floor, where her bad knees made it necessary for someone to help her get up. The blanket meant she could be warm for the ten to fifteen minutes it would take for the truck to get out to the field. She was a small woman who seemed of no consequence—laughable, really. But once we got there, she worked hard and determinedly, like everyone else.

All day I replayed the early-morning truck scene in my mind. Why had this young woman affected and touched me so? Why did I want to cry? When she had put her hands on my head, it felt like when my mother touched me in our rarest and closest loving moments. And I had never even seen her before today.

I looked for her all day in the groups of migrants. She wore faded jeans, an old shirt, and a garsolé hat just like all the other females, so it was a little hard to pick her out. When she and her mother would get close to the edge of the field where I was, I got as close as my shyness would let me.

Once she saw me and her face lit up with a smile. I felt as if the sun had just been turned on—for me. The love overwhelmed me again. It was too much. I ran back to the truck, my heart fluttering wildly. What was she that she could affect me this way?

The day seemed unbearably long. My solitary meditations left me no peace. I could only think about her. My family seemed tame and ordinary. I carried the water bucket and did my chores quietly and obediently. It seemed night would never come.

But it did.

I wolfed my dinner down. And then I waited anxiously, wanting to give her time to eat her dinner slowly. When I could wait no longer, I ran over there. The other children were already there. I cursed myself that they had been with her a moment more than I had.

She had spread a quilt and pillows on the floor. She wore a floor-length skirt and a rebozo. I wanted to touch her hair. There seemed to be a faint smell of flowers coming through the after-dinner smells.

She sat on the floor and drew another child and me to her. My breath caught and I wanted to cry again at her touch. Again the overwhelming feeling of not deserving this much love.

The other children crept closer to her.

While her mother did things quietly in the kitchen, we got quiet and she started.

"Ésta es la historia de 'La Gitana.' The tall gypsy woman walked out of the lake, her raven hair glittering wet in the early morning sun. She swirled around three times. The droplets flying all around her changed into diamonds as they fell. She picked them up and put them in a small red silk purse. All but one, that is. A fat, green frog swallowed the one she missed . . . "

I had never heard of princes, queens, fairies, giants, dragons, magicians, and rogues. She would take us to places we had never heard of or imagined. She made them real and transported us there in the circle of her embrace.

The quilt left the room and flew through the night sky. We rode an undulating magic carpet through the stars with the wind caressing our faces and our hair blowing behind us. She took us to faraway places, where we rode fast horses and magical beasts. It seemed she went on for hours, spinning one tale after another. We never wanted it to end.

All too soon, she would kiss us and send us home. No one in my experience had ever kissed me. We would stumble down the stairs and walk home, dreamy-eyed under the stars.

She wouldn't let us come every night. But she would call us to her often. Sometimes we sat under the big sycamore tree, where the summer night air and the moon and stars added to the magic. Her supply of stories seemed unlimited; I was sure that they came to her new and fully formed every time. She lived them with us.

She awoke my imagination. I didn't know other worlds existed besides my family world. I experienced my heart and soul being transported to the other side of the world while my small body remained at the migrant camp.

The only imagining I had ever done was with my doll made out of Rudy's old sock, onto which my mother sewed thread eyes and a red mouth. My sister Diamantina made a dress for her. This doll was interesting to me because it had parts of my family in it, but I never had the fascination with dolls and toys that the stories awoke in me. My brothers' cars and trucks had been short pieces of two-by-four wooden studs with bottle caps nailed on for wheels. My sisters had played house.

I grew to love those other worlds in a way that I had never loved my own.

She didn't come back the next summer or ever again. Was she working on another farm? Was the work too hard for her? I wished I could save her, save her for the world. I prayed that the world had been kind to her. I hoped that since I loved her so purely and since she was pure love, that my prayers would go straight to God through all the clouds and everything. She was a butterfly, more beautiful than the iridescent blue, green, and yellow dragonflies I loved so much. I prayed that her fragile wings hadn't been crushed by the hard work in the fields. Maybe her mother had been beautiful once; maybe she had been a storyteller. But the migrant fields had made her ugly and misshapen. Please God, save my storyteller.

I thought the flights of fancy that her stories took me on were now gone forever. I was doomed to living in this world.

But I was wrong. I found them again in books.

Now I'm the storyteller.

Her stories were grand, magnificent ones that expanded us so much that we hurt inside with a sweet, wild pain. Mine are little-girl stories, but I feel the same sweet, wild pain as I write them. I have no choice now but to write them. If I stopped, I would die.

She comes to me now in my night dreams and in my waking dreams. She smiles and touches my head again and calls me "Preciosa" in her voice like little bells in the wind. I am again overwhelmed with this love I don't deserve—could never deserve. She enfolds me in her magic and opens my heart, and another story comes out—fully formed.

They were locked in there all those years and I never knew. My days and years were dry and brittle. All the sweetness was locked up. Now I'm bathed in her tenderness and this allows me to feel the pain as I write the migrant stories—safely. So that experiencing my family's migrant days again as I write them doesn't destroy me. I am safe and deeply loved.

Chapter Eight

Querer es poder.

Where there's a will, there's a way.

(One of Apá's favorite dichos)

In September of 1958, when we came back to Pearsall from Minnesota and Wisconsin, we really had nowhere to go. My Tío Alfredo had gotten married. He and his new wife were settled in his house, so we couldn't go there, even though he asked us to.

Tía Nina's house was a tiny one-bedroom cube. In the back yard she had a one-room cuartito with broken windows where she did the wash. We chased out the pigeons that roosted there and moved in while we decided what to do next. My mother cleaned it up as best she could. Having lived in other people's houses, barns, and in migrant housing in various stages of decay and repair, it felt as though we could make a home out of anything.

One of the paradoxes of life is that when one becomes totally adept at living without something, then the universe rushes in to give you exactly that which you have learned to live without. Apá decided to take all the money he had saved and build a house that fall. He had owned a one-acre lot on the Mexican side of town for many years, but had never been able to build anything on it before. So he talked to my Tío Manuel about building us a house. Tío Manuel said it would take two thousand dollars in materials to build a two-bedroom house. His labor would be free. And with my father's and my brothers' after-school help, they could have it almost finished before the cold weather came. To add a third bedroom, my father decided to have his parents' old two-room house moved to our lot and joined to the new house. The two-room house became the kitchen and the third bedroom.

Building the house was a family affair. The boys were apprentice carpenters. There was an ancient, useless house on the property that had to be torn down, as it was mostly down anyway. The wood was saved for fires and every single old nail was to be straightened by Diamantina and me, using a hammer and a brick as a base, to be used again in building the new house.

My father thought all we needed in the new house were bedrooms and a kitchen. Tío Manuel convinced him to go with what he said was the current style, which was to have a living room and a dining room. Apá acquiesced, even though he thought it was an extravagant waste.

So it was all coming together. The new house was framed, and the two-room house was being moved. The movers had gotten it as far as the empty lot behind our house, where they had the twice-yearly fiestas.

Then I had the fight with Hilda.

Hilda was Tía Nina's adopted daughter who was three years younger than I. Nina's major goal in life seemed to be to keep Hilda happy. In their tiny cube of a house, they had an indoor bathroom—a rarity for us.

It was already dark, after dinner, and Apá had gone to the cantina. I got up to go to the bathroom and Hilda blocked my way. "It's my bathroom. You can't use it." It raised my mother's hackles and she told Hilda to let me by. "No!" she responded. Nina's hackles were raised too by now, but she wasn't saying anything. I pushed Hilda down and she started wailing. Nina rushed in like a mother wolf and gathered Hilda up.

"Get out of my house!" she yelled at my mother, "And take all your brats with you!" Hilda wailed louder as Nina yelled at us. What could we do? It wasn't our house. We left.

My mother took me by the hand and all of us walked out into the dark street. We looked like codornices (a mother quail followed by all her chicks in a line) going down the street. My mother didn't know where to go. It was our darkest time.

We followed her in shock, not knowing where to go, either. She started crying and we did too, desperately wishing Apá was there.

Finally, Rudy said we should go and stay at the two-room house, currently located on the fiesta grounds, behind where our new house was being built. Having no-where else to go, my mother agreed. We walked over there and climbed in. It was on wheels and still attached to the truck that was pulling it.

I don't know how my father found us that night, but he eventually did. We were all still awake, still in shock. He told us that we'd never have to worry about a home again—we'd have our own now.

The first day we moved in, I came home from school, took off my shoes and socks as usual, and went outside to explore. The first thing I discovered were cardillos, sharp burrs that grow on a weed that hugs the ground. They stuck to the bottoms of my bare feet and drew blood when I pulled them out.

Amá looked out the screen door and saw my bare feet. "Are you crazy, girl? There may be stray nails out there from the carpenters! And the place is full of mala mujer. Put some old shoes on!"

I hated shoes, having lived barefoot all my life except for school. But I had run into the "bad woman" weed before, and I didn't want to encounter it again. It was an innocent-looking weed, six inches tall, with soft-looking serrated leaves. But it burned like fire when it touched my skin. A patch around the touch burned for hours, then the skin got kind of numb and prickly for a day or so. I put shoes on reluctantly.

When I went outside again, Rudy had a horned toad by the tail. We called them horny toads. "Look at it from the side," he said. "If you look at it straight on, it'll spit blood in your eye and make you blind." I kept my distance and went on walking. I had a jar and a teaspoon and was looking for toritos. The sandy loam in our yard was many feet thick. When they dug the hole for our outhouse, the digger sliced through the soil as if it was butter. I found a place where the weeds were sparse and the topsoil was loose sand. Toritos leave pointers right to themselves. Instead of an anthill mound, they make an inverted cone into the ground. I took the teaspoon and dug under the center of the inverted cone. The ant lion came out of the sand to investigate. I brought the teaspoon really close to my face so I could see it up close. I collected six, leaving more in the dirt so I could find them later. Then I went and sat on the back steps just to look at them in my jar.

Our house was pier and beam construction, so there was a two-foot space between the ground and the bottom of the house. After a few weeks, a black widow spider set up housekeeping in the back corner. Her web made a triangle between the bottom of the house and the corner pier. She had chosen the remotest corner, as if she were shy or wanted to hide. But when I went to look at her, she hung on the underside of the web and showed off the scarlet hourglass that stood out brilliantly from her ebony abdomen. She was absolutely perfectly made. The hourglass looked as though it had been painted by the most careful draftsman, using blood-red paint. I never disturbed her, only looked.

When it rained, the angelitos came out. The tiny red velvet spiders only appeared when the ground was wet. My sister had worn a red velvet dress to midnight mass the previous Christmas. My little angelitos wore theirs year-round.

At night in the late spring, if I was lucky, I found luminescent green glowworms. I never touched the black widow spiders out of respect for the danger they represented. I never touched the glowworms either, but it was because they seemed strewn with fire and magic. Fascinated, I followed their lumbering progress as they lit their own way.

The wall of one of the cantinas by Tío Alfredo's house had been two stories tall, as it was part of the building that housed the Mexican movie theater. Many pigeons had roosted under the high eaves. Their cooing comforted me as I played outside. I loved to look at their soft gray colors, with shimmery pink highlights around their necks.

There was no place for birds at our new house on Dávila Street. No two-story eaves or Mulberry trees. No cooing of pigeons, mourning of doves, or squawking of urracas. Only the silent tijerinas scissoring their tails as they passed by us, flying high overhead.

The cold weather came early that year. The house was framed and enclosed and the sheet rock was up when we moved in, but we had no gas for heat or working plumbing. My father had lots of ideas that frequently didn't work. On cold nights, he took discarded two-by-four stubs and made a fire in a tub. Then he brought that into the house for warmth. The fire ate up all the oxygen in the house and my teenage sisters started fainting left and right. Then we either had to open the windows or take the fire back out. We mostly froze that winter.

We had a bathroom, but like the one at my uncle's house, it had no working plumbing. My sisters lied to their friends, keeping the door closed, and said it was broken and that's why we had to use the outhouse.

After the living room was painted, Tío Manuel took my mother to San Antonio and had her pick out linoleum and a set of living room furniture. It was his housewarming gift to us. The linoleum had big, pink, ferny designs and was really shiny. The couch was blue like the lakes in Wisconsin. It was actually two half-couches that could make one long couch or could be arranged the way Amá preferred it, with a corner table on two sides of the room. There was also a small swivel chair, upholstered in the same blue, to complete the room. The best part was two wall lamps that were frosted except for little clear stars all over them. We had gotten a little bit of the night sky that I loved so much. I sat on the little couch and marveled at how we could have all this. Every Saturday, all of the daughters waxed the floor with paste wax, even under the couches. And then we slid across it in our socks. We loved this work because the benefits were all for us.

We had a ghost in our new house on Dávila Street. Luis saw her one night, all dressed in white, and then Delmira saw her another night. I was sure it was Petra Dávila, Apá's tubercular mistress, come to see him, finally prosperous and settled with his family.

During recess at the Westside School, playing hopscotch and ring, I felt a million miles away from my family. And yet I could look up and see my mother sweeping our porch. The playground of the school was directly across Dávila Street from our new house.

The wind blew across the bare dirt playground of the school, across the street, and in through the screen door on our front porch. It drove my mother crazy that she couldn't stop the red sand from coming in and making a dull film on her shiny pink linoleum. She swept it constantly and railed loudly against the wind and the sand. I wished we could put up a wall to protect our new little house that we loved so much and wanted to keep shiny clean.

Amá reveled in being mistress of her own home. Gone were the days when she had to keep her own desires and personality in check because she lived in another woman's home.

The first spring after we moved into our new house, the Catholic church had a fiesta in our back yard. Well, not really in our back yard, it was really in the group of four empty lots that abutted our back yard. But to me, it felt like my back yard.

They started mowing the weeds several weeks before the fiesta. There weren't a lot of weeds since the area was used so heavily twice a year—once for the Diez y Seis de Septiembre to celebrate Mexican independence from Spain and once for the Cinco de Mayo, to celebrate a major battle in the fight for Mexican independence from France. The lots were mostly bare. The focal point of the fiesta was a large cement platform that was used for performances and dancing. At one end of this platform was a shed which was open on the side that faced the platform and was used for the musicians. In case it rained, the musical instruments would be safe. Surrounding the platform were low wooden benches for people to sit on to watch the dancers and per- formers. There was only one other tiny building, which had a walk-up window and was used as a concession stand. Besides these things, the lots were empty. But not for long.

People started building puestos about thirty feet back from the cement platform. These little restaurants and booths for games of chance formed a square around the platform. The effect was of three concentric squares: the inner square was the platform surrounded by benches and the bandstand, then the thirty-foot- wide empty space, and finally the puestos, surrounding everything. The puestos were frequently covered with canvas in case of rain. Multicolored streamers decorated everything. The fiesta ran for a week and a half—every night and during the day on weekends. There was a competing fiesta at the far end of town by the Buenos Aires Cantina. Some nights, we couldn't decide which one to go to first.

The first night of the fiesta, I couldn't wait for the sun to go down so the festivities could start. My father only gave me twenty-five cents because he said the fiesta would go for many more nights. As soon as the sun went down, I ran over there, but I was too early. The food sellers were unloading the cooked food from their cars and the people running the games of chance were arranging their prizes. I couldn't find any of my school friends, so I went back home through my back yard.

Standing between the newly-planted peach trees in my back yard, I could see when the parked cars and people arriving reached the point when it seemed a real fiesta. When the band started playing, I ran over there again. I found my friend Manuela and her two older sisters and we started the paseo. This meant walking in a circle around the platform on the thirty-foot-wide walkway. For the teenagers, this meant the girls walked in one direction and the boys in the other. Twice in every circle, they would meet each other and smile—or not smile and look the other way on purpose. This is the way initial courtship was done in Mexico at the central plaza of the town. But in Pearsall we had no plaza, only the fiesta twice a year.

Manuela and I ate "chili pie" for dinner. This was a small bag of corn chips with a scoop of chili beans poured inside which you could buy for fifteen cents. The adults had more interesting things like tamales or menudo. For dessert we had snow cones for five cents. I had a nickel left over, so we played manita. This was a game in which a board had a circle of nails driven in it and a wooden arrow, nailed in the middle, that you spun. Where it stopped determined your prize. Once in a while, we stopped to watch the couples dancing on the platform to the music of the band.

Then it was time for the performances to start. There was a group of kids who had been practicing their costumed dances for weeks. The girls wore colorful dresses with long skirts and the boys wore sequined jackets. Weeks before I had asked my mother to let me participate in this, but she wouldn't let me because the costumes were too expensive to make. The performers danced and paraded around the platform. A few chosen ones went to the microphone to give short speeches about the revolutionary heroes and their ideals. Each speech culminated with a shout of "¡He dicho!"

After the kids were done, the candidates for "La Reina" paraded around the platform in their evening gowns and danced with their escorts. For weeks we had been seeing glass jars with pictures of pretty girls pasted on them. These were at the checkout counters of every store in town. You voted for your favorite pretty girl with your money, each penny being a vote. The whole fiesta was a benefit for the Catholic church building fund. On the actual Cinco de Mayo night, La Reina was crowned with a rhinestone tiara.

My parents usually let me stay as late as I wanted, since it was just in my back yard. But my friend's parents took her home at ten o'clock, so I went home also. As I went to bed, I was reminded of how it used to be at Tío Alfredo's house, with the music from the cantinas on either side. Again I went to sleep to Mexican music, but now it came live from the fiesta in our back yard, the words and melodies imprinting themselves on my soul.

That spring my mother and sisters started planting plugs of St. Augustine grass at our new house which were harvested from the edges of my aunt's yard. They were hoping that this would keep the dust from blowing into the house so much. My father thought this a waste of time. He was only interested in planting, nurturing, and growing things that you could eat, and besides, he didn't mind dirt in the house. For much of his life, he had lived in dirtfloor houses.

My mother's friends also started giving her rose cuttings and geraniums to plant. My sisters wanted a boxwood hedge like the ones they had seen in books at school. This would help in keeping the blowing dust out also. The boxwood came from somewhere and we planted a boxwood hedge to form a border between our house and the street. Of all the things my mother planted that spring, the gardenia bush outside my sister's bedroom window was my favorite. It thrived and grew to be six feet tall. On the warm spring nights, the heady fragrance filled my sister's bedroom.

Since my father only planted things that you could eat, he started with pecan saplings spread all around the house to provide shade and nuts. Then he went on to citrus. We had grapefruit, lemon, and tangerine trees. Then a row of peach trees that went the 100-foot width of our property. These formed the border between the house (surrounded by newly planted trees already) and the half-acre vegetable garden. He also planted plum, pear, and fig trees. The figs were my favorite. Their dark, musky sweetness was the first of the summer fruit.

He worked the vegetable garden in the morning before he went to work and after six when he came home. He grew a bonanza of corn, tomatoes, squash, cucumbers, onions, garlic, and peppers. At the end of the season he dried seeds from the best produce and saved them. At the beginning of the next season he started the seeds in paper coffee cups full of dirt, then transplanted the strongest ones into the ground. The neighbors frequently came and offered to buy the produce.

The biggest heartache of my father's gardening was his inability to grow avocados. In his home town of Villaldama in northern Mexico, he went to sleep to the sound of the ripe avocados plop-plopping heavily onto the ground.

Avocados were contraband from Mexico into the U.S. But once my mother smuggled an avocado pit home in her handkerchief, in spite of her fear of the Federales (the name given to the Mexican army by the revolutionaries; to my mother, all men in uniform were Federales). My father planted this tiny piece of his homeland by the side of our house and tended it like a first-born son. He gave it black dirt from San Antonio and rainwater collected in barrels from the downspouts. When winter threatened, he made a frame house for it and covered it with plastic.

The avocado tree kept growing for him. He was sixty when he planted it. Avocado trees don't bear fruit for seven to eleven years from the date of planting. But my father was undaunted. He just kept taking care of it.

Pretty soon, the avocado tree got as tall as the house (in Mexico they get much taller). Now the frame house covered with plastic for winter protection got unwieldy, but he wouldn't give up. He talked his nephew, who worked for the county, into installing a telephone pole ten feet from the house. This served as the central pole from which to build his plastic tent to protect the tree.

One winter was particularly cold. He bought a used smudge-pot to put in the plastic house to provide additional heat at night. My mother ranted about how he would burn the house down. And she complained that he took better care of the avocado tree than he did of her.

The tree got monstrously huge, and still no avocados. He got lots of advice from friends: Drive a rusty nail into the trunk (this was to give it the iron it needed to make flowers), or use goat manure for fertilizer the way they do in Mexico.

The worst news he got was that some avocado trees were male, others female, and so a single avocado tree hundreds of miles from another one would never bear. This was disproved the following year.

It bore five huge, delicious avocados.

My mother, in her typical style, said it would have been cheaper and a lot less work to buy them at the Model Market in downtown Pearsall. This only dimmed my father's jubilation a little bit.

It never bore fruit again.

After five more years of mammoth cave-like plastic coverings for the tree (which my mother complained were an eyesore), my father let it freeze.

And then he cut it down, bitterly resigned to his separation from Villaldama.

After more than a year in our first house, it finally became familiar to me. I walked barefoot across the cool linoleum floor in our living room. It was shiny and smooth and my feet were slightly sandy with red Pearsall dirt.

Clutching a few nickels in my sweaty hand, I walked out through the front screen door, letting it slam since my father wasn't home from work yet. I was the youngest by far, so people were always giving me small change to buy candy.

Amá was making dinner in the kitchen. My homework finished, I decided second grade wasn't too bad, at least not the first week. I was going to Cande's store on the far corner of our block to get a treat.

The dirt of the sandy, unpaved street was hot under my feet, so I had to run from shady spot to shady spot. There wasn't much shade—a few telephone poles and some skinny trees. The sun burned into the part at the top of my head, where my hair, which had never been cut, was separated into two braids. I decided to buy a popsicle, too. I had enough nickels.

The sandy Pearsall dirt was very different from the Minnesota clay. The dirt never seemed as hot in Minnesota. I could pull up the shards that formed on top, as the dirt dried after a rainstorm, and find cool, wet clay underneath. Pearsall was just hot, unrelieved, red sand.

I went to Cande's store and let the screen door slam there, too. The floor in the store was cool, bare cement, dusty from the customers' feet. I let the coolness sink into my soles. It made me shiver slightly in the hot afternoon.

Cande came out from the back of the store, between the curtains that separated the store from the living quarters. I walked up to the big glass case and reviewed all the candy: Big Daddy caramel lollipops, sugar multicolored button dots, caramel Sugar Babies, jawbreakers, bubblegum—these were my familiar treats. I chose the candy first, letting the popsicle stay in its freezer case until the last minute. It would melt fast once it came out. I chose multicolored sugar button dots stuck on a roll of white paper, and bubblegum.

After giving Cande my coins, I put the candy in the pocket of my sundress and told her I wanted a grape popsicle, the kind that's two skinny popsicles stuck together. She handed it to me and I peeled back the paper. It was coated with frost only for a few seconds, then the heat of the day turned it to a glistening purple. I didn't separate the two halves of the popsicle because then it would melt faster. On my way out, I stood at the screen door and let my feet absorb the cement coolness for a few seconds before I walked out into the hot sand.

I ran out, biting the popsicle as I looked for the next cool place to put my feet. I could have worn my school shoes, but I preferred the feelings in my feet, as they were alternately cold, hot, sandy, and sweaty. As I stood in the shade of a telephone pole, I let the popsicle drip on them to make them even cooler. Then they were sticky too, with sweaty, sticky designs. Amá would make me wash them if she saw me.

It was only one long block to my house. I ran across the street to the final shady place before my house, the big mesquite tree at the edge of the Westside Elementary School yard. I sat in the shade of the mesquite tree to finish my popsicle, as it was melting fast and coming apart. As I worked on it, I noticed two young men walking down the street. They were going to pass right in front of me. They were pachucos. I looked for the bulge of long jackknives in their front pockets. They wore extra hair pomade and spoke their own brand of Mexican slang. They called policemen "la chota," and "¡ponte trucha!" meant "pay attention!" They were the kind of boys that dropped out of school early in Pearsall.

They didn't notice me; I was an insignificant urchin in their eyes. So I heard everything they said. They were talking about a woman who had overstepped her bounds. It wasn't clear from the conversation what she had done. What is clear is that they thought she was lower than dirt because she had forgotten she was a woman.

They called her "presumida."

I shuddered again in the cool shade. Their derision was so strong. In my mind's eye, I imagined the object of their contempt. I saw her standing presumptuously, saying loud arrogant words, her vanity obvious.

I wanted my father to like me. I wanted my brothers to like me.

Sitting at the base of the mesquite tree, I decided that no one would ever call me "presumida." I would never forget my place. I would be what the men in my life expected me to be: a poor Mexican girl who knew how to be quiet.

Long after they were out of earshot, I got up and walked back across the street into our yard. I went to the water faucet in the front corner of the yard and let the water run out of the attached hose until it wasn't too hot anymore. Then I washed my feet. I rubbed one foot against the other to get the dirty stickiness off. I pointed the hose straight up and drank out of it. I closed my eyes and squirted water all over my face to get the stickiness off there, too. Then I bent over and wet the top of my head a little. It's one of Amá's superstitions that if you wash your body in any way and you don't wet the top of your head, you'll get sick. I didn't believe it, but I did it anyway.

I sat on the edge of the cement porch to eat my candy dots, with my feet in the sandy dirt of our side yard, where there is no grass. My feet made little imprints in the sand.

By then, I could smell the garlic and cumin from my mother's dinner. It wafted out through the screen door. Tortillas too. I could hear her punching them down on the comal to get the bubbles out. I could hear it even through the ranchera music on the radio.

The candy dots tasted too sweet all of a sudden. My mouth watered for a hot tortilla with butter. I put the candy dots back in my pocket and brushed the dust off my feet before going in. My feet were always dusty. As long as I lived in Pearsall, my feet were always dusty.

Apá brought his distrust of the Catholic Church from Mexico. He would tell me bitterly that all priests were crooks. That the poor women got suckered by the priests into putting their last two cents in the collection plate rather than feeding their children. He had only set foot in the church three times: to be baptized as an infant, to get married to Amá, and to baptize his compadre's son Hugo. The marriage in the church was not by choice; Amá blackmailed him into getting married in the church long after their children were born. The church and cemetery rules in Pearsall said that good Catholics were buried inside the cemetery fence. Fallen Catholics who had broken the rules, or obvious sinners were buried outside the fence. The thought of being buried outside the fence terrified Amá, even though she would be dead by then.

So she threatened Apá. Either he was to make an honest woman out of her in the eyes of the church (they had been married by a justice of the peace originally) or she would tell us kids "the big secret." He drove her to the church and the priest married them in the afternoon—no witnesses, but duly entered in the church register. Now her place inside the cemetery fence was assured.

We never learned "the big secret." Delia was entrusted with it
and she is to tell us when Amá dies.

My father believed in God, absolutely, but not in the form
that the Catholic religion took. Amá was a lukewarm Catholic.
She really only believed in hard work—that was her credo. She
went to Mass on Christmas and Easter, and only occasionally during the year. She wanted it to appear that she was a believer and
a good Catholic, but the truth is that she preferred to stay home
on Sunday morning and make breakfast for her brother Alfredo,
who never missed a Sunday morning at my mother's table.

So when all my friends went to catechism after school, I went
to be social, not because I felt bound in any way to the church.
The nuns were all from Mexico and they wore floor-length navy
blue habits. They gave us holy cards and tiny statues of saints for
learning our prayers. I had a good memory, and I soon had a
cache of saints and holy cards that Amá displayed on a shelf hung
in the corner of the room. Mass was in Latin then. I soon memo-
rized all the appropriate Latin responses too, having no idea what
they meant. But the Padre Nuestro, the Ave María, and the songs
sprinkled in the middle were all in my childhood tongue. They
made my heart heavy with sweetness.

Children in Mexico are very much prized, loved, and respected. The nuns brought this attitude with them to Pearsall. They
taught in soft voices, which made the room full of second graders
listen quietly. I don't remember a single disciplinary action. Their
soft-spoken, kind manner drew me like a magnet. They had soft
hands and immaculately clean faces. The living room of the
house they lived in was shiny, clean, and spare. I loved the sparse-
ness; they seemed to require so little. I wanted to be around them
all the time.

Soon I started going to the rosary every evening. It was still
light at seven in the evening when they said the rosary, and the
church was only two blocks from my house. The church was so
clean, the wooden pews and floors polished to a bright luster by
the nuns. I knelt in the pew directly behind the sisters. They all
knelt in the same pew. To an outsider, they might look all the
same, but I recognized them even from the back. The Mother
Superior was slightly wider, not fat; none of them was fat. Sister

Teresita was the tallest and slimmest, and she had the softest voice of all. I liked her classes best. Sister Inocencia was the smallest and youngest, not much taller than the children. She always had a giggly smile on her dark brown face.

The rosary took so long that the whole church took on a golden glow for me. The nuns were all bathed in it. Kneeling the whole time made me tired and woozy in a strange way, bringing me close to fainting. I didn't resist this feeling of being on the edge of consciousness. It took me to a kind of ecstasy. I walked home feeling holy and pure, as I imagined the nuns felt all the time.

I joined the choir. We learned to sing the high mass in Latin for Christmas and Easter. If we wanted to receive Communion at midnight Mass, which of course we did, we had to fast before it. The empty stomach, the late hour, the clouds of incense, and the very long High Mass brought me as close to the edge of consciousness as I ever was. My thoughts would race; I could really have a lot of thoughts in a short space of real time. And there was heat, not sweaty external heat, but an intense heat that started way deep inside of me and radiated outward. Then the golden glow in the church got really strong and lasted a long time. I felt as if I could fly to heaven.

Church seemed a way to escape the common humanity of my family. But Apá didn't like this little papist in his house. My sisters were marginal Catholics like my mother. And my brothers, like my father, never went to church.

"¿Otra vez a la iglesia?" he asked as I tried to sneak out the door on my way to choir practice.

"Sí," I answered timidly, looking at my shoes.

"When you come back, you'd better help your mother wash the dishes."

"Bueno," and I'd hurry out the door, closing the screen door softly.

Then Amá had her hernia operation and was in the hospital for a couple of days. Minor, the doctor said. She was to come home Sunday morning. My regular Mass time was ten-thirty on Sunday morning. At ten, I was walking out of the house with my little circle veil on the top of my head for church. They pulled up in the yard with my mother, who was theoretically fine now.

When he got out of the car, Apá glared at me, angrier than I'd ever seen him, hating me really. "Is that church more important to you than your mother? Take that thing off and help me with your mother!" He spat the words out. I ripped the circle veil off my head and went to help Amá get in the house, my tears spilling out silently. We settled her in the bed and I was sent to get her a glass of water.

It was true. I loved God more than my mother.

Early morning noises, rattling pots and pans and voices in the kitchen floated through my early morning drowsiness. My father's footsteps coming to wake me.

"Levántate, hija."

"Sí, Apá."

I got dressed and sat down to scrambled eggs and hot tortillas. It was Saturday and it was washday.

Amá had the water boiling on the stove and Apá had made the fire outside under the huge black cauldron. I smelled the wood smoke. Amá carried water heated on the kitchen stove and dumped it into the cauldron. The fire under the cauldron kept it boiling. Then she put more on the stove to boil. The clothes were separated into colors and whites.

In the early morning, she began by scrubbing the clothes on the washboard. Standing in the dirt, I could hear the rushhh, russhhh of her hands pushing the clothes hard against the washboard. Then she put the already scrubbed white things in the cauldron to boil for awhile in the steaming water. We took them out, boiling hot, with a long, clean stick.

Then the clothes were put in the wringer washer outdoors—whoosh, whoosh, whoosh. My older sisters were up by then and helping. They talked and complained while they moved the clothes around from place to place. The clothes were individually scrubbed, boiled, washed, and rinsed. Then the white ones got bleached in Clorox and rinsed in bluing. The school pants, shirts, and dresses all got starched. We hung them up with our mouths full of clothes pins. A seven-foot two-by-four piece of wood with a notch in it was used to push the baling-wire clothesline higher so the clothes wouldn't drag on the ground as they flapped in the wind.

Six children and two parents—even though we didn't individually have a lot of clothes, it took most of the day.

Delia stood on one side of the wringer and Delmira passed the clothes to her through the double rollers. Our old neighbor Gorgonia once got her huge, fat arm caught in the rollers up to the elbow. They ran to unplug the machine while she screamed. She lost the use of her arm. Afterwards she had to wash with the other hand.

I watched Delmira's skinny arms feeding the clothes through the rollers carefully, so that the rollers caught the cloth, but not her fingers.

It was intimate. To wash your brother's pants and to pass your sister's bra through the double rollers, one item after another. We got to know each other as we washed each other's clothes. The shit-stained underwear. The blood-stained skirt from Delmira's period.

Each item was handled separately by each one of us at our stations. We rinsed in soft rain water collected in a barrel under the downspout. Back to nature.

Lourdes was matchstick-skinny. Brown, straight hair. Faded, clean dress. Big eyes, brown in a pure white background.

She came to play jacks with me. I didn't love her. I knew I was better then she was. Better clothes, better house, and better toys. And the most important thing; I knew more than she did. I was smarter. Lourdes was a simple girl—much simpler than I. She had no pretensions to anything. She just was what she was. And she never expected to be anything else. I cared about her only a little. She was a convenient playmate.

Her mother, Pepa, was large, not fat really, but with massive calves and arms and as tall as my father. She had been a cantinera at the local cantinas.

Pepa was kind and worked a lot. One of her eyelids drooped slightly and she had a mole that was all bumpy and strange. I couldn't look at anything else when she talked to me. She always looked bright and alive. She cleaned and cleaned their tiny two-room house and then swept the yard with the broom. Their yard had not one tree, not one bush, and she didn't allow any weeds to grow. It was pure, unrelieved, hot red sand.

I didn't love her either, since she had been a cantinera. She was very kind, though. Amá did love her. Amá didn't care that she used to be a cantinera. Or maybe she loved her more because of what she used to be, because they could laugh together when they told each other cantinera jokes: "She walks around like big María, with no underwear on!" And they cackled uproariously.

Pepa came to help Amá make tamales. It was a big job that took all day. They took the meat off the pork head, cooked it slowly with chiles, then spread each corn husk with the masa. Amá paid her in tamales. Pepa came to help can tomatoes, too. Amá paid her in jars of canned tomatoes.

While they worked, Lourdes and I played jacks on our cement porch. The cement was always cool. I won and won and won. Like killing a fly, hard, with the flyswatter. I got her every time. She didn't seem to feel bad about it. I expected her to show some feelings, like feeling bad, or wanting to cry, but nothing. This made me want to win harder.

We played bebé leche. For this game of hopscotch, all we needed was a rock to draw the rectangles on the soft sand. We played barefoot, and we each put our rock in the square that we jumped to last. I could jump farther than her. My legs were longer, I was slightly older, and my mother fed me better. I never let her win. I killed her in this game, too. Again she never said anything, just kept on playing and playing. It made me mad.

When I had money, she went with me to buy a snowcone at the corner store. She never had money for snowcones. I got nauseated thinking about her sharing my snowcone, mixing the spit from the inside of her mouth with mine. I was afraid that her mouth was not clean, although her teeth were big and white and looked very clean. So I put the snow cone in two little saucers with spoons. She got less than I did, of course.

When my mother made cookies, I gave Lourdes some—two for me, one for her. Never said a word, just ate what I gave her.

But when we just sat and talked, she really made me mad. "Amá is going to buy me a doll for my birthday this year, a baby doll this high. I picked it out at Danchack's already," I told her.

"I already have one of those," she answered.

"Liar!"

"It's true," she insisted.

So I sent her home and wouldn't play with her anymore that day. I wanted to be better and richer than someone else. She didn't let me.

I never went to her house. She never invited me. And I never wanted to go, anyway. Tiny. With a tiny porch. It had never seen paint, inside or out. When they all lay down, with all those children, I'm sure there was no place to step on the floor. There were only two beds; I could see them when they opened the front screen door.

I knew they had nothing. The beds looked carefully made, but there was nothing else in the room besides the rocking chair where Pepa sat in the evenings.

There was only one other room, the kitchen. This I could see when they opened the screen door to the kitchen. A small table with an oilcloth cover, two chairs, and a stove. That's all. Sometimes they asked us to put something in the refrigerator for them. They didn't have one.

Lourdes always kept some distance from me and my family. She seemed to be always observing, studying us. She watched every move silently with those big, brown eyes. Being on display, and to such a forgiving audience, I became an exhibitionist. I talked louder than normal, laughed more freely, and took more chances. After all, if Lourdes criticized me, it wouldn't mean anything. But I knew she wouldn't. She took whatever I dished out.

I had so much more than she did: a house with paint, new furniture, a grassy lawn, a car, a father. Around her was the only time I felt like a privileged princess.

Pepa and Lourdes walked to the grocery store together. They didn't have a car. The muscles rippled in Pepa's calves as she walked. She seemed to have no trouble carrying the bags home. Lourdes was light as a feather; it seemed to be no effort for her to walk, either.

When Pepa was helping Amá and my father was home, he told them cantina jokes. All three of them cackled and slapped their knees as they laughed. This was when Pepa looked the happiest, when she was laughing with her whole body at cantina jokes. I guess she remembered the good times from when she was a cantinera.

I didn't like the cantina jokes. I didn't laugh—better to go outside. Lourdes said nothing.

Eventually Pepa moved away. I guess she didn't pay the rent. When she left, the owner of the house sold it to another family. They tore the old house down and built a new one.

Pepa went back to being a cantinera again. Then, when she came to see Amá, she wouldn't come in the yard. They talked at the fence. Amá wanted her to come in the house, but she wouldn't. It wouldn't look right, she said, for a cantinera to go in the house of decent people.

When I was in high school, Amá told me that Lourdes had become a cantinera, too. Now both Pepa and Lourdes spent their nights at the cantinas, just two different ones.

I felt guilty then. She had looked at me as though I were some sort of princess. I held it over her. I wondered if it is human nature to lord one's station over another if possible, or if I was just a cruel child.

Classism was part of my existence. The white people on the east side of town had more than me. I had more than Lourdes. I wasn't allowed into the white people's world. I allowed Lourdes into mine. But both of us knew she was just a spectator.

Later, Lourdes got into boyfriend trouble. Two men fought over her. One beat her in a jealous rage. Lourdes was always skinny. Not beautiful, but simple, with her brown eyes in a clean white background, and her clean, white teeth. Even when she became a cantinera, she didn't wear makeup or low-cut dresses. She didn't look like a cantinera; she looked like a decent girl. I guess that's why the men got confused; they forgot she was a cantinera.

Then Pepa really left the cantinas. She found a church—not the Catholic one, of course, because everyone there was mean to her. Another church, a little one. She cleaned it every day on her knees as a penance. She no longer sang cantinera songs as before when she used to wash the clothes. Now she sang about grace and redemption.

Chapter Nine

*Arriba ya del caballo, hay que aguantar
los respingos.*

Once mounted on a horse, one must hang
on when he bucks.

(Mexican dicho)

It seems it would be impossible to be a dainty teenager if you're a Mexican migrant girl. But my sisters tried to be. Even in the beet fields, my sisters worried about cleanliness. They brushed the crusted dirt off the lower part of their jeans and their sneakers at night so they wouldn't look too dirty the next morning.

We had no plumbing, so one of the boys got a bucket of water from the well first thing after rising. From this bucket, a little would be poured into a shallow pan for washing your face. Delia had put a towel and soap next to the bucket. All this was done outside, in front of the house so the water spills from washing your face and the spit from tooth-brushing fell on the ground. The well water was cold and bracing early in the morning, usually before daylight. It was easy to see who had washed his face already—my father insisted everyone do it—otherwise they would still be warm and sleepy from bed and not ready to work. It was a trick he used to get everyone ready to work; he wasn't concerned about cleanliness at all.

But my sisters were. They combed and brushed their hair carefully in the morning. Delmira had learned in home economics class that you were supposed to brush your hair one-hundred strokes every night. She worked at this at night until my father made her go to bed, her hair a glossy light brown. They arranged their hair under the garsolé with bobby pins. They took combs in the pockets of their jeans to the fields.

One thing they hated was drinking out of the same dipper as everyone else.

There was frequently only one large water barrel that was kept filled for all the migrants at a particular field. From this hung a dipper much like a soup ladle. Everyone used this to drink. The truck holding the water barrel got moved down the edge of the field as the migrants worked the rows.

One summer an old man, Don Chano, came to the migrant camp by himself; he had no family to take care of him. His wrinkled face looked forlorn and sad, but he was very friendly and talked a lot. He talked in the truck all the way to the field, when all of us were still wishing we were in bed. "My daughter in Houston has five children. Her husband doesn't want to come North, but maybe next year they will, and I won't have to boil my eggs along with the coffee grounds to make coffee for my breakfast."

My sisters looked at each other as if they wanted to throw up.

The worst thing about Don Chano was that he had sores— maybe cold sores, maybe something else, who knew?—on the edges of his lips. It was hard to look at him, even though we felt sorry for him.

Delia and Delmira held the dipper in their left hand and drank out of the back side of it so that their lips wouldn't touch the place where Don Chano, being right-handed, drank from.

Once, we finished our rows at the same time as he did. Talkative as usual, he walked over to the water barrel at the same time as we did. The water barrel had been lowered from the truck via ropes in its handles and was sitting in the shade of the truck to keep it cool. Politely, he asked our family to go first while he chatted on.

"My wife was always a hard worker even though she was sick. We only had one daughter. The rest were born dead; she could never carry a live baby after Carmela. It broke her heart. I think that's what killed her."

When we were finished and it was his turn, he apologized for having to drink out of the same dipper because of his sores, but after all, there was no choice. He would, however, drink out of the back side, holding it in his left hand, so his lips wouldn't touch where everyone else's did.

My sisters ran to the other side of the truck and hid their violent gagging with loud coughs. My father laughed and we went back to work.

They stayed thirsty the rest of the day and vowed to tie tin cups to their belt loops from then on even though it would bother them all day. They tried to be dainty.

The first year we went to Minnesota, Rudy was ten, two years too young to be working in the fields legally. He had just finished the fourth grade.

My mother had thought only briefly about sending him to the nuns along with my sister and me. He was too independent and grown up for this. Besides, he insisted that he wanted to do his share of the work.

Short hoes had been outlawed several years previously. A short hoe is a hoe with a short stick; it looks like a home garden tool. This forces the migrant to bend down closer to his work and thereby do a better job. Many people's backs were ruined by being forced to bend at the waist all day.

But the short hoe was perfect for Rudy, since he had just finished the fourth grade and was only four feet tall.

He insisted on working, so my father devised a way for him to do it. The family put stakes at the ends of the rows they planned to work labeled "L. Treviño." Usually, my father worked two rows at a time, walking in between them and alternating his hoeing, left three strokes, right three strokes. Everyone else took one row.

But they didn't start right at the edge of the field; they started thirty feet in. Rudy, with his short hoe, worked the first thirty feet of everyone's rows. But he was to keep one eye out for gringos. If any drove up or drove by, he was to drop his short hoe and walk away nonchalantly, or pretend to be playing. We didn't know what would happen if my father got caught violating the child labor laws.

Rudy did his work very well. He only had to be told once how to do a job and he would be finished before everyone else. My father approved of him; you could see it in his eyes and his half-smile when he looked at Rudy. It made me jealous.

Rudy was everything I wanted to be and wasn't: handsome, strong, and arrogant almost to the point of cruelty. He carried being my parents' favorite easily. He worked harder than anyone else easily. He was disdainful of complainers, even though he sometimes silently helped them. He could get away with anything by never defending himself against my parents. It is hard to attack someone who never defends himself.

Life seemed so easy for him. People laughed at his jokes. But I couldn't resist Rudy; no one could. I wanted him to like me, to look at me, to just notice I was there. He rarely did. Everyone wanted the same things from him.

It was harder for my brother Luis to be in the same family as Rudy than it was for me. Luis always came up wanting in my parents' eyes. Immediately defensive, he had a million excuses. He was full of mannerisms and speech that my father didn't like.

He usually fell behind when we were hoeing the beet field. He tried to keep up, but he would get tired and distracted and end up at the rear with Delia, who was always last.

After Rudy turned twelve, he started working his own row along with everyone else. Once when Rudy and my father had finished their rows first, as usual, Rudy decided to turn around and work Luis's row backwards to make him look bad, to shame him into working faster. Luis saw what was happening and started going faster, making mistakes, leaving only one plant sometimes instead of two. Delia pointed this out to him and he became furious. He shouted out to Rudy to leave his row alone.

Rudy ignored him and kept hoeing. Luis hoed furiously and when he was getting close to Rudy, he ran up and hit him with the wooden part of his hoe, almost as hard as he could. Rudy looked up with murder in his eyes. Without saying a word, he coolly and deliberately swung the blade of his hoe into Luis's skinny thigh, exposing the bone beneath.

Luis howled as he fell, and everyone came running.

My father looked at the leg and then he looked at Rudy, who hadn't said anything during the whole incident. Even in his fury and his panic, my father still didn't deviate from his "an eye for an eye" philosophy, and so he said, "You did this to him, you drive him to the hospital!"

Rudy was twelve. He had never been behind the wheel of a car. The doctor was miles away in Moorhead.

My father grabbed Rudy by the collar and dragged him to the car. He threw him behind the driver's seat like a sack of bones. Rudy, red-faced, remained in stony silence, the muscles of his jaw working.

Amazingly, the wound was not bleeding very much. Luis was laid in the back of the car, my mother assigned to be with him. My father got in the front seat next to Rudy. He yelled at us to keep working. He began barking instructions to Rudy about how to drive a stick shift car, and he damn well better learn fast if he didn't want to die at my father's hands.

The car jerked away from the field, my father screaming instructions.

For the time that Luis couldn't work, Rudy had to work two rows like my father, instead of his usual one. He saw what it was like to be last. But he didn't care.

Sometimes, on Saturdays, we worked only until after lunch. Then the people went back to the camp, took a bath and went grocery shopping or to do laundry. Sunday was a workday like the rest. Our getting up time was the same every day—before dawn.

Taking a bath was a production. Water had to be brought from the well and heated on the wood stove or outside over a fire. Wood had to be brought for the fire to heat the water. The boys brought the wood, the girls carried the water, and Apá built the fire. Amá pulled the beds out from the wall at an angle so that the headboards made a "V". Then she draped sheets over the headboards and tied them. This made a mostly private corner where one could take a bath and not be seen.

One by one, we took a bath behind the sheets. I stood in the large tub while I soaped myself all over, including my hair. Then, with a tin cup, I took heated water from the bucket next to my tub to pour water on me and rinse myself off. When I was finished, we took the tub I had been standing in and dumped out the water. Each of us did this one by one, until all eight of us were clean.

Amá scrubbed clothes on the washboard while the rest of us bathed. She took a bath last while the rest of us rinsed and hung up the clothes she had washed. This was the only opportunity to do laundry. We hung up the clothes with our hair still wet from the bath.

While the rest of us took a bath and did laundry, Apá did accounts. With a pencil and paper, he figured out how many acres we had done this week, how many we had done already, how much we had spent on groceries at the grocery store, and how much money we could expect to take home. He folded the piece of paper carefully and put it in his wallet. He seemed satisfied and happy doing this work. We made much more money in Minnesota than he was able to make in Texas. As he got up from the table, he said, "The important thing is that they report my Social Security. With that we will be able to live when your mother and I are old." He was fifty-six years old, with six young children, including a six year old.

"O.K., woman, let's go!" he said to my mother.

"Quit harassing me!" she spit back as she dried her feet carefully.

Finally she was ready. She closed the front door but didn't lock it. There was not one thing of value in there. Our few clothes were the same as everyone else's, and the furniture went with the place. There was nothing else.

In the car, everyone was wearing their best clean clothes, with shiny faces and damp, slicked-down hair. We were just going to the grocery store, but it felt as though we were going to the fiesta. Not having to work for a few hours was really something. Maybe Apá would buy us a treat.

Usually we went to the small, convenience-type store nearby in Sabin, where we could get credit, but that day we went to the Red Owl Grocery in Moorhead. When we got to the parking lot, Apá gave the big kids a dollar and me a quarter. We went off happily to have a Coke at the restaurant next door while he and Amá grocery shopped.

This is what they bought: twenty-five pounds of white flour in a patterned cloth sack for tortillas, twenty pounds of potatoes, pinto beans, eggs for all week, waxed paper for lunches, coffee, and sugar. Meat was purchased just for dinner that day since more than this would spoil, as we had no refrigerator. Milk kept for a few days if we put it on the windowsill.

They put the groceries in the car and walked down the street to sit in the park for awhile. There were lots of migrant worker trucks lining the street next to the park. Amá had bought two strips of licorice and she ate one happily. She hid the other one in her purse like a secret. In the middle of the week, when no one would be looking, she would eat it and think of sitting in the park, resting. Apá didn't care for sweets of any kind.

We finished our Cokes and walked to the park to see if Apá was ready to go. "No, hijos, go for a walk, we're not in a hurry." So we went and bought popsicles and walked around happily. Once, Apá let us go to the movies to see *Lady and the Tramp,* which had just been released, while he and Amá waited in the park.

When we came back to the park the next time, Apá was ready to go. "What did you buy?" we asked Amá. "Same as always," she said. "Except I got some meat to make tonight." We salivated in anticipation. It had been a week since we had had meat.

Amá's life was the hardest. She gave and gave and gave. "May God give me patience!" she would exclaim when it got to be too much for her. One time she quit eating tortillas. Said she was on a diet. When we finally caught the rat in the flour bin, we realized what the true story was. She couldn't bear to throw out twenty-five pounds of flour, but she couldn't bear to eat the tortillas, either.

We couldn't have a bath every day, since it was such a big production. But she made us wash our feet every night. It was a rule. One night she seemed especially tired. She was still cleaning up long after everyone else was in bed. Finally she turned out the light and was headed for bed. She stubbed her toe just as she was about to get in bed and let out an exclamation. Luis rushed to turn the light back on. "AAAMMMÁAAA!" he said and woke everyone up. She hadn't washed her feet and they looked filthy in the light of the naked bulb. But that wasn't the worst part. She had a peeled orange that she apparently planned to eat in bed. Fruit was an extremely rare treat. She had waited until everyone was asleep so she wouldn't have to share it eight ways. Poor Amá.

After beet thinning season in Minnesota, Wisconsin was next every year. In contrast to Minnesota, where we stayed in the stop-sign-shaped house every year, we never knew where we'd end up in Wisconsin. This was terrifying and wonderful too; I loved the travel and the excitement of new, unknown places.

One of the houses was completely ours for the summer. It was a small house, complete with a yard, picket fence, and everything. At one time, it had probably been a working farmhouse, but now it was old and run-down, so the migrants got to stay there. The pump in this house was inside the huge kitchen sink. We didn't have to go to the well to pump water. There was a second pump in the back yard, about twenty yards from the kitchen door. It was in the middle of a grassy yard. The grass was a deep green color and deliciously soft on my bare feet. Diamantina and I would play in the sunshine with the water from the painted-red pump while Amá hung clothes on the line. She was wearing shoes in the soft grass while she hung up the billowing clothes in the wind. I tried to convince her to go barefoot, but she wouldn't. She rarely relaxed, working hard all the time. She loved the perfectly clean clothes though, and got much pleasure out of getting them that way.

To Apá, the accommodations didn't matter; we were there to work and make money. A bed, a stove, and a table were all he needed. We never had a refrigerator, but no one missed it. The water typically came from a well via a hand pump.

But to me, those August months in Wisconsin were like vacations. One of a child's favorite things to do is explore the surroundings. And I did. The places where we stayed in Wisconsin were much more interesting and varied than the Minnesota house. We only stayed in housing built for migrants one year. The rest of the time we stayed in places that had originally been something else.

I wanted to explore everything—the kitchen cabinets, the attic, the basement, the closets, the barn, the copse of trees outside, the indoor water pump, the outdoor water well, the wheat field at the bottom of the hill. It was all thrilling and new every August. For years, these were the only things I remembered: the excitement, the newness, the discovery, the fun. I had forgotten the shame that goes with that life.

In Wisconsin, the work was sporadic and unpredictable. Sometimes we would work many days at a stretch, sometimes there were no fields that were ready to pick. On these days, we did the laundry or went swimming or fishing at Lake Holcomb, the Chippewa River, or one of the many other lakes in Wisconsin.

Poison ivy was a problem. For several years, Luis and Delmira hung their swollen feet out the car windows all the way back to Texas to cool off the burning poison ivy rash.

At the end of August, many of the migrants went back to Minnesota to work on the beet harvest. Apá took us back to Texas. He didn't want us to miss school. His dream was for all of us to graduate from high school. So he left the money there that we would have made by staying another month.

In Wisconsin we always went to different farms. We never knew from one day to the next, from one year to the next, where we would go or live or what we would do. The word about what kind of work was available and where came by word of mouth and by chance. This was distressing for my father because he would have liked consistent work every day, and great for the kids because they worked less.

For me it was a big adventure. Moving into new houses, going to the lake, swimming, fishing, or canoeing. Rudy would make eight-inch birch bark canoes with a needle and thread.

On free days, such as when there were no fields that were ready to pick, everyone excitedly got ready to go to the lake. My father would get fishing line and find a pole. He and my brothers would have melted lead over a wood fire the night before to make lead weights for the fishing line. Hooks and a float ball were the rest of his equipment.

He and Rudy were the fishermen. But once, at the river, I wanted to try. Apá hooked the line to a pole, put a lead weight and a hook on it for me, and I was set. I wanted to please him. I wanted him to respect and like me as he did Rudy.

The sunlight shimmered on the water and my sisters laughed on a blanket by the car. All was right with the world and we were on vacation. I caught a flat sunfish. I loved all the colors on it.

My father said it wouldn't have a lot of meat, but he still seemed pleased with me. His being pleased with me was something I constantly sought. Rudy didn't seem to seek it; it just came to him.

That night we had fried fish dipped in cornmeal for dinner. My father sat at the table. There wasn't room for all of us at the table, so some of us stood up and ate or sat on the floor with the plate on our legs. Apá was ravenous after a wonderful day in the sun at the river. He ate the fish too fast. A bone got stuck in his throat.

As he gagged, his terror filled the room. His eyes got big and red. Rudy knocked over his chair to get to him. Apá pushed the rest of his food out of his mouth onto the plate and furiously worked his jaw and massaged his throat. Rudy slapped him on the back as hard as he dared.

Then it got noisy. My father's gagging, Rudy's slapping, my mother screaming "¡Ay Luis!" and our own terrified silence deafening us. Apá finally got it out by sticking his huge finger in there and pulling it out. More than a little blood came with it. He ran outside to hide his fear from us, but we had seen it. He rinsed his mouth and gargled over and over with the water from the water barrel outside. We bunched up watching from the doorway.

"Nada, it's nothing, I tell you," he said between mouth rinses.

He came back in and sat down and picked up his fork determinedly. But he couldn't do it. Big, macho Apá had been hooked by the fish, right in the throat. He just chewed on some tortilla and swallowed over and over and kept drinking water. The rest of the fish stayed on his plate and in the skillet.

He made us all go to bed early because he wanted the lights out. What he said went. But we didn't hear his snores right away as usual. All of us lay there with eyes big as quarters, looking at the ceiling in the dark.

I saw us fatherless, like Marielena and her mother, dependent on others' kindness and good will. Who would drive the car? My mother had never driven except on the farm in Texas, and that had been years ago when Diamantina was a baby and drank gasoline. Amá had to drive her to the field where my father was working and together they took her to the doctor in town to pump her stomach. Luis? He was only sixteen. Could he drive us all the way to Texas? Luis was the oldest son. Would he have to quit school and work with Tío Alfredo at the Willie McKinley farm? I guessed the girls would have to quit school, too.

Finally my father started snoring. The snores were big and strong. But I imagined the fragile, pink softness of his throat. A little fish bone in just the right place . . .

Since all my siblings were teenagers, there were lots of crushes and romances. Rudy went for the morenitas. Luis went for the gringas like Mary Lou, Jackie, and "La Gordita," who was the town operator. Delia would meet Adrian, "El Prieto," by the water well to talk in secret. Delmira snubbed them all; she was saving herself for someone with clean fingernails. Diamantina was too shy. I was too young.

The last year we went north as a family, Rudy was fifteen years old. He had left Carolina behind at home. He had carved her nickname "Caro" on the marbleized plastic side of his pocket knife that he always had with him. I would ask to look at it when he took it out to peel an orange for me. I would ask questions about Caro, but he would brush me off.

The García family was staying in the house next to ours at the migrant camp in Wisconsin. They had come from Midland, in west Texas. The father, Epifanio, and Apá became fast friends. They would pick beans working side-by-side rows so that they could talk all day. They called each other "compadre" and told stories about the old days in Mexico.

The Garcías had a dark-skinned daughter, Amalia, who had brown curls all around her face. When she smiled, she got deep, cute dimples in both cheeks. She was a year older than Rudy. The two of them started picking green beans and working next to each other.

The rows of beans in Wisconsin were much shorter than the half-mile-long sugar beet rows in Minnesota. Because of this, my father would let me be in the field with them instead of waiting at the edge of the field with the water bucket.

I saw the way Rudy and Amalia looked at each other and smiled secretly. Everyone else noticed it too and let the two of them fall behind the rest of the two families. No one said anything or asked questions. It was some sort of unspoken agreement to let the young people woo each other in peace.

I didn't like it. I was jealous. Rudy was the closest to me in age, albeit seven years older. He wouldn't really play with me, but he would harass me, tickle me until I cried, and call me names like "greñas" and "costra." It was negative attention, but I wanted it anyway.

He was handsome and strong and I didn't like sharing him. Especially not in this new, unfamiliar way. Their new feelings of adolescent hormonal lust seemed to create a circle around them that other people respected and expected. I resented it.

I caught up to them on their row. Rudy looked murderously at me from his squatting position between the rows of beans. "¡Qué quieres!" he barked.

Amalia looked at me, too. I looked at her while I asked, "Rudy, why do you have 'Caro' carved on your pocket knife?" He lunged at me from his squatting position, almost knocking me down. He grabbed a chunk of my tangled curls with his right hand and bent my arm behind my back in a wrestling hold with his left hand. He did this as he propelled me back to the car. "It's none of your business, mugre. Stay away from me!"

At the end of the season, we were packing the car in the early evening. We would be leaving at three the next morning. There was talk of this being the last time we came north as a family. Next year only Apá, Luis, and Rudy would go to work in the Wisconsin canning factories. Amalia and her family came over to help pack and say goodbye. She mostly hung around Rudy while he carried out bundles.

When the trunk was full and our room almost empty, all the adults were sitting around on chairs and bare mattresses, talking about how the season had been and the prospects for the future. Rudy took the cardboard box that had our tacos for the trip to put it in the back seat of the car. Amalia followed him out. I watched them through the screen door. He went to one side of the back seat and leaned in to push the box in. She went to the other side of the car and pulled the box into place in the middle of the back seat. Their hands touched on the box. They both reached farther and kissed—a long, slow teenage kiss. I thought inside me that it was their first.

He got to hold her hand by the car for only a minute. Then the adults dispersed, said goodbye and good luck, and everyone went to bed.

Rudy was quiet and looked out the window the whole trip back to Texas.

We went north six years altogether. It became a familiar routine. But then Delia and Delmira graduated from high school. They moved to San Antonio to live with Tía Chela and find jobs. With only four kids, there was a lot more room in the car, but we missed Delia and Delmira a lot.

Then Apá changed directions. He decided to go to the Wisconsin canning factories and take only Luis and Rudy with him. It was terrible work, but it paid well. Only men were hired, so Amá, Diamantina, and I stayed home.

They stirred the ten-foot-high vats of cooking yellow corn or green beans with giant boat paddles, standing on a scaffold. The steam and the heat changed the way the body cooled itself, which made it hard to sleep at night. They lived in a camp that was made up only of men, and that included Tío José, my mother's brother, who went with them.

Then Luis graduated from high school and left Texas to seek his fortune in Wisconsin year-round. He left the day after graduation with several of his buddies in an old, beat-up car. He worked in the foundries there.

A couple of years later, Rudy graduated, got married, and went to work in the Wisconsin foundries, too.

Now there was only me to support. Apá stopped going north. He started drawing Social Security when I was twelve and he was sixty-two.

Chapter Ten

*No hay mal que dure cien años, ni cuerpo
que lo resista.*

There is no ill that lasts 100 years, nor anyone who can resist it.

(Mexican dicho)

It was Sunday morning in Pearsall. Amá heated the menudo she
had spent hours making the day before. My brothers, who had
been out drinking on Saturday night even though they weren't
supposed to, ate the menudo sprinkled with raw onions, a squeeze
of lemon, and fresh cilantro. The menudo, slightly slimy with the
protein from the lining of the cow's stomach, helped their hang-
overs and made their eyes less bloodshot.

Tío Alfredo came for breakfast every Sunday until he died.
He sipped his coffee loudly, aspirating air with it to cool it down.
I loved my Tío Alfredo; he was handsome, witty, and always generous. But I hated his coffee-slurping habit. He told us about la
canícula, a time in August that foretells what the weather will be
like for the next twelve months. He told chistes, jokes in Spanish
that he heard at the cantina Saturday night or from his friend
Arturo. I loved to look at his face. To me, he looked more handsome than the stars of the Mexican movies.

Apá came home with a cabeza, a whole cow's head that had
been steaming in a pit in the ground all night. It was so well done
that the meat fell off the cheeks. We all watched as Apá carved the
steaming cow's head into a platter of barbacoa. This was a regular Sunday morning ritual. The white kids across town had French
toast dusted with powdered sugar. We had menudo and barbacoa.
The brains, which looked like dirty cottage cheese, were set aside

to be scrambled with eggs. Apá reserved the eyes for himself. He didn't even hide them in a taco, just popped them in his mouth like olives, one after the other. The meat from the cheeks was the only thing that looked to me like something I could eat. In my mind, I tied to disconnect the meat in my flour tortilla taco from the empty sockets in the cheeks of the cow's head. Unbidden, scenes came to me of this particular cow mooing contentedly in the pasture and then screaming in the slaughterhouse covered with blood.

Later, at dinner, Amá made a separate pot of carne guisada for me without garlic, cumin, onions, chili, or pepper, because my child's tastebuds couldn't take all the spices. Amá had no concept of nutrition. If I wanted to eat Fritos and gravy for dinner and that was all, it was fine with her, as long as my belly was full. She lived for filling people's bellies. Three times a day, she made mountains of fragrant, brown and white, perfect-circle tortillas.

Amá catered to my eating tastes from babyhood. I didn't like the yellow part of my scrambled egg, only the white, so she separated it for me. I didn't like beans. In Mexican families, beans are an absolute staple. But she never once asked me to eat them. She was my short-order cook for breakfast. I could choose whatever I wanted from her small repertoire: scrambled eggs with bacon, soft-boiled eggs, skillet-sized pancakes made in a cast iron skillet, tortillas with butter, tortillas with cheese. She really had only a small number of dishes that she knew how to make. I was a child when she got a cookie recipe from my tía. She never learned another one. She continued making that same recipe her whole life.

We rarely purchased meat at the grocery store. During deer hunting season, Rudy brought his trophies home and hung them by their hind hooves from hooks installed just for that purpose on the roof of the back porch. After disemboweling the deer, he pulled the skin off, all in one piece. Apá frequently brought a small cow home and after killing it, laid it on its side on a picnic table to cut the best pieces up into steak and grind the rest into hamburger to be frozen. Amá participated in the slaughter also. She cornered a squawking chicken in the coop and took it firmly by its two legs with one hand. Then she walked it over to the tree stump. She grabbed the ax with her right hand as she arranged the chicken's neck into the middle of the stump, still holding it by its legs. One whack of her strong arm and the head rolled off the stump. Sometimes the struggling chicken got away from her at this point and ran around the back yard, crazy and headless. When the chicken finally died, she again grabbed it by its legs and dipped it in a pot of boiling water. This loosened the feathers, which raised an awful stink all over the back yard. She sat on the back steps to pull the feathers out. Naked, the chicken looked cold and goose-pimply.

After the migrant years, Apá tended bar at the Buenos Aires Cantina on summer weekends. On Wednesdays after dinner, Chilino and Manuel Tafolla came to pick up my father. The three of them went to the Buenos Aires to play cards and dominos and have a few beers. The cantina was closed to the public except on Friday and Saturday, so they had the place all to themselves. They seemed to enjoy it so much, driving away laughing together. I don't think they actually drank much; Apá never came home drunk from these Wednesday outings. They just laughed and talked a lot. Their friendship was old and deep. Apá and Chilino had picked cotton side by side in Arizona long before either of them was married. The hardships and common history had bonded them like a vow of brotherhood exchanged with blood. They were true compadres even before Amá and Apá carried Hugo, Chilino's son, to the baptismal font. This made them compadres in fact as well as in feelings.

When Chilino came to pick up my father, he dropped off his wife, Amparo, and his daughter, Margie. Sometimes Tío Leonides dropped off Nina and Hilda and joined them at the cantina.

Amparo and Tía Nina sat in lawn chairs on the front lawn with my mother. Hilda, Margie, and I spread an old patchwork quilt on the grass and lay down to look at the stars and talk. Streetlights had not come to Dávila Street yet, so on clear summer nights, the dark, starry sky hugged our house and lawn. Those gentle evenings colored my girlhood with magic. The big dipper looked like the long-handled pot that Apá melted lead in over the campfire to make sinkers for his fishing line. The little dipper looked like the smaller dipper I carried with the water bucket to the beet fields. With the mothers close by talking about familiar things like births, deaths, marriages, and affairs, the girls, Margie, Hilda, and I, felt safe, told secrets, and giggled by starlight.

On one of those evenings, Margie took me behind the house and told me how babies are conceived. I laughed out loud. "That's the dumbest thing I ever heard," I said. "Whoever told you that was pulling your leg."

The next day, in the cold light of morning, she showed me cartoons she had stolen from her older brother that showed people "doing it."

Not my parents. Surely not my parents. My mother was so asexual. She stopped bathing me when I was three; it seemed she was embarrassed to look at me. She told me to scrub the "dirty places"—my feet and between my legs—really well.

The next day I told my friend Manuela what Margie had told me. She confirmed it and added more details. I went around in shock for days, looking at the adults in a new way. I stared at my mother sweeping the porch. Was it possible? My aunt and uncle too? All of them?

I didn't like the slimy underbelly of the face these people showed during the day. It seemed impossible to reconcile the two.

Margie came the closest to being a pampered child of anyone I knew in Pearsall. Her mother had named her Margot, which was French, like her brother's name, Hugo. She had a set of the *Book of Knowledge Encyclopedia* that I never got enough of. I would read happily alone while she took long baths. They had a cooler in their living room window which made the air cool by evaporating water. It was the only cool place I had access to in the hot Texas summer. She went to tap dancing school and wore tap dancing shoes, click, click, clicking through the house. My mother wouldn't let me take lessons. Two dollars a week was too much. I only got to go to the first lesson, which was free. Margie had a fat-wheeled red bicycle that we both learned to ride on, taking turns going around the block. I had never had a bike, and I knew I never would.

The day before Chilino and Amparo's six-year-old son Hugo was to have his tonsillectomy, their whole family came to our house. Hugo was wearing new cowboy boots. He walked in proudly and my sisters laughed because they were on the wrong feet, the toes pointing away from the middle.

The laughter reverberated in my brain the next day when I found out he had hemorrhaged to death alone in his hospital bed. I wanted the moment back, to hug his small body and fix his shoes. I wanted to silence the loud laughter of my sisters in my head.

They came to get Margie at school.

"Your brother is dead."

I watched the car drive away, Margie a big howl. Her open screaming mouth as big as her face. Her screams mixed with my sisters' laughter that wouldn't go away in my head. Chilino, her hard, proud father, crumpled with pain.

They took me over there after school. I could hear Amparo screaming before we, horrified, got out of the car.

"The doctor, he killed my baby! my baby! my baby! ¡Mijito! Why didn't I stay with him! The doctor told me to let him rest. ¡Ay Dios mío, no!"

They were senseless with grief, all of them. We couldn't help them, being raw wounds ourselves now.

We had to be with them. They were part of our family even though we weren't related. We stayed with them almost around the clock until the funeral. Amparo never stopped screaming. We endured it all, whatever she needed.

I had been jealous of Margie and wanted to be her. Now I was glad I was me. My family was all healthy at home. My mother was sane and held me close occasionally. Her mother was crazy with grief and lost to everyone.

Death was an integral part of my growing up time. Tía Chela died on the same day as my sister's baby was born. Tío Blas, Tío Rey, Tío José, Tía Sofía—I was constantly at wakes and funerals.

PART TWO

Farther Migrations

*No le tengan miedo al chile, aunque lo
vean bien colorado.*

Don't be afraid of the chile pepper even
though you see it's so red.

(Mexican dicho)

Chapter Eleven

La esperanza no es pan, pero alimenta.

Hope is not bread, yet it nourishes.

(Mexican dicho)

Mrs. Frances, my third grade teacher, let the class vote on who should get the "Honor Pin" for being the best student in the class. They nominated and voted for me. It was the first time I had been singled out as a good student.

Mrs. Winters, my fourth grade teacher, had the reputation of being the meanest teacher in the school. She taught the "A" group of fourth-graders. The school administration unabashedly divided each grade into A, B, C, and D rooms, the "A" room being the brightest kids and the "D" being the kids who didn't do so well. I wanted to be in the "A" room, but I was afraid of her reputation. She had an angular body with sharp edges, a pointy nose, and corners for shoulders.

But I had been taught by my father how to be around mean people. I decided to work hard, lay low, and be quiet. This worked and she liked me right away. I never raised my hand, speaking only when I was called on. And I usually knew the answer.

The year of my fourth grade was a series of turning points. It started with my hair. Scissors had never touched my hair when I started the fourth grade. My braids were long and heavy. Every time my curly hair was washed, it took an hour to untangle and braid.

Diamantina tried to convince me that braids were boring; I could do so much more with my hair if it was short. Amá said she worried that the weight of my hair was what made me so thin and that it was the reason for the new headaches I occasionally got. If my hair wasn't combed, Rudy still tortured me by calling me "greñas."

The migrant years were over. We lived in a new house. I decided it was time for a change, so I told Amá I was ready. She said there was a traveling photographer in town. She wanted to have my picture taken with my hair long so we could remember it. The next day she dressed me in my best dress and went to the photographer. He said the negatives would be ready in a week.

That night, Diamantina sat me in front of a mirror and got Amá's sewing scissors out. She put a rubber band at the top of one of my two braids and crunched through the thick hair with the scissors, just above the rubber band. The hair on the right side of my head sprang out wild and free. The sight of the unruly short hair shocked me. I burst into tears and ran from the mirror. I cried inconsolably for two hours.

I couldn't form the words, but I knew this was a watershed. Children had braids. Adults had fashionable hair that they messed with for hours. I couldn't bring myself to touch the hair on the right side of my head that I knew was flying about wildly unanchored. It felt like it was bleeding, as if it were a severed limb, traumatized in agony.

At the end of two hours, Amá came and yelled at me. "Don't be such a baby! It's too late to change your mind! Let her finish the job so we can go to bed."

Sympathy would have made me cry all night. But anger and reason made me resolute and stoic. I dried my tears and went back to sit in front of the mirror. When she sawed through the second braid, I showed no feelings at all. She continued to cut until I had short curls all over my head.

In the morning, my eyes puffy and red, I went to school embarrassed, feeling like some huge layer of protection had been stripped away, leaving me raw and vulnerable. So I started to build another one, inside.

A week later we went to see the proofs. When the photographer told my mother the price of the photo package, she was shocked. She told him we'd have to think about it, and she pushed me out the door. We never went back.

In the fall of that year, the high school band director came to talk to us about playing an instrument in the band. Those of us who were interested were taken on a bus to hear the high school band play. They played a piece from *Marriage of Figaro.* Jukebox and "conjunto" music had always been a part of my life. This music was different and otherworldly, and I fell in love with it.

I told my father that the open house at the band hall was the following Saturday from one to four in the afternoon. I had never asked for anything like this. There would be money involved—a lot of money. He understood this without my saying anything.

On Saturday he came home at lunch after orchestrating the orders, deliveries, and chilling of the beer for the Buenos Aires Cantina that he ran on weekends for my Tío Manuel. He took a bath while my mother made lunch for him. I paced up and down on the front porch, hoping he'd remember and want to go, but not wanting to remind him.

He had his lunch and then sat down to sharpen kitchen knives with the whetstone. My father was never idle. At two-thirty I started to cry softly on the front porch. The time and the opportunity were slipping by. I could never ask him again for that much money. I really had no idea how much a flute cost, but I knew it was a lot more than the two dollars a week that my mother had refused to spend on dancing lessons for me.

My silent weeping drew my mother to the front door. She looked at me and walked away without saying anything. She walked to the kitchen and told my father I was crying. He put down the knife and whetstone and put on his Stetson. He walked out to the porch and said, "Let's go."

I dried my tears quickly with the underside hem of my dress and ran to get in the passenger seat as my father got behind the wheel.

He and I went alone to the band hall. Most of the parents had left by then. My father spoke no English and the band director spoke no Spanish. My father didn't know about band instruments either. I translated for Apá. The music company representative looked at us and said that possibly he could find a used instrument for me that would be a lot cheaper.

He walked down through the glittering array of gleaming new silver and brass instruments.

"Which one do you want?"

I tentatively pointed at a shiny silver flute.

"How much is it?"

I translated. The band director and the music company representative were staring intently at us. "One hundred fifty dollars cash or twenty-five dollars down and ten dollars a month in installments," the salesman replied. I explained it to Apá in Spanish.

"Tell them we'll take it on installments."

I translated and they rushed to get the papers. He took twenty-five dollars out of his wallet and signed everywhere they told him to, not being able to read a word.

We walked out. Spoken appreciation and gratitude were rare in our family. I was full of them and I had no model for how to let them out.

"¡Apá . . . muchas gracias!" It came out mixed with tears, past a lump in my throat.

He patted me awkwardly on the back with his huge brown hand. "I just want you to be happy, hija."

We rode home in silence, probably both thinking about the money. I didn't know how much he made now, but my sister had told me that on the farm, he had made five dollars a day. That meant that two of his long, dusty hot workdays a month would be for my flute.

I shouldn't have asked, but it was done now. I felt greedy and demanding.

When we got home, my mother asked me what happened. I told her. She rolled her eyes at the amount, but she didn't say anything.

A week later, it was waiting for me at the school. A shiny brand-new flute. It was the most glorious thing I had ever owned. I wished I could wear gloves to protect it from my sweaty little brown fingerprints.

The sound carried for blocks. When I practiced my scales, my friend Irene could hear every note a block and a half away.

My sisters had only two dresses for school when they were my age. Luis had gone around for years blind for the lack of eyeglasses. I had gotten a silver flute from heaven through my father's hard work and generous heart. I was luckier than the rest.

Every month he gave me ten dollars and fifty cents in cash. I walked downtown to the post office, bought a ten-dollar money order, and put it in a stamped envelope along with the payment stub.

My music made no sense to him, but he accepted it as part of my gringo school education. I loved my flute and the music it made as I had loved the storyteller in Minnesota. Like her, it made shimmering, otherworldly magic. I cleaned and polished it every day after practice and reverently put it in its velvet case.

Not a lot of money was spent on the janitorial services for our school. That year the school began a new program of having the students pick up trash on the playground. The duty rotated from class to class, just as the safety patrol did.

I loved the safety patrol. In the third grade I got the end-of-year honor pin for being the smartest in the class, but I would have preferred the safety patrol pin. I didn't like being intelligent; it was presumida. When you were chosen to be in the safety patrol, you got to wear a wide strap that went around your chest and around your waist that identified you as a crossing guard. You also got to wear a huge four-inch silver badge that said "Safety Patrol" and had scrolled designs all over it. Only the third and fourth graders were allowed to be in the safety patrol. The third graders were the doers and the fourth graders were the leaders and the captains.

I had been a doer for a long time—I was ready to be a leader and a captain. Soon it would be our class's turn and my turn. We went alphabetically and since my last name was "Treviño," I had waited impatiently through most of the alphabet.

For the trash detail, we were given a stick with a nail on the end of it for skewering the trash, and a paper bag. We went out to the playground first thing in the morning while it was still cool.

My brother Rudy was a senior in high school that year. As most seniors are, he was arrogant and thought he knew everything. It didn't help at all that he had been elected "Most Handsome" the previous year.

I saw him walk out of our house, across the street from the school playground. I turned away from him, hoping he wouldn't recognize me, but he did. He was walking to school because the previous week he had wrecked our car while fooling around with his friends. My father hadn't yelled at him since he had earned the money for the car at the canning factory in Wisconsin the previous summer. He saw me picking up trash and decided it was his job to save me from this filthy work (some of the trash was used toilet paper) since my parents spoke no English and couldn't help me themselves.

So, full of hormones, six feet tall and muscular in his football jacket, he walked around to the other side of the school, into the principal's office, without asking the secretary if he could.

"My little sister, Elva Treviño, is in the back of the school picking up trash. She's not a janitor and you can't use her that way. It's dirty work and she's a child. You gringos think you can use Mexican children to do your dirty work. If I ever see her picking up trash again, I'll be right back here in your office, and then I'll be MAD!"

And he walked out, leaving Mr. Ward speechless. He hadn't said one word.

That afternoon, I was informed by Mrs. Winters that the next time our class picked up trash, I would stay in the classroom alone. I would not be allowed to do safety patrol duty either, since that might be considered "work" by my family.

I felt that this was the worst thing Rudy had ever done to me. He had brought attention to me when I had been trying to fade into the woodwork. Mrs. Winters felt betrayed and said, "Why didn't you tell me you had a problem with picking up trash? I would have excused you. Instead you had your family go to the principal." I stood there silently, wanting to die.

I didn't cry until I got home. "Stay out of my business! I can take care of myself!" I yelled at him, choking with tears and rage.

He grinned gleefully—he had won another battle against the gringos—and he didn't care that it made me unhappy.

My parents seemed disoriented about the whole incident. They certainly didn't want me picking up other people's trash, but they would never have walked into the principal's office to complain about it, either.

I spent the rest of the school year working harder than ever on my studies and being quieter.

When people first told me that Rey liked me in the third grade, I was disgusted. At the time, I wanted nothing to do with boys. He sat at the opposite end of the room in the row in front of me. I felt his eyes on me constantly. When I looked up, he turned his head quickly.

In the fourth grade, Mrs. Winters devised a seating chart for the classroom. Rey was assigned a seat next to mine. We were constantly and intensely aware of each other's nearness. He passed papers to me, laying them gently in front of me. He paused just the right amount of time after I read before he started reading. If I dropped my pencil, he picked it up and ran to sharpen it for me.

Rey woke me up to boys.

His starched shirts were neat and crisply ironed. His jeans were starched too, the crease line ironed sharp so many times it was faded. He used hair oil with a slight flowery scent and it was neatly parted on the right. I loved to smell him and listen to his rustlings as he moved next to me.

He lived two blocks away. If I had walked through my back yard and then across two empty lots, I would have been at his house. My mother's most successful flowering bush was a five-foot gardenia outside my window covered with fragrant white blossoms. I dreamed waking dreams about Rey on hot nights with the intense smell of my mother's gardenias wafting in on the breezes through the screened window. I wondered if he was also lying awake, thinking about me.

I imagined myself getting out of bed in my white cotton nightgown. I would walk barefoot through my back yard with the moon lighting my way, feeling the heat of the day still in the sandy loam under my feet. He would get out of his bed and walk toward me, too. Our desire for each other drawing us both like sleepwalkers. We would meet in the middle of my father's six-foot-tall corn field, walking between the rows. No one would see.

"I knew you'd come," I'd say quietly as he reached for my hand.

"I knew you'd come too," he would answer.

I had no idea what we'd do next.

My frustrated yearning for Rey had me in a constant state of longing. He was so close and yet so far away. We touched each other only by accident. I was ripe for Manuel.

I met him at the Cinco de Mayo Fiesta in the spring of my fourth grade. I bought my twenty-five-cent ticket to go on the swings, which hung in a circle around the ride operator. I sat in my swing, waiting for the ride to start. My friends hadn't wanted to ride, so I went alone. I heard him yell to a friend on the sidelines and I turned around to look at him. He met my eyes and casually said, "Want me to push you?"

My heart leaped into my throat. I had seen other couples playing this way. The guy would grab the girl's swing and hold on to it until the ride got going really fast. Then he would push it forward as hard as he could. This would propel the girl forward and him backward, then the two swings would swing back toward each other. They would clasp hands to keep from banging into each other and then start all over, laughing gleefully.

"Sí, bueno," I answered nervously, my heart hammering. He was handsome and his smile warmed me like a hot sun.

"What's your name?"

"Elva."

"Mine is Manuel."

The ride started and he reached for my hand. I reached for his and heaven started. His hand was strong, firm, and gentle. He held me with his smile the whole time.

"Scared?" he asked as he pulled my swing close. Yes! I was terrified! But not of the ride.

"A little."

"Don't be afraid; it's nothing."

And he shot me forward. Explosions, sparkles, and rainbows happened. Then he reached for my hand again as I careened back to him. And I reached for his.

"Faster?"

"¡Sí!" I said. Wild feelings galloping through me.

And we went flying. Together, apart, together, apart. The ride was over much too soon.

We got off the swings and walked toward the exit together, and I was afraid to look at him.

"Later we ride again?" he asked when we got to the exit gate.

"Sí, bueno."

I stumbled around on shaky legs, trying to find my friends Irene and Rosemary. They were playing "manita."

"Your cheeks are all red and your hair is wild. What happened?" Irene asked.

"Nothing, I just rode the swings," I answered, avoiding her eyes.

When we passed each other on the paseo, he smiled. I smiled back that I liked him too, then quickly lowered my eyes, suddenly shy.

"Who's that?" asked Irene.

"I don't know," I answered, not ready to have them share him with me.

My mother found me and said I had to go home because it was getting late. I protested, but she was firm.

The next night was the last night of the Fiesta.

He found me and asked if I wanted to go on the Ferris wheel. He had already bought two tickets. This was more dangerous—kisses happened up there. I had never ridden the Ferris wheel with a boy. But I remembered his touch from the swings and I trusted him.

We got on and they closed the bar over our laps with a loud click. We sat not too close and not too far apart. He looped his left arm over the seat behind me, not really putting his arm around me, but almost. They took us up one notch and stopped to load the next seat in front of us. A little boy and his father got on. Apparently they knew Manuel.

"Hey, Meño!" the little boy yelled. "Riding the Ferris wheel with a girl!"

I blushed and pretended to be very interested in the fiesta. Manuel laughed nervously and said nothing.

It started going again and we rode up into the stars together. I knew life would never be the same for me. When they stopped us at the top, the little boy called to him from below. He leaned over the back and made the seat rock upwards. I panicked at the sudden motion so high up and let out a little scream. Concerned, he touched my shoulder. "Don't be afraid, it won't fall," he said quietly. I wanted to slide over and have him hold me, but the little boy was watching. He smiled at me, his face framed in the dark sky, and I smiled back gratefully.

"Want to go on the swings again?" he asked.

"Sí."

We walked from the Ferris wheel to the swings again. I was terrified that someone I knew would see us. My brother Rudy would be the worst one. I would never hear the end of it. But no one in the crowd seemed interested in us. When he pulled my swing to him, it seemed he pulled it closer than he needed to, and I liked it, terrified and exhilarated.

It seemed the rest of the world disappeared except for his swing and mine. He pulled my swing so that my face was right next to his. He squeezed my hand on the bar and then he pushed me away hard. I flew back to him harder. We both laughed out loud.

Again I wasn't ready for it to be over. As we walked away, he lit up in a smile for me again and said, "Bye." I waved even though I wasn't ready to let go. I didn't even know his last name. It seemed as if it had been a dream. Not one of my friends had seen us in the crowd or met him.

I didn't see him again all summer. My longings for Rey were nothing compared to what came next. My hands burned when I remembered Manuel's firm, gentle touch. My whole body burned when I remembered how he pulled me to him in the swing. The memory of his smile on the Ferris wheel, with the stars and the midnight-blue sky framing his face, made my knees weak.

"What's wrong with you?" My mother woke me out of my daydream reverie.

"Nada."

I found out later that he was two years older than I, his last name was Madrigal, and he was poor. But to me he was a brilliant smile, firm and gentle hands, and a feeling that drew me irresistibly like a moth.

I had been drawn to Rey, but Manuel was my first love.

Rudy graduated from high school at the end of my fourth grade year.

My sister Diamantina made a blue chiffon dress and a ruffled petticoat to go underneath for me. She was a born seamstress and dress designer. The dress had gathers at the hem with tiny daisies holding the gathers. I walked out into the living room proudly. Apá was sitting there dressed in his best black slacks, ready to go. He said, "You have some gathers there on your dress that don't look right. Fix them before we go." What did he know about fashion, anyway?

There was a lot of excitement in the Mexican community because the valedictorian that year was Dolores Treviño. She had the same last name as ours but was not related to us. It was the first time a Mexican woman had been valedictorian. The only thing I remembered about her speech was that she said she was going to college at the University of Texas.

I sat there in my chair between my mother and father in my blue chiffon dress. Dolores's family wasn't any better off than ours. I had gotten the honor pins, both in the third grade and in the fourth grade, for being the smartest in the class. Maybe I could go to college, too. That would be the biggest turning point of all.

To my father, and therefore to me, at that age, graduation from high school was a big achievement for a Mexican migrant. The drop-out rate on our side of the tracks was high. Working seemed easier than competing academically, past the language barrier and the discrimination. But I was doing very well academically. And it seemed easy to me—much easier than working for my father in the fields.

On the way home, Apá talked proudly about how now five of his children had graduated from high school; there was only me left. He hoped I would graduate, too.

"Apá, I would like to go to college like Dolores when I graduate from high school. Do you think I could?"

He didn't respond right away. He seemed to be taken aback by this startling possibility. We each replayed the scene of Dolores giving her valedictory speech in our minds, weighing the possibilities that it seemed to hold for me. Apá knew that my grades were good.

"Do you really think you want to go to college? I think it's probably pretty hard."

"Sí, Apá. I really like to study. I think I can do it. But college must be very expensive."

"Well I think it probably is, hija, but let's see if I can save a little to help you."

Then I felt guilty. He was already working two days a month to pay for my flute. Now it seemed I was asking for more. None of my brothers and sisters had gone to college; they had all started earning their own way immediately.

I knew I was no better.

Chapter Twelve

Del dicho al hecho, hay mucho trecho.

It's a long way from word to deed.

(One of Apá's favorite dichos)

For four years, all my classmates had been pure Mexicans at the Westside Elementary School. Across town, all the students at the Eastside Elementary school were white except for two or three blacks. In the fifth grade, we were integrated for the first time. There were girls with blonde curls sitting next to me in class. Even then, we divided the playground on our own between the Mexicans and the white kids; no one had to tell us.

My parents started giving me money for the cafeteria. None of my siblings had ever eaten in the cafeteria. The cafeteria ladies served me pork and boiled white rice. I was used to arroz con pollo, so I doused the white rice with sugar and milk. I made pudding out of it so I could eat it.

Our teacher, who was the Eastside Elementary School principal as well as our classroom teacher, had his office across the hall from our classroom, so that he could go back and forth easily. We had lots of in-class assignments that we were to work on quietly while he worked across the hall in his office. We had art every day at the end of the day. Sometimes the end of the day came very early if our teacher needed to be in the principal's office. Our class consisted of the bright kids and we were usually quiet and well behaved. I made a huge number of art projects that year: collages, elaborate popsicle stick lamps, papier-mâché dolls, etc. Amá ran out of shelf space to display them.

Gilbert sat next to me for part of the year. The Pearsall Volunteer Fire Department announced an art contest: a $100 first prize and second and third prizes for art related to fire prevention. Gilbert drew as naturally as he ate.

Gilbert used a white poster board, and with nothing else besides a number two pencil, he drew a burned-out forest. Looking at the charred stumps made me want to cry. They evoked pictures of green, thousand-year-old trees killed by the fire. I decided I would never let my father toss a match out of our car window again.

We all clustered around him and raved about his talent and his art, proud that the Mexican community had produced him.

He was disqualified.

They said he couldn't possibly have drawn the poster. It was too good; someone must have done it for him. This Mexican kid was a liar.

Gilbert didn't protest. And we didn't either, even though we knew a whole host of ways to prove he had actually drawn it alone. They didn't want proof, and they probably wouldn't accept it, anyway. They saw what they wanted to see.

A Mexican artist would not get far in Pearsall.

A couple of years after Delia and Delmira moved to San Antonio to work, Delia got married. It was traumatic for all of us when she and Chale eloped. We hadn't even known she was dating him.

The next day they drove up to the house, where Amá and Apá were sitting on the front porch. Delia told them that they were married, and showed them the marriage license to prove it. "What does a damn paper mean to me?" Apá yelled. Then he told them to leave. Delia shook with sobs as she got in the car. The rest of us watched from the bedroom window.

Amá cried for a day or two until Apá relented. Delia and Chale were invited to be part of the family.

They rented part of a big white house for awhile. Then, when Delia got pregnant, they moved in with Chale's mother, Victoria, who lived deep in San Antonio's west side, right on the edge of the Arroyo del Alazán creek. I felt very comfortable walking around the west side of San Antonio. The residents were almost all Mexican American, the restaurants sold mostly Mexican food, the cantinas only played Mexican music, and the children all spoke Spanish. The drugstores sold herbs as well as pills, and candles with pictures of saints were everywhere.

Victoria was tall and shiny dark brown like polished mahogany, with laugh lines around her eyes and mouth. I never heard her speak a single unkind word. Victoria's husband had died when Chale was a freshman in high school. Chale had quit school to support the family. Victoria's house was humble but sparkling clean and neat. It had a tiny front yard where she grew oleander and crepe myrtle.

Directly across the dirt street from her house was the Arroyo del Alazán. This creek was usually a trickle, but during a flood, it could crest to a dangerous roar. But floods were rare. The weed-covered sides of the creek were a place for the neighborhood kids to play. And play they did, with wild abandon and frequently without shoes. Carlos, Delia's oldest, would frequently come home with cut feet from the broken glass hidden in the weeds. She couldn't get him to wear his shoes.

When Delia started having babies, we really looked forward to her visits. When we knew she was coming for the weekend, we went from window to window on Saturday morning, hoping to be the first to run out to the car and carry one of the babies.

At Delia's house, the entertainment for me was her babies. She had six in all, one after the other. So there was always a baby for me to carry around or tickle or feed. I had never had a real doll, and real babies were much better, anyway. I learned early to change the umbilical cord dressing and change diapers.

Rarely, very rarely, we left the babies with Victoria and went on the city bus downtown. There we either shopped at the Solo-Serve or went to a matinee at the Alameda, which showed Mexican movies in Spanish. A couple of times, we went to the Majestic for an American movie. The Majestic Theatre really was majestic. The ceiling was covered with shine-in-the-dark stars. The massive velvet curtains opened when the movie was about to start.

Sometimes we visited our city relatives: Tía Chela, Tía Adela, Tía Sofía, Tío Rey. They all had tiny, dark houses with tiny yards covered with trees. I liked living in Pearsall's open spaces much better. The cousins were the ones I envied. They got photographed in studios with frilly white dresses, their bodies draped against Roman columns. They took piano and tap dancing lessons. Some of them spoke mostly English. This was hard for my mother, so she just smiled a lot when they came in the room.

Delmira told me about menstruation. She was the guide that led me through all the significant events in my life: menstruation, sex, surgery, marriage, adoption, divorce. I was probably too young to know. I was not yet in the fourth grade and none of my sisters had started having periods before age fourteen. A girl-friend had told me about it, but I didn't believe her. But I believed everything that Delmira said; she was my idol. So she told me. Maybe she needed to tell me for herself.

My parents had taken me to San Antonio to spend a week with Delia. At the end of the week Delmira picked me up in her boyfriend's long, brown, two-seater Jaguar. She was taking me back to Pearsall as well as visiting my parents overnight. The boyfriend that came with the Jaguar was new, a soldier from one of the many air force bases in San Antonio, and one that really adored her, she said. She had picked this one because the last one had hurt her badly.

Carlos had been her first boyfriend in San Antonio and the only Mexican that I ever remember her dating. She was besotted with his looks, his soft-spoken charm, and his easy grace. He had jet-black hair, white porcelain skin, and a to-die-for smile. I had met him the previous month. He wore slacks and cardigans—unheard of in Pearsall. I liked him, although I didn't see how he would ever fit into our down-to-earth Mexican family, who ate with their fingers and used an outhouse. He seemed so clean and suave, a city boy whose feet had never touched dirt.

But he was a dirty liar and a cheat. He had to marry the other one—the one he was dating at the same time as Delmira. The one who got pregnant.

So now she was driving me home, full of hurt feelings and pride. And so she told me about menstruation and the other time—the time she'd been hurt.

She said that Amá hadn't prepared her for womanhood; no
one had. So she would take it upon herself to prepare me even
though maybe I was a little young. She had gone from being a
tomboy, nicknamed Pongui because she was always climbing on
things, to bleeding between her legs and feeling betrayed by
growing up. Even Delia, only two years older, hadn't told her
about menstruation.

We were driving through Lytle and I was being absolutely
quiet, afraid that she'd stop talking. She looked at me and her eyes
narrowed, as if trying to decide whether to go on or not.

"I'm going to tell you something that I've never told anyone—the way it really happened. Think you're ready to hear it?"
I nodded my head.

"About two months after having my first period, I could feel it
was time for it again. My breasts were hard, swelling new nubs. I
hated them and the painful tenderness. I had to do everything
more slowly, because they hurt when my dress brushed against
them. I wasn't wearing a bra yet.

"We went to visit Tío. We sat in the living room and they
offered Amá coffee. They sent me in the kitchen to get it. When I
went in the kitchen, there was the cousin, big and strong, fully a
man. It all happened very fast. I saw he was looking at my new
breasts pushing my cotton dress out. I froze. 'Look what pretty
little lemons,' he said as he took each of them between his thumb
and forefinger and twisted them hard.

"'¡Ayy!' I stifled a cry while he ran out of the room laughing.

"'¿Qué tienes?' Amá yelled from the other room.

"'Nada! I . . . I . . . I burned myself with the coffee.'

"I wobbled out the back door to the outhouse. I couldn't stop
crying as I locked myself in. I wanted to cry a grito abierto. But
I bit my fist and swallowed the screams instead. Wave after wave
of shame washed over me. When my face was covered with tears
and snot, I felt the red wetness between my legs. Chingao—the
last straw.

"I fixed myself up the best I could with toilet tissue. They
were waiting for the coffee."

I tried not to move a muscle while the car rolled toward Pearsall. She seemed to have forgotten that I was there.

After Delia got married, it didn't take long before Delmira moved out of Tía Chela's also. She moved into a big white house on Quincy Street. She and two roommates had half of the house, with their own entrance, kitchen, and bathroom.

And my forays into the world alone started.

Delmira worked it out with my parents. They put me on the Greyhound bus in Pearsall. I rode the fifty miles to San Antonio alone, and Delmira waited for me at the San Antonio bus station.

I dressed myself in my best church dress, white socks, and my Shirley Temple school shoes. I put some clothes for the weekend in a paper bag and was ready.

On the way to the bus station in Pearsall, my mother kept telling me not to leave the San Antonio bus station in case Delmira wasn't there. I was to call Delia from the pay phone. I promised.

I liked to sit in the very front of the bus so I could see out the big front window as well as the side ones. The bus stopped in Moore, Devine, Natalia, and Lytle on the way to San Antonio. Delmira was there waiting even though it was three-thirty in the afternoon. She had skipped her lunch hour and breaks at her job working as a secretary for the city of San Antonio to come and get me. We went back to her office and I sat quietly by her desk until five o'clock.

We took the city bus to her apartment in the big white house. The house had a grassy lawn and a large, wooden front porch. The ceilings were nine feet high. The house was shaded on all sides by huge sycamores. The porch, the shade of the trees, and the high ceilings all combined to make the house seem cool and dark, very much unlike our house in Pearsall. Our house had no shade trees yet, no insulation, and low ceilings. It baked in the sun, surrounded by hot, red sand.

That night, she had a date with her boyfriend, Carl, the brown Jaguar guy, and I was to go along. I watched, fascinated, as she and her two roommates walked around the house in their bras and half-slips getting ready to go out. In my house, everyone was always fully clothed except behind closed doors. Delmira asked me to repair the hem of her skirt while she put on her makeup. I sat in a chair in their giant bathroom with a working toilet while she put on her mascara in her underwear and joked and laughed with her roommates. They told each other dirty jokes and laughed uproariously, then apologized to me after each one. I blushed, said it was O.K., and kept sewing.

Her makeup finished, Delmira stuffed a cotton ball into each cup of her bra to make the points stand out. I told her the skirt was finished and asked if she'd like me to iron it. She said yes and set up the ironing board for me.

Then the men started arriving. The dates. I got really scared then. At our house, dates weren't allowed except on prom nights. Girls had to date surreptitiously: to go out with their girlfriends and then meet the guy at the hamburger joint. Intimacy happened in parked cars on country roads in the dark. Here the dating was totally in the open: they kissed, sat together on the couch, and told jokes. On the one hand, I liked all the seemingly dangerous excitement. On the other hand, all this open intimacy scared me.

After Carlos, Delmira stopped dating Mexicans and started dating soldiers. The U.S. Air Force brought them for her from all over the country. Her two roommates were still dating Mexicans.

Carl came to the screen door and knocked, then just came in when he saw that the room was already full of people. The other two guys were nice looking, but Carl was stunning. He was six foot two inches of long, sinewy muscle. His swimming-pool-blue eyes caught and held me when he realized who I was. I tore my eyes away from him and looked at my shoes—feeling like a fish in a room full of land animals—completely out of my element.

He led us out the front door to the long, brown two-seater Jaguar that I had already been in. Delmira and I shared the passenger seat. I was not surprised that Delmira had a handsome, blue-eyed boyfriend. I had known she would someday.

He took us to a drive-up hamburger joint. We sat there with the top down, eating our burgers and onion rings under the bright lights. Elvis sang "Love Me Tender" through the loudspeaker. Then they took me to the go-cart place. Carl and I raced each other in the go-carts while Delmira watched behind the chain-link fence. He was fun and I liked him a lot.

I couldn't meet his gaze, though. His blue eyes bored into me like the aliens with glowing eyes at the Saturday matinee. When he looked at Delmira, I let myself stare at that incredible aqua color.

They decided to get married. What a brother-in-law I would have! He would wear his air force dress whites to the wedding. The picture staggered my mind. Dress whites covering all that muscle, showing his golden-brown tan and making those eyes even more startling.

When she brought him home to introduce him to my parents for the first time, my father was uncharacteristically quiet during the whole thing. He gave his blessing for the wedding. My mother said not one word; she wasn't expected to.

But after they left, she said a lot. She didn't like this guy. She had a bad feeling about the whole thing. She worried herself into a lather.

The night before the wedding, as we feared, she went over the brink. She became trastornada. Hysterics, screaming, paralysis, the doctor, Amá lost to the world. When she screamed, the screams were about Delmira and this doomed marriage she was embarking on. Delmira had to be called in San Antonio. "Come home! Amá está trastornada. Yes, it's about the wedding."

Delmira called the whole thing off and came home. We all sat around Amá in a darkened room, sure she was going to die. Rudy cried big macho tears in the doorway.

Amá recovered, of course, and Delmira never married Carl.

After Carl, the next boyfriend was Al. Al was a Boston blueblood. He was serving his country after graduating from Yale Law School. When he was finished serving his time, he would go back east and join the family law firm.

By now, the bus trip to San Antonio was routine. Instead of Delmira coming to get me at the bus station, I walked to her office alone, with my paper bag of weekend clothes. My mother didn't know, of course, that we had this arrangement. Delmira understood and trusted my capabilities and independence much more than my mother did.

I got off the bus and walked to the corner that had the big clock on it, then I turned right and walked to the city hall. The whole walk was only eight blocks or so through downtown San Antonio.

Al came to the screen door in a white shirt and narrow tie. He drove us to the restaurant in a four-door sedan. The waiter in the French restaurant put the linen napkin on my lap. Delmira whispered to me to leave it there. Al ordered for all three of us, as the menu was in French. He quietly asked me about my school work while the violins played in the background.

Al flew Delmira to Boston to introduce his future wife to his mother. His mother lived in a stately Boston brownstone. Delmira told me the story when she got home.

When Al had gone upstairs to dress for dinner, his mother and older sister had a little talk with Delmira. "Don't you realize you can never fit in here? This marriage is impossible. You must convince Al that it could never work. You must allow him to marry someone of his own class." She didn't respond, not knowing what to say. She just let them go on and on. When she heard Al coming down the stairs, she swallowed the lump in her throat and stood up to go to dinner.

She never told Al what had happened. She just broke off the engagement. My parents never heard about Al. For my part, I was not sorry to see this one go.

The Jewish dentist, raised on Flatbush Avenue in Brooklyn, was next. Kal was a captain in the air force. He had put himself through Yeshiva University.

He took us to an Italian restaurant with loud music. I had never heard of pasta, so again, someone else ordered for me. Kal could have been a stand-up comedian as easily as a dentist. He dangled a piece of pasta from one nostril and talked about having a bad cold. We laughed the whole time over dinner as I watched the other patrons, some slurping, some rolling, and some biting their long spaghetti.

When he took us home, Delmira snagged her hose on his car door and got a run. The next morning he had twelve pairs delivered to her door. I liked this guy, and so did my parents. Delmira was twenty-seven, practically an old maid, but they decided to get married.

Delmira came to Pearsall on the morning of their wedding day. She wanted Apá to be certain that she was really getting married—no recriminations like when Delia got married. She was lying on the front bedroom bed, looking out the window, wanting to catch the first possible glimpse of his car coming down the street. Straining with all her body to hear the familiar car motor even before it came into sight.

She was waiting to be married. That afternoon she had been waiting twenty-seven years. The courthouse closed at five. At two she started to be anxious, combing and recombing her hair in place. At three she lay on the bed, every muscle taut, no longer caring about wrinkles in her clothes or perfect hair, just wanting a bridegroom.

I alternated between being in the bedroom with her and walking out to the curb, where I could see further down the street.

Having aged years, at four o'clock she got up, smoothed the wrinkles on her skirt and patted her hair, preparing herself to be a jilted bride. She started to visualize going back to work at San Antonio City Hall, trying to act nonchalant between waves of cold shame. Would she be able to hold the tears back?

At four-fifteen, when we had both given up, he drove up without our noticing. Amá told us he was here. She ran out. He had lots of excuses. They drove away and got married with half an hour to spare. While they were in Acapulco I wondered what kind of marriage this would be.

Chapter Thirteen

Caballo que vuela, no quiere espuelas.

A horse that soars doesn't need spurs.

(Mexican dicho)

I was walking to Danchak's Department Store on the day I saw that the public library had opened. I was in the sixth grade. Before I started school, I had no books. I neither read nor had books read to me. For me, this was the worst part of our poverty. At the Westside school, there was no library. In the fifth grade, they had finally started taking us to the junior high school library.

The double front doors of the public library were open to the street. It had been a department store in the past. The two display windows on either side of the double doors were draped with cloth and books were featured.

The new sign read "Pearsall Public Library." Did that include me? I walked in and spoke to the librarian. "Can anyone check books out here?"

"Yes, anyone that lives in Pearsall," said the middle-aged white lady. She was sorting through stacks of books that had been donated to the new library. The air was thick with book dust. The books were aged, with yellowed pages. I walked between the piles on the unfinished wood floor under a high ceiling.

"How much does it cost?" I had to ask so I wouldn't be embarrassed later.

"It's free; you just have to fill out a library card."

Almost directly behind her and to the right were The Hardy Boys and Nancy Drew. Up to then, what I mostly read outside school were my sister's *True Confessions* magazines and comic books from the grocery store.

"How many can I take at once?"

"Three."

I took two, not wanting to seem greedy.

When I got home, my mother wanted to know where they came from. I explained. She had never heard of a public library.

On the third day, during my sixth public library book, my mother started yelling at me. She had only gone as far as the third grade. She didn't know what to do with a voracious reader. "You're going to go blind reading those books!" she said. "You're going to go crazy reading all those books!" That was my mother's reaction.

The books threatened her because she didn't know what was in them. And I was clearly and absolutely obsessed with them. So I started hiding them. I would go to the opposite end of the house from where she was working, feeling guilty that I wasn't helping her with the housework, and read in secret, always listening for her footsteps so I could hide the book. Reading became my adolescent rebellion. I read under the quilt at night with a flashlight after they had gone to bed, I read out in the yard behind the outhouse until she came to find me, I read on the steps of the Westside school, wherever I could get out from under my rattled mother's worried eyes.

My plan was to read everything in the library. I wasn't too selective. I went from Nancy Drew and The Hardy Boys to Arthur Conan Doyle's Sherlock Holmes. I began to hope that someday I would be able to figure out life the way they solved mysteries. After mysteries came Frances Hodgson Burnet, with *The Secret Garden, The Little Princess,* and *Little Lord Fauntleroy.* I continued with Louisa May Alcott's *Little Women.* Being a poor Mexican child in an arid landscape, these children seemed to lead dream lives.

At first I avoided the books with big words. Then Delmira gave me a dictionary for Christmas. This made it harder to hide, because I would have an open book, an open dictionary, and a paper and pen to write down definitions.

To assuage my guilt, I split my time between reading and helping my mother around the house. Also, this way she tended to leave me alone more during my reading time.

My head swimming with visions of Victorian England, I did the dishes. I imagined myself in flouncy Victorian dresses and bloomers, riding sidesaddle through the misty English countryside. I left the black and white movie of my childhood and escaped into the Technicolor of books. Pearsall became too small for me, like an outgrown dress.

Up until the summer after the sixth grade I had explored the world, safe in the bosom of my family. Then Delmira and Kal got married and moved to the Queens borough of New York City. When the airlines instituted "youth fares," Delmira and Kal offered to pay for me to come to New York to visit. Kal came back to Texas to take the dental license exams. That way, in case they ever moved back to Texas, he could practice there. We flew back to New York together.

Delmira was working for PepsiCo on the corner of 59th and Park Avenue in Manhattan as a secretary. Kal was working for another dentist in a Park Avenue penthouse office that only took executive clients. The office looked more like a well-appointed library than a dental office. It had leather chairs, Persian rugs, and a garden terrace that overlooked Park Avenue. I felt like Alice in Wonderland, and I expected to wake up in Pearsall any minute.

Delmira and I rode the subway from Queens to Manhattan in the morning. We went to the door of her building together and I promised, in response to her worried entreaties, to stay close to 59th and Park and meet her for lunch.

Of course, at first, I stayed close, but the city called to me and I felt perfectly safe responding. No one even seemed to notice me. The streets and avenues were easy to figure out, and I had a map, anyway.

At the Horn & Hardart Automat, my favorite place to have a mid-morning snack, I put coins in the slot to get lemon meringue pie or cheesecake. Window-shopping at Tiffany's was next. I never dared go in, afraid they would recognize me as a poor Mexican migrant and throw me out. I tried to get lost on purpose in Bloomingdale's. All the half floors and twists and turns in the departments were endlessly fascinating.

I was always back to the lobby of the PepsiCo building by noon. We had a light lunch with Delmira's friends—soup and half a sandwich. Then we window-shopped together for half an hour. It seemed that Alexander's was the only place we ever bought anything; all the rest was window-shopping and dreaming.

The other place I loved to go alone was Grand Central Station. Everyone was in a hurry there and I didn't recognize one single person among the thousands that hurried by. In Pearsall, no one was in a hurry and I knew them all. I made up stories to go with the people's facial expressions at Grand Central: "Her husband just left her last week. Her mother makes her feel guilty about wanting him back . . ."

At five o'clock we took the subway home.

On weekends they took me to the Guggenheim, the Met, and on the five-cent ferry to Staten Island. One Saturday we took the bus tour to Chinatown, Little Italy, and Wall Street.

Coney Island was pure excitement. I learned to love knishes with mustard there. A huge black man bumped into me and said, "Excuse me, cupcake." No one had ever called me "cupcake" before.

We went to see *Oliver!* on Broadway and walked through Greenwich Village afterwards.

When I got back to Pearsall, I tried to tell my friends what it had been like. They had been bored all summer. They listened politely, unimpressed with the wonders I was describing

I soon learned to keep New York to myself.

The next summer, Rudy and Luis, who by now were married to Consuelo and Dolores, were living in Wisconsin. They worked in the steel foundries in Waukesha. The two of them, along with Delmira, made a deal for me. I guess they felt prosperous now that they were all out of the fields, and they wanted to share their prosperity with me. Luis paid to fly me to Wisconsin since the airline "youth fares" were still in effect, Rudy paid to fly me to New York, and Delmira paid to fly me home. They did this every summer until I graduated from high school.

As their world opened up, they opened up mine.

Chapter Fourteen

Quien siembra vientos, cosecha tempestades.

He who sows the wind shall reap
the whirlwind.

(Old Testament, Hosea 8:7)

In the seventh grade, I discovered the scientific method. The science fair was announced with lots of fanfare. The projects were to be judged by visiting dignitaries from San Antonio. I stayed after school to talk to my science teacher about possible projects. He suggested several alternatives, one of which I latched onto immediately.

Planaria are flat little worms that live in water and look like tiny arrows. They have a head, a tail, a gullet, and not much else. What's fascinating about them is that they have the ability to regenerate severed parts of their body. If you cut off the tail, they grow a new one. If you cut the tail in half, they grow two new tails. They are so insistent on living, that even if you behead them, they will grow a new head.

I proposed to cut up the little creatures in ways I was sure no one had thought of, pushing the frontiers of basic science out to where they had never been before. I imagined I could sew several heads together or cut one head three ways and make four. I proposed to do all this following the scientific method exactly, varying only one factor at a time while keeping all others constant, taking extensive notes in a lab notebook so that other scientists could follow my groundbreaking work.

The science teacher showed me how to order the planaria and petri dishes from a catalog. My father didn't mind at all giving me the money for my experiments, since planaria didn't cost much.

When I laid out all the experiments I wanted to try, some that had predictable outcomes and many that did not, I realized that I wouldn't have enough petri dishes. My science teacher came to the rescue with a few more. When the planaria arrived in the mail, I fed them right away with raw liver rescued from my mother's dinner plans. They live in water, and they're fastidious little things, wanting their dinner removed as soon as they're done eating. I changed the water three times until it was clear.

Then I got a razor blade from my father's shaving kit and started the surgery. I figured they would be less likely to move a lot if they were full of liver. First I performed the predictable experiments to make sure I had a good batch of planaria. Cut off the tail, it will grow a new one. Put the amputees in a separate dish with a piece of numbered masking tape marking the dish. I really couldn't imagine that new heads would grow when I beheaded some, but the guillotine fell on three of them to make sure. A third set got both their head and tails cut off, leaving only the midsection with the gullet intact. Of course I saved the tails and the heads in separate dishes to see if they would grow new bodies. I recorded all of this in my lab notebook, noting the day of the surgeries and the number of the petri dish for each experiment.

There were two last predictable experiments. If you take a triangle cut just behind the head, you should get a smaller head growing there. If you split the tail in half, you get two fully developed tails.

Then I went wild. First I tried to sew two heads together. I sterilized the smallest needle in my mother's sewing box by passing it through the blue flame on our gas range. That's the way our neighbor sterilized needles for piercing baby girls' ears. I used red thread so I could see what was happening. It was a mess. The initial surgeries had been easy, as I made the cuts right in the petri dish, having dumped most of the water out. But to suture the little buggers together, I had to take them out and handle them.

Each day that passed brought new ideas for how to cut and/or paste. What was the tiniest piece of head that would grow a new body? Could I split the tails of a two-tailed planarian and get a four-tailed planarian? I had to go to my father for more money as I had run out of petri dishes again. He seemed less willing to give it to me this time, but he did, anyway. He had seen me moving the petri dishes around and thought I had too many already. I called Delmira in San Antonio and she brought them for me on the weekend.

The directions said to keep the planaria in a cool place. Cool places are hard to find in a South Texas house when it is spring and you have no air conditioning. I kept changing my mind as to where the coolest places were. Under various beds, under the couch, on top of the refrigerator. I considered putting them under the house, as our house was built with pier and beam construction, but I was afraid that my mother's outdoor cat would eat the tender little morsels tasting of liver.

After observing their progress one day after school and recording changes in my lab notebook, I decided to put them under one of the twin beds. As I was pushing them way under the bed to the darkest corner, I saw a triangle of green sticking out between the headboard and the box spring. I investigated and pulled it out. It was a book—a brand-new book. It had no dust jacket, but it was obviously new. The binding was totally unbroken and it smelled just like the books at the book fair, fresh off the press.

I had never seen a book in our house before. School books of course, battered books covered in brown paper with lots of doodling and brown smudges from previous students. But this book was pure, pristine, untouched.

In my mind I went through all the people who lived in or came to our house to see if I could fathom how this stranger had gotten in our house and been so well hidden in the bed, wedged way down between the headboard and the box springs. Amá? Apá? Ridiculous. Rudy? Dee? Delia or Delmira? I had never seen any of them with any book other than a school book.

I started reading on page one. It was obviously a novel, but it read like pure drivel to me. The guy had an attitude; he didn't like anything, and he wrote paragraphs that went on for pages. I leafed through it to see if it got any better toward the middle. It didn't. I decided I must be missing something. The book must be important somehow or else it wouldn't be in the house, brand new, and hidden so well. I started again on page one and read ten pages. Gobbledygook. I leafed through it again more slowly and hit upon the phrase "Egyptian fuck."

The book was Henry Miller's *Tropic of Capricorn*. I had never read or even heard of Henry Miller, but now I knew why the book was in the house. I got up and made sure there was no one in the house besides Amá. She was busy in the kitchen making dinner. Then I sat in the front bedroom by the window so I could see immediately if anyone came to the door. I got a piece of paper and went back to page one. I turned through the pages of gobbledygook and interminable paragraphs fast, skimming the words until I got to another hot passage. I read it and noted the page number on my piece of paper. The passages varied in length from half a page to several pages. It was amazing how the writing got clear during these passages. The writer seemed to slow down and finally write in a language I could understand.

I wasn't finished when Amá called me to dinner. I hid the book in a new place, in the bedroom closet under Amá's suitcase where she kept Apá's naturalization papers. If anyone asked about the book, I would know who the guilty party was. I still didn't know if I would tell that I had it or not.

Over the next few days, when still no one had asked for the book, I read the passages over and over, getting more and more titillated each time. After I had decided to tell no one, my friend Manuela told me a dirty joke one day at lunchtime.

"I have a book!" The words burst out of me like a little explosion before I could catch them.

"Book?" she asked, alerted by the tone of my voice. She made me tell her the rest.

"Bring it to school!" she said.

"Are you out of your mind? I'll get expelled!"

"Who would ever know? We all carry books around all the time."

I covered it in brown paper just like my textbooks, and then doodled all over the cover to disguise it further.

My planaria were all but forgotten. Oh sure, I fed them, moved them to cooler places, and desultorily recorded which ones had made progress and which ones had died in recovery. The day before the science fair project was due, I stayed up all night making a three-sided stand-up poster to display at the fair, along with a few petri dishes that displayed the most dramatic results and my lab notebook.

The next night I didn't sleep either, as I had to catch up on homework that had been postponed because of the planaria and Henry Miller. By now, the book and the list of page numbers had circulated all through my friends and were in the hands of friends of friends. My constantly growing anxiety had demanded it back many times, but it always had to go to just one more person.

At ten that morning, a page on the intercom interrupted my English class to call me to the principal's office. I knew my goose was cooked. I knew of two boys that had been expelled for having half a bottle of beer, but I knew of no girls that had ever been expelled. I wondered who had turned me in.

But the principal was smiling. He extended his hand to congratulate me on winning first place at the science fair. I burst into loud, uncontrollable sobs. He led me to a chair and said maybe I had been working too hard.

After a while, I wobbled out of the office and went to the girls' room to splash water on my face. At lunch I demanded the book back and wouldn't take no for an answer. On the way home after school, I walked out of my way to throw the book into the garbage behind the grocery store.

No one at my house ever mentioned that it was missing.

Chapter Fifteen

Mestizo educado, diablo colorado.

An educated mestizo is a red devil.

(Mexican dicho from the colonial days)

O n the morning of my first day of high school, I sat on the porch and waited for my friend Manuela to walk by so we could go to school together. I wore a new outfit that I had made with Diamantina's help, and I also wore white bobby socks and canvas sneakers. My mother had scrubbed the bobby socks on the washboard to get the red Pearsall dirt out. She had bleached them and rinsed them in bluing. They blazed startlingly white against my brown legs. She had scrubbed my canvas sneakers too, trying to get them white again after I had walked through the mud in them.

When Manuela came by, I fell into step with her and her two sisters. On the next block, Irene joined us. Two blocks later, we picked up Rosemary. We walked a mile to school because buses were only for the farm kids and for the kids who came thirteen miles from Moore, an even smaller town than Pearsall. Except for two of the main streets, the streets on the Mexican side were not paved. I was glad that the weather had been dry lately, because when it rained, the streets ran like muddy red-brown rivers, making deep rifts. The cars picked their way slowly around puddles of unknown depth. When it dried, the city grader tractor came and leveled the dirt streets somewhat. Of course, no storm drains existed, so the really big storms caused major damage.

Our little group walked across the railroad tracks to "el otro lado," the other side of town. The railroad tracks divided the town like the Río Bravo. It might just as well have been the Río Grande River because Pearsall was really two towns. The gringos lived on the east side of town and the Mexicans lived on the west side. That's just the way it was. The Mexican side of town was euphemistically referred to on surveys as "Spanish Acres." The downtown, the junior high school, the high school, and the post office were all on the gringo side.

The downtown consisted of a few stores, the bank, and the post office. There was no mail delivery on the Mexican side, so Mexicans had to have post office boxes. Our whole family shared Tío Alfredo's post office box. I had gone with my father to the bank often. He went there to borrow money every time we went north again. We bought cheap trinkets at the dime store. And we liked the clothes store downtown because we could buy on credit. For the rest of our needs, we stayed on our side of town. We had little grocery stores called "tendajos," except for the big one owned by my father's oldest brother, Tío Blas. We also had the Mexican movie theater, the big Catholic Church, and lots of cantinas.

In Pearsall, even the cemeteries were segregated. There might have been one or two Mexicans buried in the gringo cemetery, but the Mexican cemetery was pure. No gringo in Pearsall would allow his body to rot for eternity among the Mexicans.

The halls of the high school were shiny with new summer wax. The students were shiny with a first-day-of-school polish: scrubbed faces, new clothes, new shoes. The inside of the dark school building felt cool in the south Texas September morning.

At the end of the previous school year, at the eighth-grade graduation, I had gotten the "High Point Mexican Girl" award. In Pearsall, there wasn't just one award for having the highest grades. There was "High Point Girl," "High Point Boy," "High Point Mexican Girl," and "High Point Mexican Boy." No one ever said whether the grades of the other winners were better than mine or not. I determined to do well in high school also, even though my parents had low expectations for me. They signed the back of my report card without looking at the front. My "A+'s" and my angst over the one "B+" meant nothing to them. They couldn't read the English or understand the grading system. They hoped I wouldn't get pregnant and that I stayed in school long enough to get a job that didn't involve dirt or being someone's servant.

At the high school, benches surrounded the trees. No one told us to, but we segregated ourselves on the schoolyard, waiting for class to begin. The white kids had their set of benches and we had ours.

Teachers in Pearsall came in two basic flavors. One was the out-of-town teachers, who frequently came only for a year and were never seen again. Most of the imports were just well-meaning teachers who couldn't find a job anywhere else. The other variety consisted of locals: farmers' wives, bankers' wives, and male teachers who had family in town. The great majority of the teachers were white; you did not need all the fingers on one hand to count the Mexican teachers in the entire school system.

My first class in the morning was freshman English. When the late bell rang, our teacher walked into the classroom, sat on top of the desk, and looked at us. I had never seen him before, so I assumed he must be one of the one-year imports. We looked at him. His dark eyes examined us out of a shiny, dark brown face. His clothes, a brown coat and tie and brown pants, were unusual in Pearsall, especially in the hot months. He looked the way I expected my college professors would look someday.

When he had had a good look at us, and we at him, he went to the perfectly clean blackboard and wrote "Mr. Derderian, English Composition and Literature." He said he was from Brooklyn and had gone to NYU.

"Now, if you'll take out a clean piece of paper," he started. Rustle, rustle, rustle.

"Ey, Elva. Can I borrow a sheet of paper?" It was just like Robert to come to the first day of class with no paper.

"And for the next ten minutes, tell me about the last book you read," he continued. I waited for someone to say, "But what if you haven't read a book?" But no one did. Maybe they said it on paper. We all scratched away for ten minutes.

My favorite book then was *Bulfinch's Mythology.* I read the tales over and over. Persephone and I descended into the underworld together even as I grieved with Demeter. Every time I killed a spider, I thought of Arachne. I flew with Icarus every time he got too close to the sun and melted his wings. I despaired with Sisyphus. In my dreams, I flew heavenward with Pegasus, the horse of the Muses.

When the time was up, I wasn't done. But I wrote a closing sentence and passed it in. "Next, I want you to tell me a fairy tale on paper. Any fairy tale—your favorite will do. But I don't want you to use perfect English to write it. Tell it using Mexican slang words, black jive, teenager parking-lot words, business memo language, or Bible verse language . . . For the rest of the class, write down some ideas for this project—or even write the project."

We sat there stunned. What happened to diagramming sentences? Subject, predicate, verb, adverb? Mexican slang? Anathema in the Pearsall schools. Worse than profanity. Obviously this guy was new. He probably wouldn't last the year that most of the non-resident teachers did.

I wrote the Three Little Pigs using King James Bible language. It was as far out as I could go. Then, within the new bounds he had set for me, I had a good time with it. Writing the fairy tale felt like eating candy. I felt a sweet excitement when I turned it in the next day. I knew it was good. It had come from a place in my soul that was joyful and free and that rarely found expression in my Pearsall life.

The following Monday morning, he walked in and sat on his desk as usual. He laid the stack of papers next to him and asked, "Which one of you is Elva?"

I flushed red as everyone turned to look at me. He took my fairy tale off the top of the stack and handed it to me. "Will you stand at the front and read this, please?" He looked at me with that half-smile of his. All the blood had gone to my head and was making my face burn. My legs and arms were filled with molasses. I got up to the front and someone started reading my story.

"In the beginning, God created three little pigs. Now their minds were formless and empty. Darkness was over them . . ." It didn't seem to be me. It was a Bible scholar reading at the lectern at church, except she was reading about pigs.

When I finished, the class clapped. I looked up and everyone was smiling. My story had made people smile. And their smiles were the same as the smile I felt when I was writing the story. Transference had happened.

Mr. Derderian clapped too and smiled broadly now. He asked me to tell the class my "experience" of writing the story. But the experience was over for me; I was tongue-tied and nervous now. I said I didn't know and sat down fast. He seemed disappointed. The class kept looking back and forth between us. Desperately, I wished I was somewhere alone with a book instead of here. He left me alone and went on.

Later, as we were working quietly at our desks, I looked at him out of the corner of my eye. He wasn't handsome at all, at least not to me. But he was very alive. He seemed to be thinking and creating every second and he pulled us along with him.

Our next assignment was to write a diary entry for someone we admired: a famous person, a family member, or a character in a novel. My heroes then were dancers, especially ballerinas. They practiced until their toes bled. Bathed in beautiful music, they danced through their pain, making their movements look effortless and graceful.

Being tall for a Mexican girl, I rarely got asked to dance. When I was ten, I wanted to take dancing lessons, but my mother said we couldn't afford the shoes or the two dollars a week for lessons. I wrote all my longing into my piece, along with my admiration for and love of hard work and beauty.

At the end of the period, I walked out of English and down the hall to algebra. In math there was only one right answer. Mr. Jiles would have a hard time giving Ruth a better grade than he would give me if we both had the answer right. At least this way, I could come out even. I made sure there was no possible way he could take off points: I copied the problem down neatly, showed every single step neatly, and put a box around the answer neatly.

In math I could always make 100% if I just worked hard enough, long enough. My history teacher could judge me less than the white kids, as could my English and band teachers, but I could fight the system in math and win.

So, even though I loved English and reading best, I gave my all to math. Nothing would satisfy me except to get every single problem right on my homework and on my tests. I hated to fight for grades. In math, if I just did my very best, then I didn't have to fight, and I could get the best grade. I had finally found a place where being Mexican didn't matter.

During math, Mr. Jiles was telling us about the previous night. He had been visiting a friend. Mr. Jiles, his friend and his friend's daughter, Marjorie, had watched as a mare delivered her foal. Marjorie, blonde, beautiful, and talented, was two years older than I. Her family was wealthy by Pearsall standards; they could afford pregnant mares and veterinarians. Mr. Jiles was singing Marjorie's praises, saying she had such a strong stomach, she was so brave, so calm, so . . . I gritted my teeth and thought that I would be brave, strong, and calm too if I had a stable of horses and a rich daddy.

The next day Mr. Derderian wasn't there. The top of his desk was clear and empty. My dancer piece burned in my notebook. Toward the end of the period, the principal came to our room. He said he would be announcing some terrible news over the loud-speaker about Mr. Derderian. He wanted to tell us first because we were his class. Mr. Derderian had been found dead at the side of the major highway between Pearsall and San Antonio. This was all he knew. Further details would be forthcoming.

I never knew the real story. Rumors were that he was naked and several miles from his car. There was evidence that someone else had been with him—there was possibly foul play, possibly he had been hit by a car, possibly he was homosexual.

The desk sat empty for several more days. We did math homework in English class. A local matron replaced him. She asked us to read *Great Expectations* and write a book report. She had us write about our summer vacation. Ruth wrote about going to summer camp and swinging from a rope into the cool water of the Blue Hole at Wimberley. I wrote about visiting my sister at the edge of the Arroyo del Alazán, deep in the Mexican west side of San Antonio, and the joy of playing with my new baby nephew, even though it was among the broken glass and weeds. I was afraid the subject matter would influence the grade, but anything else would have been fiction.

Mrs. Ballard, my sophomore-year geometry teacher, was the best. She was severely handicapped, which is probably the reason she ended up in Pearsall. She walked slowly, moving her deformed legs and arms carefully. But this didn't stop her from much. She was cheerful, married, and had two babies. She couldn't make her arms work to write on the board, but she could make her hands work on an overhead projector.

She loved geometry, teaching, and kids, and she pushed us to the limit. But my limit was miles above that of anyone else in the class. Working geometry problems in clean bobby socks and a dress was trivial compared to working for my father in Minnesota. The perfect logic and symmetry of geometry proofs appealed to my sense of order.

Her grading method was to give everyone longer tests than anyone could possibly finish in a one-hour class. And then she graded on a curve. I worked at home for days before a test as if training for a marathon. Every problem in the previous chapters, even all the ones that had never been assigned as homework, became practice exercises for me. Changing the most difficult ones, I worked those. I pushed myself to work harder and harder geometry proofs faster and faster.

By the time the test was handed out on test day, every single problem was trivial to me; the only thing that mattered was speed. I worked like a madwoman.

I beat her system. I finished her monster tests and still got every single problem correct. If she graded on a normal curve, I would get 100% and everyone else would fail.

She asked me to separate myself from the class. She asked me to work ahead in the book alone. She would get James, a teacher's son in another class, whose only interest in the world was math, to work with me.

I tried it. The work itself continued to be no problem, but I was paying the lonely price of succeeding too well. Before this, my friends would ask to see my geometry homework in the morning before class. They copied my answers to the problems they hadn't been able to work on their own. Now they looked at each other's work. In the past, I could amaze everyone and get huge satisfaction by proving a complicated problem on the board. Now I was no longer part of the class.

I couldn't do it. The loneliness of the new regime devastated me. I requested permission to go back to working with the class with the understanding that I would be graded separately from them.

The truth was that what I loved was not so much the geometry. What I loved was clearly being the best—not in anyone's opinion, but in fact. I had finally found a place where I could not only be equal to the gringos, but clearly better.

It was at this time that my first writing muse came to me. I called her a muse because she inspired me to write, but she was really more of a mentor, mother, and supporter all in one. She came to me through the written page and very much encouraged me to write about everything. Her name was Soledad (Solitude). I addressed all my diary entries to her. She comforted me in my aloneness. She understood everything I said in English, but she answered me mostly in Spanish, which I loved.

Journal entry:

Me: Soledad, where are you? Here I am alone again, looking for you, as always.

Soledad: Aquí estoy, Preciosa. Ya no estás sola. Ven aquí, cuéntame donde has estado, cuéntame tu vida. Aquí estoy. Sólo para ti, mi amor. Cuéntame.

Me: Today my Algebra II teacher invited me to be on the Number Sense team to compete in the InterScholastic League.

Soledad: Ay qué bueno, mija. Ha de pensar muy bien de ti. Cuéntamelo todo. Dime qué es "Number Sense" y cómo van las cosas.

Me: Well, to participate in Number Sense competitions, you learn how to do math problems in the shortest amount of time. You learn hundreds of shortcuts and clever ways to do math in your head. The more shortcuts you learn, the faster you can work math problems in the Number Sense competitions.

Soledad: Qué bueno, hija. ¡Eso lo podrás usar toda la vida!

Me: Yes, I know, but I'm afraid. I prefer to think on paper, the way I do with you, rather than just figuring out everything in my head. And also, I have to come to school half an hour early and only take twenty minutes for lunch. That cuts out most of my social time with my friends.

Soledad: Mira en tu corazón. Allí está la respuesta.

Me: Yes, I see. I have to do it. Thanks for talking it out with me.

Soledad: Aquí, en el otro lado del papel, estoy siempre para ti. Háblame seguido.

Sometimes at night, after my homework was done and my parents were in bed asleep, I wrote to Mr. Derderian, telling him how much his half-smile and his encouragement had meant to me. When he had smiled at me, he had looked straight into my face. I was a real person to him, not a Mexican, not a non-gringo, but a real person with a life, hopes, dreams, and expectations. I had things to say, unspoken opinions, and creative juices. He saw all of that in me, and his seeing it made me bigger than I was.

As a tribute to him, I wrote journal entries for him. In them I described why I had left Brooklyn and come to this dusty south-Texas town. I told how I had come by my dark, shiny brown skin. I described my death.

So my sleeping parents wouldn't hear, I cried quietly into my pillow. I cried for all the affirmation I wouldn't get, for all the hopes, fears, and opinions I had inside that no one would ever hear.

One afternoon after school, Tío Manuel came to talk to my father about some business at the Buenos Aires Cantina that Apá managed for him. But my father was out, so he sat in a lawn chair to talk to me instead.

"Your father tells me you're an excellent student," he said.

"Everyday I fight the good fight, Tío."

"What's your favorite subject?" he asked.

"I enjoy English best because I like reading and writing, but my best grades are in math."

"Is that so? I'm starting a big new job soon, and I'm going to use a lot of math. Maybe you could help me figure some of it out."

I quailed deep in my stomach. I was great at academics but poor at life.

I remembered a time when the whole family had been in the car going to visit some farm relatives. The farm gate had been latched and I had begged to be the one to jump out of the car to open it. This was normally Rudy's job. Apá let me go. I jumped out and ran to the gate. I fumbled with the latch until Apá lost all patience. He yelled something about "muchacha inútil" and sent Rudy to open the door. I walked back to the car in disgrace, knowing I would never be as good at life as my brother or my father.

Another time, when Rudy was out with friends, Apá had asked me to dice the jalapeños for the salsa. Normally Rudy diced jalapeños, onions, and tomatoes for the salsa. In the midst of the job, I accidentally rubbed my eyes and they caught fire. I ran, crying and half-blinded, to the faucet. I tried to wash my eyes with the backs of my hands. All I succeeded in doing was turning up the fire with soap in my eyes. Everyone in the kitchen laughed.

"¡Qué muchacha más inútil!" Apá had said amid guffaws. It was only one of many times he had called me a useless girl. In my father's eyes, Rudy was the useful one. He was the one who got to work with Tío Manuel on Saturday as a carpenter's apprentice. When Apá had a job that required dexterity and common sense, he gave it to Rudy. I was sent to fetch water when he was thirsty, and I was the go-for-this and go-for-that one.

If I failed at this project Tío Manuel wanted help with, he too would think of me as a muchacha inútil. This hurt particularly because Tío Manuel was my favorite uncle. He was the man I most admired.

Tío Manuel was Apá's most successful brother. The two of them grew up in Mexico and no one in the family had gone to school past the fourth grade, but Tío Manuel had wanted to very badly. In his school days, he had boarded in town with a childless couple. They grew fond of him and recognized his potential. Finally this couple went out to the ranch and tried to convince Manuel's parents to let them adopt him and send him to school in Monterrey. Alarmed at the prospect of losing him, his mother Sarita pulled him out of school and put him to work on the ranch.

So Tío Manuel educated himself. He learned enough math and reading and business to be a prosperous carpenter who bought plots of land, built houses, and sold them at a nice profit, which he then reinvested in more land. When we visited him at his house, he was frequently reading with a dictionary at his side, or filling pages with sums and figures for his work.

On weekends, Rudy and Luis went to work with Tío Manuel as carpenter's apprentices. His apprentices buzzed around him amid mounds of fragrant sawdust. He insisted that the workers around him hum with activity, that they work as hard and as consistently as he did, which was at a furious, nonstop rate. He barked out orders to his minions, wanting it done *pronto!* And they got busy, running, not walking, to their tasks, the way he liked it. Sawhorses were set up everywhere at his work sites. The sounds of hammers and saws filled the air. Biting into the wood. Making it into a dwelling. Slackers could expect a clod of dirt to hit them hard as a reminder to pick up the pace. Pearsall dirt is soft, sandy loam, so the indignity hurt a lot more than the blow.

I've heard of a Protestant work ethic. I've heard Mexicans are lazy; they'll do it mañana. But I never saw anyone work harder, more diligently, or with more ganas than my Tío Manuel.

My two brothers learned carpentry at Tío Manuel's side, as did his children and grandchildren. He drove them hard. "Want me to cut it off?" he would ask Rudy if he held the hammer by the middle of the handle, instead of by the end of the handle, which is the correct way. He made me want to be a carpenter. It seemed like the most honorable, clean profession in the world.

I didn't like housework, laundry, the hot kitchen. Watching my Tío Manuel sharpen his flat carpenter's pencil and then whip out figures and sums right on a wooden plank, I became envious of his apprentices.

"Don't get too close, mija; you could get hurt." A building site was no place for a girl. I was the one who got out of the car to deliver the hot lunch. The bringer of hot tortilla tacos and cool salsa.

Tío Manuel finally brought me the problem he was having trouble with. It had to do with cone-shaped holes in the ground, cubic yards of dirt, and the amount of cement needed for the job. It was a huge job he was estimating, probably the biggest of his life. He was to build the Morales feedlots. They would be massive cement cattle feedlots, where hundreds of cattle would be fattened. The

cow manure would be mixed with water and fed out through giant
sprinklers to fertilize the surrounding pastures.

But what I had learned in school was plane geometry.
Solutions for a two-dimensional world. He was working in the real
world, with real shovels and real money to be estimated for the job.
I couldn't solve his problem. Oh, I worked at it mightily. Research
at the library. Ciphering into the night. But it seemed my brain
wasn't big enough to hold all the parameters of his problems.

The disappointment on his face devastated me. What good
are math whizzes then, if they can't figure out everyday practi-
cal problems? No, he didn't say it, but it was written on his face.
He never asked for help again. And he figured it out. The best he
could. By trial and error, partial figuring, and a lot of intuition,
he learned and did things his fourth-grade education didn't help
him with.

By the following spring he had finished the project success-
fully. The meadows around the Morales Farm turned a deep, lush
green, dotted with yearling calves.

Even in math, where I was most successful in school, I had
failed in the world. I really was a "muchacha inútil." Well then, I
would focus my attention on academics even more. I had wanted
to go to college since the fourth grade. Now I decided everything
I did would be aimed at that goal.

Chapter Sixteen

El que mucho abarca, poco aprieta.

He who tries to hold too much, grasps little.

(One of Apá's favorite dichos)

I wanted to give my all to school, but teenagers are all too human. And my humanity kept surfacing.

The day after I graduated from the eighth grade, I had my first date. The only reason my father said I could go was that I had just received the "High Point Mexican Girl" award at the eighth-grade graduation.

He was in high school and drove a car. He took me to the movies, the only place to go for a date in Pearsall. A week later, he wanted to take me out again. Like a fool, I asked again. My father hit the ceiling. "What do you mean you want to go out again! Are you going to marry this guy or what? The answer is no! Absolutely not! And don't ask again!"

I didn't ask again for two years.

With no possibility for a date again for the summer, I decided to look for a way to earn money. My father found someone who supervised the cantaloupe pickers. The truck would pick me up at five in the morning so we could get a head start on the sun. I wanted to see for myself what it had been like for my brothers and sisters.

But the experience was impossible to duplicate. The shame that they had felt was much less for me. It was true that I didn't want to be seen on the back of the truck by my friends or by the white people who knew me, but for the most part, I had a ball.

The teenagers I went to the fields with were not my regular friends. They were the "at-risk" kids who might drop out of school or get in trouble. But I was just as comfortable with them as I was with my "well-dressed, get-good-grades" friends.

We joked with sexual innuendos and flirted with each other all day. We were young and strong and the work seemed easy. No physical challenge was too much for us. All the laughing and comradery in the absence of parents made it seem more like an outing than a job. At the end of the day, I had more energy than I had had in the morning.

The truck would drop me off to my mother's cooking, clean sheets, and a comfortable home. I knew that this was not my life, but only a way to earn money. My parents let me keep all my money, whereas all my brothers and sisters had worked as my father's slaves; he kept all the money.

Trying to duplicate their experience didn't work. I seemed doomed to an easier life.

Music had always been a part of my life ever since we lived at Tío Alfredo's house between two cantinas that had their jukeboxes going until midnight. Then the fiestas came into my life, with Los Nietos playing every night for a week at the fiestas in the empty lots behind our house, again until midnight. Some of the little girls danced with each other or with boys. The dance platform was the very center of the whole outdoor fiesta; absolutely everyone could see you.

When I was an adolescent, our little group of about twelve or so girlfriends from the seventh and eighth grades got together and danced in Aurora's garage. We danced rancheras and boleros to forty-fives that we all brought from home. We took turns leading and following. My usual dance partner was Manuela. She was my best friend and forgave all my missteps. We got all dressed up for these affairs in the garage, wearing chiffon and petticoats and patent leather shoes. We made canapés to snack on.

On Saturday mornings in high school, we watched *American Bandstand* with Dick Clark. Saturday afternoons we listened to the Beatles on the radio. But Saturday night, we danced corridos, rancheras, cumbias, and boleros. The quinceañera girls had a dance for coming into young womanhood, and the young bride and groom had a dance to celebrate their marriage, and it was all Mexican music. The music of our souls, of our rites of passage, and of our mating rituals was in Spanish.

I was president of the Catholic Youth Organization that year. The other officers and I usually met at the church rectory with the priest to plan the activities for the following Monday's general meeting. One particular week, the priest was to be out of town. One of the other girls offered to host the meeting at her house instead.

I was immediately threatened. I knew I would have to walk much farther at night. The church was two blocks away, while her house was seven or eight blocks away. In Pearsall there were a lot of loose dogs. My parents would be suspicious. But of course I couldn't refuse.

It was a miserable evening for me. They just wanted to party, not conduct business. I prayed that it would be over soon, so I could get home at a reasonable time without my mother asking too many questions.

But they wouldn't stop laughing and joking. Finally, I had to leave or be in a lot of trouble at home. "The guys will walk the girls home," one of them said. "There may be loose dogs."

I was horrified but tried not to show it. My parents would kill me if they thought I had been out on a secret date. Their ideas about dating were not only Mexican but Victorian. But I couldn't tell that to my friends, so I let them walk me home.

I should have been thrilled: the guys were both tall, good-looking, and popular at school. They obviously liked me enough to want to walk with and talk to me. But I was nervous and jittery the whole time.

When we were within a block of my house, I said, "This is great; thanks for doing this. I'll be O.K. from here."

Being the gentlemen that they were, they insisted on taking me right to our front gate. I didn't see my mother in the shadows when we walked up.

"Thanks, see you tomorrow," I said.

"It was fun, see you tomorrow," they responded.

Then Amá came out of the shadows and started screaming. "Where were you? What were you doing? Who were those guys?" She fired the screaming questions at me, one after the other, without giving me a chance to answer. They weren't really questions, but accusations. She thought she already knew the answers.

I was shocked speechless. She yelled at them, too. She told them they were *never* to come back to our house. There was no way to be rational, to convince her that I had been at a meeting. That no one had touched anyone, that this wasn't that kind of thing. She was too far gone for that.

I went in the house and left her out there screaming at them. My sister was in the house with her new baby. She was shocked and speechless, too.

My social life at school was hard enough without what this would add to it. I felt my life was over; no one would ever want to date me or be my friend again. My mother had seen to that.

On the days when there were to be elections at the high school, we tried to make all the decisions on the playground before school started. Our freshman year, we weren't too good at this, but by our senior year, we had it down pat.

The Mexicans made up about sixty percent of the class. We could elect our candidates easily if we were smart about it. But what would happen is that the gringo kids could nominate a second or third Mexican kid at the last minute, besides the one we had already nominated. Of course, that person's friends would vote for him or her. That meant the Mexican vote would be split and the gringo candidate would win.

So before the bell rang in the morning, we would decide who would accept the nominations for what office and who would decline. Of course, not everyone agreed with the playground decisions, so sometimes the system would break down. But usually it worked.

"Elva, will you be an officer?"

I hated that question. I was already the tallest girl in the class and my grades were too high. That made two reasons for the boys not to ask me out. Being a class officer would be a third. But they expected me to be a leader because of my good grades, and I had a strong sense of duty.

It seemed there were some activities that were the exclusive province of the white kids, usually things that required special lessons or summer camp. During our four years, there were no Mexican cheerleaders. We were all thrilled when a Mexican girl, Irene, against all odds, through sheer determination and strength of will, became a twirler. She was our hero for that. Barbara, the only Mexican girl on the tennis team, was another personal hero for me. Then the couple elected to be "Señor and Señorita P.H.S." refused to have their pictures in the yearbook across the page from "Mr. and Miss P.H.S." Gloria and David went to the principal's office and denounced this tradition for the racist practice it was. They were our heroes, too.

There were a lot of lines that you couldn't cross. We would be shocked to learn that one of ours had gone out on a secret date with someone from the other side of the tracks. The shock waves would ripple through both sides of the tracks.

It wasn't that we hated each other. There were very few of them that I hated, and then only for specific bigoted acts. I truly liked some of them. We would joke in the flute and clarinet section of the band and laugh uproariously together. We had secret jokes together about the physics teacher. But at the end of the school day, we went across the tracks and they stayed on their side.

They went to summer camp at the blue springs around Wimberley. Most of the Mexicans worked or did nothing in the summer. They were in the Allied Youth Club. We were in the Catholic Youth Organization. The white priest taught us table manners and the proper way to bathe. They had been Bluebirds in elementary school and Girl Scouts in junior high school. We went to the fiesta to celebrate Mexican national holidays twice a year.

I left all of this behind in the summer. By the time I was sixteen, the three-legged summer trip from Pearsall to Wisconsin to New York had been happening for four years. My eyes were opening to a whole big world outside Pearsall.

In Wisconsin, on weekends we went to someone's cottage at the lake. That's right, here the Mexican Americans had summer cottages on the lake in addition to a nice house in town. Sometimes on the weekends, Rudy, Luis, Consuelo, and Dolores would take me bar-hopping in Milwaukee. This was not at all like drinking in Pearsall. In Pearsall, the men went to the cantina alone, while the women sat at home and talked. I was tall, almost as tall as my brothers, and no one questioned my age. The waiters took my orders for a Manhattan or a Tom Collins without blinking. We sat around the piano bar and I mused about how far we had come from living in the stable while we worked in the fields, probably not too far away from here.

Luis had given up his job at the foundry and was now working with other migrants. He was a counselor and supervised other counselors. He wore a starched shirt, tie, and dress pants. They encouraged migrants to get out of the fields, off the road, and into permanent, mainstream jobs.

He used my visits as excuses to travel. On weekends we went to the Museum of Science and Industry in Chicago, across Lake Michigan from Wisconsin to Michigan on a boat, to the hothouse gardens in Milwaukee.

Sometimes his friends would go with us. He had friends that were black, white, and non-Spanish-speaking Mexicans. Luis's wife was one of these. She looked as Mexican as I, but she spoke not a word of Spanish.

When I was sixteen, I tried to find a summer job in Wisconsin. No luck. In New York, Kal had a friend at an employment agency. They got me a job working as a clerk for Dun & Bradstreet at 99 Church Street in Manhattan. Since it was the sixties, I ironed my curly hair straight and backcombed it high. I put on spike heels and a miniskirt and walked to the subway, feeling like something out of *Vogue*. Delmira had a baby by then, so she walked me to the subway stop with the baby in the carriage and then went home.

When the coffee cart came along, I took a break and looked around the office. I could see myself coming back here with a university diploma and getting Mr. Sloan's job and having the corner office, or even being his boss. Yes, I could leave dusty old Pearsall. I could come to New York and make big bucks. Spending my days in expensive clothes running a company while I hung out all night

in trendy bars on Bleecker Street, dressed all in black with a ciga-
rette in my left hand and a drink in my right.

That summer, we saw The Doors, Joan Baez, and Simon and
Garfunkel at the Forest Hills Amphitheater. We saw *Hair, Zorba,
Oliver!,* and *Fiddler on the Roof* on Broadway. I looked around
the theatre and wondered how I could be in this world when I
belonged in another.

One Saturday, Delmira and I decided to go into the city just
to play. We put the baby in the carriage and went on the subway.
We walked around all day, buying knishes and falafel from the
street vendors, window shopping, and trying on miniskirts. By
the time we went home on the subway, the baby was sound asleep.
The subway car was almost empty. I looked up to see a really cute
boy sitting across from us. He had been staring at me. I lowered
my eyes, feeling my face flush. When I looked back up, he was
still looking at me, but with a wide smile now. He said, "Hi."

"Hi," I responded, and then felt that I shouldn't have. I lowered my eyes again.

He came and sat in the empty seat next to me. I leaned toward
Delmira and looked at him, more curious than wary. "What stop
are you going to?" he asked. I couldn't tell if his accent was
Italian, Jewish, or just New York. His manner was so friendly and
nice, so I told him. He said his stop was one before ours. He went
on to ask me how long I had lived in Queens. We talked all the
way home. Right before we got off, he asked if he could call me.
I turned to Delmira questioningly.

"I don't care! Don't ask me!" she said, but she looked
alarmed. Being sixteen, I gave him our telephone number anyway.

He called that night. And the next and the next. Delmira
looked nervous every time, but she bit her lip and didn't say anything. By the end of the week, he was telling me how great Jones
Beach was on the weekend, and asking if I would like to go there
with him on the subway on Saturday morning. Before I talked to
Delmira about it, I consulted the subway map. Jones Beach was
an awfully long way from Forest Hills in Queens.

On the other hand, I rode the subway alone twice a day to
Manhattan. I was making my own money and surely I could get
myself out of a jam if I got into one. What was Jones Beach like?

I wondered. The only ocean beach I had ever been to was at Corpus Christi in Texas. First I imagined us on an almost empty beach under an umbrella with him asking me to spread suntan oil on his back. Could I do it? Then I imagined a beach full of derelicts, drug addicts, and trash. What if I got mad at him for some reason and had to come back alone? What if I got lost in a seedy neighborhood or accidentally got on a train that went to a place I had seen on the subway map called Flushing? Nothing good could be happening there. I decided to make it Delmira's decision.

When I asked her, she looked away nervously. "Well I'm not your mother, and I can't tell you what to do. But if it were me, I wouldn't go out with a boy who was shorter than I was."

I was stung to the quick. Yes, now that I thought about it, he was slightly shorter than I was. All the old, familiar feelings washed over me—of being too plain, too tall, and too smart for the boys. She went on and on about how it really didn't look good for a girl to be taller than the guy. The guy was supposed to be taller than the girl so she could then wear high heels and still look feminine.

I didn't go and I didn't talk to him anymore. He seemed sincerely hurt when I said goodbye on the telephone. He had liked me a lot and I had liked him. I had never met a boy in Pearsall who was more genuine and warm.

I had to find a tall guy, no matter how much of an asshole he was. So I could look feminine.

At the end of the summer, Dun & Bradstreet offered me a promotion. I told them they would have to wait six years or so while I finished high school and college. They were sorry to see me go.

Chapter Seventeen

*¿Dónde es tu tierra? Donde la pases, no
donde naces.*

Where is your land? It is where you pass your
days, not the place where you were born.

(Mexican dicho)

After we stopped going to Minnesota and Wisconsin, the high-lights of my father's life were his trips to Mexico. When a friend invited him to Mexico, he would come home full of excitement. "Ándale, mujer, give me some clean clothes. I'm going to Mexico!" My mother rushed around laying out his best khaki pants and khaki shirt and his going-out khaki-colored felt Stetson. He bathed and shaved extra carefully and used lots of Old Spice. They honked in the street and he'd be gone.

The next day or several days later he'd be back with two fifths of rum añejo for himself and a bag of Mexican candy for us: caje-ta, the burnt milk and sugar caramel in the round wooden boxes with colored tinsel around them; coconut tri-color candy, pale red, white, and green, the colors of the Mexican flag; and the chunky candy made from squash which I didn't like, but my mother did.

Once a year or so, we would all go together, but only as far as Laredo.

By the time I was seventeen and he was sixty-seven, Apá had been on Social Security for five years and only worked sporadi-cally. One day Apá's nephew, who was in his fifties, came and told him about driving into Mexico and visiting relatives, some of whom Apá hadn't seen since he left Mexico when he was eleven. Apá started dreaming about his boyhood home. He asked me if I thought the two of us together could find the places. His family had lived on a working ranch in the country. He had gone to school in a town named Villaldama for three years. Sabinas was the closest big town. When I expressed confidence that we could, we made plans for where we would go and who we would look for. Amá rushed around packing for the three of us. She put her and my birth certificates, the car title, and my father's naturalization papers in a special black bag. She wanted no trouble with the Federales.

My father had a first cousin in Sabinas named Alejandra that he hadn't seen in fifty-six years. His cousin in Villaldama he saw often, as she visited us. He also had a long-time friend in Monterrey, who had been a friend in his young adulthood. This friend had married a woman from Monterrey and gone to live there. We gathered addresses, phone numbers, and directions from the people who had them.

Sabinas is about eighty kilometers south of Laredo on the main road to Monterrey and Mexico city. Today it is a major pit stop for travelers. In my father's youth, it was the city that was closest to their ranch. My grandfather would go there to transact business and get supplies. We arrived there easily, after navigating through Laredo. The directions indicated we should turn off the main road onto a side street named Zuazua. We followed it to the end, at the far edge of town. Since most of the houses were unmarked, we asked a passerby if he knew Alejandra. He indicated the right doorway to us.

We hadn't let her know we were coming, as she had no telephone and was illiterate, so she couldn't read a letter. She opened the door and screamed and cried big, heaving sobs when my father told her who he was and she recognized him. Apá smiled a huge smile and patted her back awkwardly as he held her while she finished crying.

Alejandra was Mexican-Indian, dark, and big boned. My father was six feet tall, and she stood shoulder to shoulder with him. When they posed for pictures, they looked as though they had just walked off an Aztec pyramid. You could tell they were related. They had the same high cheek bones and red-brown Indian color. She was poor and humble and had lots of children and grandchildren. She carded wool with hand cards as she talked to us. My father had only one sister, who had died, so he claimed Alejandra as his own.

Even though she looked Indian, she claimed to be Mexican. She told stories about the true Indians shooting at her family barricaded in their adobe farmhouse. Her father shot back through the slots left in the adobe walls just for that purpose.

Alejandra literally had nowhere for us to stay. She lived alone in a tiny two-room house with only one bed. Her son lived next door. They lived at the end of a street that was not paved, but still had huge potholes. We promised her we would visit again on our return trip home several days later.

We stayed at a small hotel right on the main highway. Our room was directly above the hotel's neon sign, which blinked on and off through the thin curtains. The trucks roared by, only feet from my pillow it seemed, all night.

The next morning, we drove off immediately after showering. Apá said we should stop for breakfast on the road to Villaldama. He thought the road would be the same as the main road that led from Laredo to Sabinas, dotted with restaurants and places to stop for gas. He was wrong.

Once we left the outskirts of Sabinas, we entered another world. The houses stopped and the hills and small mountains started. We crossed the rivers, creeks, and valleys on one-lane bridges with no guard rails. Someone had put rough, six-inch stones all along the edges of the bridges so the tires would tell you if you were getting too close. We marveled at the cave openings high on the mountainsides.

My father was beside himself at the bucolic beauty of the scenery. And at the closeness of his childhood haunts. It was as if his nose detected long-ago familiar smells, smells that had been dear to his heart. He had navigated this same route with his father when he was a boy, but that had been on horseback. I drove carefully along the winding roads. For the next hour, we passed almost no cars. Apá's face and childlike joy were as fascinating to me as the scenery.

Needless to say, there were no restaurants of any kind on the way. The only people we saw were a few goat shepherds. When we arrived at Villaldama, we decided to have breakfast before going to Englentina's house. We had called several days earlier to say we were coming, but we hadn't said what time we would arrive.

We asked and people directed us to a restaurant on the corner of the main town square. It was open, so we went in and sat down. We were the only customers. When the waiter came, Apá said he didn't need a menu, just bring him huevos rancheros and coffee. The waiter looked around the room as if searching for something and apologized sheepishly. He said huevos rancheros wouldn't be possible as they only had one egg in the kitchen. My father looked dismayed and confused, and then he laughed. How was it possible for a restaurant to only have one egg at breakfast time?

It was decided I would have the solitary egg. Apá ordered machacado beef and Amá only wanted tortillas with butter.

After breakfast we navigated the streets as directed. The house was only about three blocks from the main square, but we had to turn several times on narrow streets bordered by sidewalks that were two feet high in some places. The adobe houses were all joined together, separated only by a change in paint color. Englentina had told us that the birth, death, and baptism records at the main church in Villaldama dated back to 1780. For several blocks around the square, the houses and buildings appeared not to have changed at all in two hundred years.

Unlike Alejandra, Englentina was very well known to us, as she had visited us in Pearsall regularly. She had eyes the color of green sea water and brown hair lightened by years of smoking unfiltered cigarettes. Her regular visits to the U.S. meant she was financially comfortable by Mexican standards and even by ours. She would come loaded down with Mexican candy, sweet bread, and handicrafts. Her husband had been killed in one of the copper mines he owned in the Mexican highlands. They had one son who had his mother's sea-green eyes but his father's dark skin. He gave me chunks of raw copper ore that shimmered blue, purple, and amber.

But this was the first time we had visited her. When we found her street, we asked a shy-looking adolescent girl walking on the sidewalk about the exact house. She pointed to a door of a residence painted an ochre color. She said Englentina was her aunt and then disappeared inside to announce us. Englentina ran out laughing to hug my father and mother.

The young girl was named Leti, and she was promptly assigned to be my companion during our visit, since she was only two or three years younger than me. She smiled shyly at me out of a broad, light-skinned face. The brown ringlets that covered her head bounced as she walked.

The adults spent the morning talking. Apá talked animatedly about how he and his father would ride horses to Sabinas, about how his brothers carried guns at their hips. He asked how his local childhood friends had fared. Leti and I hung around the fringes. The house was a comfortable size, even by U.S. standards. Twelve-inch-thick wooden beams supported the twelve-foot ceiling. The adobe walls were three feet thick. Even when the sun baked the street outside, we were cool inside. Except for the main entrance, all the other windows that faced the street had vertical bars. The windows started at the floor and were taller than I was.

In the afternoon, Apá wanted to visit his childhood friend Macías. I had heard of Macías before. He had dark blue eyes and was fleet of foot. He did especially well when the challenge at school was "Who can reach the top of the mountain first?" Macías always won, and then he blew a trumpet to announce his victory to the whole valley.

Englentina took us to his house. We walked since everything was so close. He looked much older than my father's sixty-seven years. He was smaller than Apá and thin, although still strong. His skin was dark and heavily creased, which made his indigo blue eyes all the more startling. He and Apá talked of their years together and their years apart. Macías and his wife had twelve grown sons and one daughter, who were all married and gone. I watched them talk and tried to discern from their faces which man considered himself luckier, the one who left Villaldama or the one who stayed. But their faces kept changing, as if sudden dark clouds passed overhead and then the bright sun returned.

As they talked, a grandchild of five or six came and worked his way into Macías's lap. He waited politely, as Mexican children do, for a break in the conversation. When he heard a pause, he asked his grandfather if he could be taken for a ride in the carreta.

Macías said he would be glad to do it, but later, close to sunset, when it was cooler. Macías turned to Leti and me and asked if we would like to go. We both said yes, although I had no idea what a carreta was.

Late in the afternoon, Macías and his grandson came to pick us up in the carreta. It was a square wagon drawn by a huge, old mule. The bed of the wagon was unpainted wood and the dimensions of the wagon bed were maybe six by eight feet. Macías sat on the driver's bench and held the reins. Apá got up next to him. Leti, the child, and I dangled our feet from the rear end of the wagon.

As he pulled us out to the countryside, surrounded by mountains and magueys on the edge of the road, I felt transported to another century. The sun setting behind the hills colored everything mauve and a soft orange and made the shadows long. I felt immersed in my father's childhood. I wondered if this feeling of simple freedom and simple beauty was what he remembered when his eyes misted over with memories.

In the center of the old towns of Mexico, everything looks hundreds of years old. The adobe is patched and the paint is peeling. From the street, it looks as though all the houses are the same. But when they open their doors, you can see into the inner courtyards—beautiful, cool, distinctive. Some have a multicolored bird in a cage, some a bubbling fountain, some are covered with flowing bougainvillea, in others a rubber tree fills half the courtyard and towers over it.

At night we set up cots to sleep on the open-air patio. While there was still light, I could see ants crawling around the patio. I worried that they would climb up the legs of my cot and nibble at me while I slept. The light from the kitchen door made a yellow rectangle on the floor of the dark courtyard before it was turned off. Later, a crescent moon watched me as I tried to go to sleep. I heard dogs barking somewhere. I examined the legs of my cot with the flashlight my mother had given me to take with me to the bathroom at night. No ants yet.

The next morning, I awoke slowly. Keeping my eyes closed, I listened to the sounds of small-town Mexico, brooms swishing and water splashing. The women swept the sidewalk and the street in front of their houses and then sprinkled them with water; at that time of the very early morning when the sun is not yet up, but there is enough light to be assured that the sun will come up yet another time. The creaking of a barred windowsill opening to let in the morning air, dissipating the sleep of the night. A car could be heard through the broom strokes, coming to life in the distance. Later the cars would bring the dust of the countryside to the streets and the sidewalks, but for now they were scrubbed clean, ready for the feet of passersby.

The bells of the main parish church began to ring, insistent and loud in their call to prayer. But I knew only the old mothers heeded them. Only they pulled their dark rebozos over their heads, hiding their faces completely as they walked past to church.

A cock crowed. I opened my eyes and saw that he was ten feet away from me, perched on the back of a chair. The chickens roamed free in the courtyard, which was attached to the back yard. One of them proudly cackled that she had laid an egg. It occurred to me that that might be my breakfast. A dog began to stir and loped away to an early-morning errand.

Here, as in Pearsall, my parents got up before daylight. And so did our hosts. As I left my bed in the courtyard, I could smell coffee and hear the tortillas being rolled out.

Later we drove to the ojo de agua. It was a natural spring that had been captured and made into a huge, square swimming pool. I expected stagnant water, but it was the dark blue-green color that water fresh out of deep earth seems to have. It was cold and deep and wonderful.

The local ranchers brought their horses in to be ridden for a small fee. No marked trails, no trail guide, no horse in front and one behind. Just "Here are the reins and see you later." I rode the brown gelding with wild abandon across the valley and around a small hill, disappearing from view for awhile. I waded him across a small stream, probably the overflow of the water from the spring.

Now I knew why my father loved riding in Mexico. I felt free and alive, all my pores open and drinking in the countryside, the dry, clean air and the sun very close. Silverio, the horse, responded to me easily. He was having a holiday, too, not having to work in the fields. I let him gallop, canter, and trot as he chose. I only chose the direction. I loved his horsey smell and the way his muscles worked under me. And I loved being alone with him. I trusted that even if I got lost, he would not. Like my father, this was his land.

That night, Leti and I went to the movies at an ancient theater. Like most of the houses, the entrance belied the interior. We had passed the entrance earlier; it was just another closed door on the sidewalk.

But when the sun went down, the entrance was transformed with vendors, and inside was a whole magic world. The vendors sold slices of peeled jícama sprinkled with chili, salt, and fresh lime. Others sold candy and peanuts.

We went in and sat in the courtyard, open to the sky, on wooden seats that folded down. They weren't painted and I imagined that they had been rained on over and over. There were covered porches behind arched doorways on three sides of the courtyard that held more chairs. Above these were covered balconies, also with chairs.

The movie was an old black and white one with Pedro Armendáriz riding a horse across the Mexican desert. I remembered my ride of the morning and all the feelings came back. I looked up at the stars. At the movie theater in San Antonio, they had fake stars on the ceiling. Here the stars were real and the ceiling was the midnight-blue sky.

When we went home, Leti's sister was sitting at the barred window of her bedroom talking to her fiancé, who was standing on the sidewalk outside. Her mother sat in the bedroom with her sewing, pretending not to listen to the conversation. The only reason they were allowed to talk like this was because they would be married soon. I saw where my father's ideas of dating came from.

They treated us as though we were the fancy Americans. I had never been treated so royally. Years later, I realized they treated everyone like that.

From Villaldama, we drove to Monterrey to visit Apá's friend Chema. Monterrey is a large industrial city, but Chema lived in a nice, quiet neighborhood. Like my father, Chema was retired, and the only work he did was collect rent on the first of the month from all his rental properties. They had one unmarried daughter, María, who was several years older than I. Like Leti, she was assigned to be my companion during the visit.

Early the next morning, we walked to the local market. I saw an ancient woman come out of a side street and walk toward the market across the street from us. She wore lots of thin cotton layers. She still seemed cold, in spite of the layers and the sun shining down on us from a cloudless sky. Her rebozo was a thin, threadbare, dark brown. Her shoes had soles that were barely there. When we crossed the street to get to the market, she peered at us out of filmy eyes surrounded by dark, creased brown skin.

Startled, I realized she looked like an old version of my mother. The same little flat nose and angular bones around her eyes. When she extended her hand to beg for coins, I wanted to take it. I wanted to take it and hold it to my cheek and say, "It's all right, madrecita." Instead I blinked back tears as I took the Mexican coins my father had given me and put half of them in her hand. I gently folded her tiny hand closed with both of mine. Aloud, I said, "May God bless you, little mother." The word "madrecita" caught in my throat.

"Que Dios la bendiga," she said as she attempted a puckered smile that showed her sparse teeth. My mother's mouth was puckered like that also when she took her dentures out. But this woman had no dentures. I imagined that she moistened her tortilla in soup before she ate it. Her smile didn't reach her eyes. Her tiny eyes were profoundly sad, and I imagined they no longer saw very well. But perhaps she no longer needed them; she could see another way besides with her eyes. As she walked away, I saw that she had a slight hump in her upper back. It seemed it was her years, that she had in a bundle, and they pressed her face toward the ground.

"Por favor, a charity." I heard his voice before I saw him. He didn't look like my father, but his voice was my father's. It could have been my father, easily, but my father without luck. My father had escaped this fate. His luck and his strong body had helped him. His health had never failed. And life never took away his ganas!

This man's knees buckled as he tried to walk. I could see his flaccid arms under the thin shirt. One eye was half closed and the other was a great rheumy one. If he had sons, they had abandoned him.

I wanted to take him to have breakfast. To a bath and a shave. To buy new clothes. I wanted to see how he would lick his lips over oxtail soup with hot tortillas—and don't forget the chile! I wanted to see the years and the cares fall away for a time.

But nothing. I gave him the remaining Mexican coins that my father had given me for Mexican coconut candy. I no longer had a taste for candy.

The man behind us gave him no money. In my father's voice, the old man cursed the passerby for being an uncaring brute.

The children didn't cause me so much pain—the ones who sold gum or merely worked at begging. I had worked as a child and it hadn't hurt me. They still had their lives in front of them, and the health and life of youth. But the ancient ones had nothing left, not even hope.

The next day, María and I went to mass at seven in the morning. As I got near the church, I looked up to watch the bell ringer as he furiously pulled the bell rope. At the door of the church, just inside, was the old woman that I had given coins to the day before. She didn't go on to sit in one of the pews. She heard the mass from just inside the door. The padre gave a long sermon, much too long for a midweek mass, I thought. Occasionally I looked back to the door of the church. She was still there, just inside. As if the church were the province of another class of people, those with a cooking fire at home. I have felt like her before, as if I want to be in a place, but I don't know if I belong. A beggar in a room full of moneyed gringos. I wondered if she had a fire someplace to cook her tortillas, or if she was forever cold.

When the service was over, she went to kneel in front of the painting of Nuestra Señora de Guadalupe at a side altar. Guadalupe predates Christianity. She was Tonantzín to the Aztecs. She is the compassionate mother of all Mexicans, but especially of the orphans and the disenfranchised. The old woman spoke to

Guadalupe softly, but out loud. She seemed to be telling her all her troubles. When she was finished she put a coin in the box in front of Guadalupe. Probably one of the coins I had given her the day before. I was pleased that the coin went from my hand to hers to Nuestra Señora de Guadalupe.

It was the Feast Day of the Holy Innocents. To commemorate this, the priest had a huge basket of rolls called bolillos, and he was passing them out to whoever would take them after Mass. Timidly, the old woman went to the end of the line. The priest had three rolls left, and he gave them all to her. When she turned around with the bread in her two hands, I saw her face clearly. Now her smile revealed all her teeth and gums and extended all the way through her eyes. She was beaming as if to burst. As if in these three pieces of bread, God had given her all she had ever prayed for and more. Then I knew I had been wrong: she still had hope.

My father was transformed when he went to Mexico. Here he needed no one to translate for him, no one to interpret road signs or maps. There were no gringos here to bow before. He was in his element. He was like a fish that had lived in a bowl for years, all of a sudden dumped back in the ocean. He became ultra-confident, giving big tips and talking to everyone. His eyes sparkled and he soaked up everything like a sponge.

He wanted to take our Mexican relatives on trips to the ojos de agua, to Lampasos, to Monterrey. He paid for everything recklessly and laughed and told jokes constantly. He was the local boy who had gone to the U.S. and done well. He was home.

We visited Alejandra on our way home, as promised. Alejandra's son drove us out to the ranch where my grandfather had lived. It took hours to get there on bad dirt and gravel roads. Only the walls of the stone and adobe house were standing.

My father had never set foot in a church for as long as I had known him. Now he walked around and touched things reverently, as if he were in a holy place.

When it was time to go back to Texas, he gave his cousin Alejandra fifty dollars cash—American money, secretly—and he felt like a philanthropist.

Apá let me drive almost all the time. He seemed to have absolute confidence in me. On the day we left for Texas, we stopped at a Sabinas tortillería to buy a half-kilo of hot corn tortillas. I loved the squeaky sounds of the tortilla machine and the smell of the hot cornmeal. Then we bought avocados, limes, tomatoes, and salt. This was our lunch. Hot tortillas with slices of avocado and tomato sprinkled with salt and lime. The food of the gods. Apá used the huge pocket knife that he always carried to cut up the ingredients. He made the tacos for us joyfully while he told us about the avocado trees that grew in his back yard in Mexico.

When we got to the border, I spoke to the border patrol in perfect English, putting on my American persona again. I had spoken only Spanish for days. I had dreamed in Spanish, eaten in Spanish, prayed in Spanish. Suddenly, talking to the American guard in English, I felt like a gringa with brown skin.

A few miles north of Laredo, there was another inspection point. The guy poked his head inside the car window and asked, "Y'all American citizens?"

"Yes, Sir," I answered, the way Texans expect you to.

But inside I wondered who we were, and especially who I was.

Chapter Eighteen

El que adelante no mira, atrás se queda.

He who doesn't look ahead remains behind.

(Mexican dicho)

When the high school principal called me out of study hall in the library, I had no idea what he wanted me for. Janice had been called also. He told us I was to be valedictorian and Janice would be salutatorian. We congratulated each other and left the office in shock.

I went back to the library, took a book down from a shelf and sat apart from my friends, pretending to be reading. There alone, I thought about where I had come to. The announcement was bittersweet for me. Sweet because it was an affirmation that all my hard work would be recognized. Bitter because it meant that yet again I would be singled out as different. Different from my peer group, different from my siblings, different from my community. I wanted nothing more than to be one of a group. A student among students, a sister among siblings, a Mexican among Mexicans.

It seemed I had been singled out for aloneness my whole life. In the womb was the first time I was unwanted, not part of the family. Five children were enough; my mother hadn't wanted another one at her breast. Then I was separated by age. My brothers and sisters were all teenagers, one or two years apart. I was like an only child, separated by seven years. I spent much time feeling that I bothered everyone; the only time I was all right was when I was alone. And now it looked as though there was more aloneness in my future.

I still felt like a Mexican migrant child with dirty, bare feet playing at the edge of the field. I remembered spending entire days alone almost all day at the edge of the migrant fields while my family worked. I learned meditation and communion with nature because there was nothing else to do. Sometimes they were so far away that I could barely see them through the wavy lines of heat rising from the beet field.

Through most of my adolescence, my older sisters shared a room, my older brothers shared a room, and my parents shared a room. Every night I made up a place to sleep on the four-foot couch in the living room. Alone.

In my aloneness, I discovered that I liked to read. But when I got to high school, I discovered all my reading wasn't enough. I was Mexican in south Texas. And that meant I was less than. Less than my white peers, less than the people on the other side of the tracks. But I found places where I could win: science and math.

All through high school, I had doggedly worked to get myself ready for college. I took two years of Spanish! That was because it was the only foreign language offered and I knew any college I applied to would have a foreign language requirement. I felt so silly repeating the trivial phrases after the teacher, but I did it. I took all the math and science offered. My friend Ninfa was already at the University of Texas, and she guided me through the application process. I used my summer money to buy a portable manual typewriter to type my essays and my financial aid applications.

Occasionally I had escaped to New York City with my sister, to the Midwest with my brothers, and into my father's Mexico. My experiences had shown me that I didn't have to be the person that growing up in Pearsall circumscribed me to be. I had choices.

My father's dream for his children was that all six of us would graduate from high school. On my graduation night his dream was realized.

He had only gone as far as the fourth grade in Mexico. Then his family moved to the United States and his school days were over. When I was in the fourth grade, I told my father that I wanted to go to college, not just graduate from high school. For some reason, he believed me.

On graduation night I delivered the valedictory speech, enti-tled "He Conquers who Conquers Himself." I wish now I had said "she," but it has remained the theme of my life nevertheless. Apá came up to me afterwards with big macho tears in his eyes. I had never seen him even close to crying before.

He pressed two thousand dollars in cash into my hand. "I have been saving this for you, mija. It's your money to go to col-lege." From talking to counselors and applying to universities, I knew that this money would only be enough for about one semes-ter, but I didn't tell him. Instead I hugged him, crying violently. He had never had a savings account. I wondered where all this money had been stashed. My mother thought he just carried it all in his wallet, since he carefully put his wallet under his side of the mattress every night.

My high school years had been full of paradoxes and contra-dictions. I wanted to be like everyone else, to fit in, to be liked. I didn't want to stand out. But circumstances seemed continually to push me into the spotlight. When I left for the university, my brothers and sisters seemed happy for me, but I also sensed a quiet distance. It was clear I was embarking on a life path that was very different from that of my family.

By the time I graduated from high school, I had no idea who I was or could be. A Texas Mexican American. A Mexico Mexican. A scholar. A New York career woman.

I saw that once I finished high school I had to leave and prob-ably not come back except to visit. My parents expected no more of me than to be a local Mexican girl who married a local Mexican guy and became a mamacita, a comadre, a tía, and final-ly, an abuelita. If I stayed in town and made tortillas every day, tamales at Christmas, menudo late on Saturday night, and barba-coa on Sunday morning, it would be fine with them.

I admired people who could stay connected to the family and the local support systems. They never had to feel alone.

I had to sever all ties and try my own wings—alone.

PART THREE

Returnings

*El que habla del camino es porque
lo tiene andado.*

I can talk about that road because
I've walked it.

(Mexican dicho)

Chapter Nineteen

Qué bonito es ver llover y no mojarse.

How beautiful it is to watch the rain and
not get wet.

(Mexican dicho)

Summer of 1993. It had been exactly forty years since the first time my family went to Minnesota. I spoke to my husband about going to the Fargo/Moorhead area before I left. I said I didn't expect any disagreeable surprises there. I was going with an open mind and fully aware of the way things had been there. Fargo would be easy for me, having traveled to exotic places all over the world. The easy epilogue to my story.

Before going, I wanted to meet Chachi because she still goes to Minnesota to work in the beet fields. Chachi is not an illegal alien; she is as American as Hillary Rodham Clinton. Lupita is her thirteen-year-old daughter. I have changed their names, but they very definitely exist.

It may seem that the life I tell about happened long ago. But for some people it may still be happening in very much the same way. Stories in the newspapers tell about Mexican migrants in South Carolina, Mexican American migrants in California, African American migrants in Florida, and Native American migrants in the Midwest. If you eat a fruit or a vegetable that is fragile like strawberries or grapes, it is a safe bet that it went through a migrant worker's hands on its way to your mouth. The migrant worker usually only has work in good weather, gets paid by the piece instead of the hour, and makes less than minimum wage.

Chachi is a beautiful young woman with creamy, pale skin and long, wavy hair that is silky and very black. She is five feet tall, thirty years old, and has seven children. This is hard to believe, as her body is that of an attractive teenager. I thought of my mother making tortillas for eight three times a day. They live in government-subsidized housing in San Antonio. She is quite shy. We invited her to swim at my sister's pool. She declined, saying that she was not a "descarada," meaning that she didn't parade her barely clad body in front of strangers.

Lupita looks older than thirteen most of the time, except when a vulnerable look crosses her face, revealing the scared little girl that she is. She doesn't look like her mother. Her features are Mexican-Native American, like my father's. She has a long, angular nose and high cheekbones. Her skin and hair are dark brown, and her hair is poker-straight. She is wearing black plastic shoes and a slightly dirty pink jacket.

Chachi and Lupita have been going to the Minnesota beet fields since Lupita was seven. "We go there," she says, "because there is no other way for us to make that much money." It sounded like my father talking.

"How much?" I ask.

"Fifty-five dollars an acre," she responds. I wonder how much it was in 1953, forty years ago, when we first went. None of my siblings remembers. An acre consists of ten rows of beets, each half a mile long—five miles of beets to be hoed in return for fifty-five dollars.

"And how is the housing?" I ask.

She smiles and looks away. "You take what you can get," she responds simply.

There is daycare now for the younger kids. I thought the short hoe had been outlawed, but Lupita has used it for several summers.

Lupita says she's tired of school; it's not cool. My sister is alarmed at this. She tells Lupita that education is her ticket out. Lupita doesn't look convinced. Her mother makes her help with the little ones when she comes home from school. She is tired of this.

She wants freedom.

My son went with me to Minnesota. I was taking him back to my past, revealing a side to him that he had never seen. He knew me as his career mom, who wore suits and called him on the telephone from all over the United States. No problem, I thought, this is just one of the other sides of me.

I looked out the window as the plane started to descend. Lots of green fields. Overcast in the middle of the day. The fields were all wet. It looked as though it had rained that morning and might rain again soon. We landed abruptly right in the middle of the fields. The tiny airport was carved right out of the countryside.

By the time we got into the rental car, the clouds had parted and everything was glittering from the morning rain. I expected to ride awhile to get downtown, but we were already there. The realization wouldn't come to me for several days yet. The realization that Fargo and Moorhead were nondescript small towns in small-town America. It was only in my mind that they loomed large because of what I had experienced there.

Before I left home, I had called several people and told them what I was doing. I called one of El Indio's sons and some of his cousins. They had all continued going to Minnesota long after we stopped. They offered directions, road markers, and blessings.

After my son and I checked into a hotel, we took off armed with maps, verbal directions, and a camera. We had a couple of false starts, and then, although the landscape looked exactly the same as everywhere else, the hair on the back of my neck stood up and I shivered with a sudden chill. "What's wrong?" my son asked.

"I think this is it," I answered.

Initially I saw no landmarks that told me this was it. Only the feelings that took over my body. The barn looked too big. The road that used to go through the farm now made a right turn. There was no migrant housing. But my body was right; this was it. When I saw a pony come out of the barn, I screamed. "What, what?" asked my son.

The pony had markings identical to those on Star, the pony Kit and I had ridden thirty-five years ago. I searched through my mind to see if I knew how long ponies lived. I have a friend who has a forty-year-old horse. Could it be possible?

The migrant housing seemed to be all gone, replaced with a beautifully large log cabin home. Where there had been dirt and weeds in front of the migrant houses, there was now a grassy lawn surrounded by a cedar rail fence. The gringo's house was still there by the road. It looked like a mansion to me thirty-five years before. Now I saw it for what it was: a modest, middle-class farm house.

I was disappointed that there was no one home. And even more disappointed that the building we had lived in had disappeared.

I made several phone calls, trying to find someone to talk to about the current migrant situation. The people I spoke to told conflicting stories, some saying that the migrant circuit had been unchanged for forty years and others saying that it was now non-existent. All the phone calls pointed to Pedro. He had been working with migrants for twenty years. I heard that his office opened at seven-thirty, so I was there a little after seven the next morning. The sign on the door said eight o'clock. But fortunately, there were two men waiting also, so I talked to them while we waited.

As I expected, the two lone men were reluctant to talk to a single woman, especially before eight in the morning. But I used my best people skills to gently draw them out. They were both there hoping to find work in the beet fields. One man was Mexican from Oaxaca, Mexico, and he was there alone. The other was Mexican American and he had come from Houston with his wife and five children, plus one son-in-law and a grandchild.

They talked about the difficulty of finding housing. They said only a very few migrants, the lucky ones, stayed on farms anymore. These were the ones who had long-standing relationships with the farm owners. For the rest, it was apartments in town or tiny hotels. The problem with the hotels was that city ordinances prohibited cooking in the rooms, and the rent was $800/month. The man from Houston had been going north every summer since he was a child. He used to come with his father, and now his children and grandchild came with him. It was the first time for the man from Oaxaca.

The doors opened at eight and they went in, along with several others who arrived right at eight o'clock. I hung back. I decided that getting a job was more important than research for a book.

When the initial flurry was over, I went in and told the receptionist who I was and why I was there. I asked for an appointment with Pedro. She asked me to wait and, after a minute, she asked me to go on back.

There were no questions I had that he didn't know the answers to. He had been a migrant and he had worked with migrants for twenty years. And besides, he liked to talk. Any question would set him off, telling stories and philosophizing.

From talking to Pedro and from reading in the library later, I pieced together the story of how it used to be. In the years before the sugar beet, the area used to have a lot of livestock—pigs and cows and chickens. Then the sugar beet came and changed everything. The farm where we used to work had converted from livestock to beets in 1948. The buildings that used to house livestock were changed to house Mexicans.

Now the books in the library don't talk about Mexican migrants. They talk about "tonnage," "hand-labor," "finger work," and "short hoes."

The problem was that the sugar beet seed was a multigerm seed. Where you planted one seed, several plants came up. The job of the migrant was to thin the plants, leaving the strongest to grow by themselves. But since several plants grew from one seed, the plants were bunched together. Hence the necessity for short-hoes and "finger-work" to do a superior job of thinning. During this pass also, the migrants hoed the weeds. It took a practiced eye to distinguish between the seed leaves of the beets and the seed leaves of red-root pigweed. If you didn't do a good job, a month later your rows would be full of three-foot-tall pigweed. The Mexicans called this weed "quelitre."

So, because of this, the migrants carefully staked out the rows belonging to a particular family. My father would step off the rows from the edge of the field and write, with a stubby pencil, the numbers of the particular rows our family would work on a little pad he carried in his shirt pocket. Then he would put sturdy stakes in the ground labeled "L. Treviño."

A month later, we would make another pass through our rows for weeding. The weeds robbed the beets of moisture needed to grow. If we had done a particularly good job on the first pass, the second pass was easy. It was easy to tell who had done a good job on the first pass. The tall pigweed, or the absence of it, told the whole story.

Then the fields were left alone for the month of August while the beets got huge. During this month, the migrants found other harvesting work. Our family typically went to Wisconsin to pick green beans, cucumbers, and occasionally tomatoes.

In the fall, the migrants came back to Minnesota for "el tapeo," the beet topping season. The beets were pulled out of the ground, the top of the beet was cut off, and the beet root was thrown into a truck. The beets varied in size, which made machine harvesting impossible, but were mostly around a foot across. This work was slow, tedious, and hard. It went on for a month or two and then the season was over. The migrants went home, mostly to Texas, in late October.

My father never allowed us to stay for topping season. He always insisted that we go back to school when it started in September. Our friends would go back to Minnesota and enroll their kids in the country schools there. The kids helped the adults after school and on weekends.

That was in the fifties.

Now the need for migrants is almost nonexistent, although many still go there hoping to find work. A monogerm beet seed has been developed, and it is drilled into the ground at evenly spaced intervals, so no thinning is required. Chemical herbicides are used to prevent weeds. The beets are now a uniform size, so machine harvesting is easy.

The only use a farmer has for migrants is if the herbicides fail. Then the migrants go into the fields to weed. My son and I saw a few migrants in the fields, but for the most part, the fields had no weeds. The herbicides had worked.

Migrant housing at the farms is now inspected and certified by government inspectors. So, with as little need for "hand labor" as there is now, the farmers have torn down the migrant housing for the most part.

There is little money to be made there by migrants. But they still go, hoping to better their lives as we did forty years ago.

I had always wondered why the building we lived in was stop-sign-shaped. It was all one big room with a pot-bellied stove in the middle. When I finally got to visit with the farmer that we used to work for, he told me. The reason that it was shaped like that was that it used to be a sow farrowing shed in the days when the farm still had livestock.

He told me that in the days of livestock, the shed had eight pens around the perimeter, big enough for eight sows to give birth at once. They and the piglets were kept warm by the pot-bellied stove in the middle of the room. He assured me that it was a great place to live because of the double-walled insulation. The pens had been removed and beds put in for the migrants.

I quickly went on to the next question, as I knew that if I dwelled on this, I would be moved to bitter, violent words. And I wasn't there for recriminations, only to gather facts. My next question was what had happened to the building where we used to live. Had he merely torn it down?

He said that the building had been used for a while as a sort of daycare center. A central place where the migrants could leave their children for the day. Then one day, without his knowledge, some migrants who were passing through stayed there overnight. Government inspectors made a surprise visit the next morning and cited him for letting people live in what they considered a building unfit for human habitation. He bulldozed the building and later set fire to it.

I had never felt shame about being a migrant before, as my brothers and sisters had. My parents told us it was honest, clean work, working in the fields with the vegetables. We didn't clean white people's homes as maids, and we weren't allowed to be waitresses. Now for the first time, knowing the history of the stop-sign-shaped building, I was ashamed of the life we had led.

Chapter Twenty

Quien con la esperanza vive, alegre muere.

He who lives with hope dies happy.

(Mexican dicho)

When he was past ninety and glaucoma had stolen his sight, Apá still loved to tell me about his youth. His eyes would get animated and brilliant. Not able to see the present anymore, they would look clearly into the past.

"When I was a young man, I liiiked to fight," he would tell me, dragging out the word "gustaba" as if he was eating a delicious morsel that he didn't want to swallow yet.

By then, we had a billy goat with curly ram horns and three nanny goats in the back yard. The half-acre plot that Apá used to garden in had become a pasture. The ram kept the nanny goats constantly pregnant. He never let them get near the food until he was done, and he would butt anything in sight, just because it was there. He butted my mother to the ground three times the first time she went inside the gate to feed them. The neighbors had to rescue her. My brother would stick a shovel or his boot in the air and the ram would back up, paw the ground, and charge to butt it. He would fight anyone or anything, seemingly just for pure pleasure.

That's the way my father was. Maybe that's why he didn't get married until he was thirty-five; he was too busy with women, brawling in bars, and drinking. He carried a jackknife with a six-inch blade.

He reformed when he got married, but the urges still called to him. He was jailed for "cutting" a man when I was little. This was a common occurrence in Pearsall. Apá was let go because the man was sewn up and wouldn't press charges—the law of the barrio. This man had drunkenly insulted my father—who was theoretically above reproach—and therefore he deserved to be "cut." Apá never wanted to talk about this particular incident; he was ashamed of having been jailed.

Apá was sick only once. He had a double hernia that went untreated for a long time because we couldn't afford the surgery. When he finally scheduled it, the doctor asked him if he wanted general or local anesthesia that would only deaden the lower half of his body. He opted for local and asked to watch. The doctor rigged up a mirror so that he could watch as they opened up his abdomen and sewed up the muscles. He loved every minute.

Then he had the run-in with the African American man. We didn't call them "negros." We called them "negritos," as if they were diminutive, somehow.

The African American school in Pearsall was closed by the time I knew what it was. The tiny one-room schoolhouse sat all by itself in the middle of a weedy lot a block away from my friend Margie's house. The African American church was right next door to Margie's house. On Sunday, thirty or forty African American people congregated there. I wondered where they came from. I didn't see any African American people the rest of the week except for "La Negra María" that lived on the same block as my Tía Nina. Their clothing was much fancier than that of the people at the Catholic church that I went to. The men all wore suits and ties and the women all wore hats with ribbons and lace that matched their dresses.

Apá tended bar at Tío Manuel's Buenos Aires Cantina on Friday and Saturday nights. The law in Frio County was that bars closed at midnight on Saturday night. Apá always closed the Buenos Aires cantina promptly at midnight. By 12:15, all the drunks had driven away in their pickups and he was cleaning up the place. He put all the empties in a locked warehouse behind the tavern.

The African American guy arrived about then. He was big, and my father had never seen him before. "Una cerveza," he said in Spanish. Many of the African Americans in south Texas spoke

Spanish then. This one looked as if he had already been drinking quite a lot.

"We close at twelve," Apá answered.

"I'm not leaving without a beer," the man said as he put a five-dollar bill down on the bar.

"I'm afraid you'll have to, because we're closed."

"I told you, I'm not leaving without a beer," he said as he walked around the bar to help himself in the cooler.

Apá, mad now, grabbed the baseball bat that he kept under the bar for occasions just such as this one. "Leave! Now! or there's going to be a fight!" Apá was still fearless, tall, and strong, although he was in his early sixties.

But he was no match for this man, who had wrestler's forearms and who looked to be in his forties. Easily, he wrestled the baseball bat from my father. When Apá still lunged at him, he brought the bat down on Apá's temple.

When Apá woke up, there was blood everywhere. The man was gone and the five dollars was still on the bar.

By this time, Amá was going from door to door, window to window, looking for my father to come home. I was watching the late show on our new black-and-white TV.

Apá didn't get out of the car, he just honked and honked and yelled for Rudy to come out. Rudy ran out to the car to see what he wanted. Apá told him to get the paper sack of money that he had under the mattress and drive him to the hospital. Rudy ran in the house with his eyes huge and scared.

"¿Qué pasó?" asked Amá.

"Nada," he said as he ran out the door clutching the paper bag in his hand. Rudy got in on the driver's side and peeled out with the sand flying from our unpaved street.

Now my mother got out her rubbing alcohol and her wet hand towel that she draped on her neck when she was really upset. I turned off the TV. "I don't know why that old man doesn't quit that job!" she said as she inhaled the fumes of the rubbing alcohol. She thought inhaling the alcohol calmed her down. It looked to me as if it made her more upset.

When they came home from the hospital, Apá had his head wrapped in a huge bandage that the blood had already leaked through. He looked like a mummy on the late movie, except in Technicolor. Laughing, he said, "There is nothing wrong with me, mujer! Just that a cabrón hit me with a stick. But I'm fine."

The next day, Rudy went out, wrathful and bloodthirsty, as a good Mexican son should, with his jackknife in his pocket. But he couldn't find a trace of the man from the night before. He was probably passing through on his way to San Antonio from Laredo. It was my father's last fight.

I had never told Apá that I loved him. And though he showed it, he had never told me, either. He was in his late eighties and his glaucoma was so far advanced that he had to give up gardening because he could no longer tell the weeds from the plants.

I told my therapist about his calling me a "useless girl." She suggested I imagine him in the other chair and that I tell him how I felt about it. I couldn't do it. The imaginary father in my head, the one I pretended was in the other chair, was so strong and domineering that I still cowered under his gaze.

But he was getting old. Whatever conversations I needed to have with him, real or imagined, needed to happen soon.

I knew in my head that Apá's determination and the way he drove his kids to work so hard didn't come from cruelty. It was his only ticket to see us through school.

In high school, I filled out forms for him. Occupation: laborer. He thumped watermelons in the field walking ahead of the truck so the pickers would know which ones to harvest, he worked on the railroad, he dug ditches, he was the rod man for a surveyor, he was a carpenter for Tío Manuel, he tended bar for Tío Manuel, and on and on and on . . . I wasn't ashamed of his being a laborer. I was proud that he worked so hard. I didn't resent the fact that he hadn't made more of himself. I wondered what I would say someday on a form that I filled out for myself.

I eventually had the conversation with the imaginary father in the therapist's office and then I made a reservation to fly to Texas, determined to have my first real conversation with him. All I wanted was to let him know, in words that I actually said out loud, that I loved him in spite of it all.

I led him by the arm out to the car, having told him that we were going for a drive in the country, just he and I. I drove slowly, the air coming in gently from the open windows. He talked easily, as he always does, about his younger days. I swallowed hard and started, "Apá, I want you to know that I appreciate very much all that you have done for me. You made many sacrifices so that I could finish school, and although I have never said anything, I appreciate it very much."

"Pos hija, I just wanted you to finish school and get a good job. And then, if you didn't marry, or your husband didn't turn out right, at least you would be able to support yourself."

I swallowed again. "And I also want you to know, Apá, that I love you very much. I have never told you, but it's true. You have been the best father for me. At times I have been ungrateful, but you have always been good to me."

"Well, I also love you very much, hija." Clearly it was hard for him to say it. But also, clearly, he meant it.

There, it was done. Although I visited often, it was years before I was able to take the next step.

I often dreaded visiting Amá and Apá. Whenever I went there, I still turned into an eight-year-old child, cowering and ready to do my father's bidding. And Apá turned into the domineering, arrogant, "I don't need anybody and I'm in charge" macho man. Even at ninety, he slipped into his old persona easily.

"Bring me some water, cold and without ice."

"Wait and take the glass with you."

"Call Rudy on the telephone. Tell him I want him to come over here."

"Go get me some string and some tape at the store."

On and on and on. I ran to carry out his demands and wondered how I could have thought I would last a week there. I timed his demands. Maximum two minutes before the next demand.

Finally I sat down in a chair next to Apá.

"Apá, I'm not used to being ordered around. Not even my husband orders me around. At my house, people say 'Please.' They respect me and appreciate me. I wish that you could do the same with me."

Although I said it as quietly as I could, I saw a look of fear come into his blind eyes. His forehead furrowed and he didn't respond. He was still six feet tall and still weighed over two hundred pounds, but his body all of a sudden looked smaller.

The next time he asked me for something, he started, "When you have time . . ."

I ran to do his errand, thrilled that he had heard me.

That night, when we were about to go to bed he called me to him. He asked to take my hand—a first for him in my lifetime.

"Hija, I know that there have been some hard things between us. Forgive me. I always wanted the best for all of you. I want you to know that I love you very much in spite of what there may have been between us. And I appreciate everything that you have done for us. I appreciate it with my whole heart."

I squeezed his huge brown hand with both of mine, glad that he couldn't see my tears. I knew that at that moment he could see me better than he had his whole life. And I was seeing him more clearly than I ever had before. I felt loved and appreciated.

I had stepped out from under his foot to talk to him person to person. This allowed him to step down off his pedestal and be merely human in response. I broke out of my role, and this allowed him to break out of his role. What a relief for both of us.

After that, when I visited, I didn't have to position myself under his foot when I first got there and stay resentful the whole time, wanting it to be over.

My husband and I visited my parents on the way to a driving trip in Mexico. When Apá found out where we were going, he said he would like to go with us. My husband and I exchanged worried glances, as Apá occasionally got disoriented when he got too far from home. But his voice had the quality of a last wish. We knew and he knew that it would be his last trip to the place of his birth. He could still see dim shapes and bright lights then, but no more. We couldn't refuse him. So we took him. He visited his last remaining relative from his generation. They talked about the old days for the last time.

On the way home, he was very quiet. I worried that he was over-tired. We stopped for the night at a motel in Laredo. We got adjoining rooms, but my mother asked me to sleep in their room. "Sometimes he gets crazy at night and I can't handle him," she said. So my husband slept alone and I slept in the other bed in my parents' room.

I woke up to find my father fingering his jackknife. He had always carried a huge pocket knife. In his youth he had carried it for self-defense. Later, he would peel oranges for me and slice avocados with it.

Now he sat on the edge of his bed, his feet on the floor, and gripped the knife as if ready to lunge at an unseen enemy. His eyes were wide, staring, trying to make out something. I knew that if I breathed, if I spoke, if I moved, he would lunge with all two hundred of his pounds at me, not knowing who I was.

I barely breathed for many long minutes, maybe twenty or so.

Finally he blinked, sighed, and started moving slightly. He calmed down enough to ask, "¿Quién está allí?"

"It's me, Apá, your hija."

"Where are we?"

"In Laredo in a motel room. I'll have you home by tomorrow."

He relaxed. He folded his knife and put it under his pillow. I stayed awake the whole night.

The next time I went to visit him, he had become incontinent and we had to change the sheets every morning. At ninety-two, he still weighed over two hundred pounds. His arms were still hugely mus-cled even though his hands had no fine motor control anymore.

"Elva, help me get to the bathroom," he said as he groped his way along the hall wall going the wrong direction, away from the bathroom. I took his arm, led him to the bathroom door, waited until he was fully inside and then firmly closed the door.

But his huge brown hands couldn't work the zipper anymore.

"Elva, help me undo my pants."

"Can't you do it?" I pleaded desperately through the door.

"No, I can't," he said, an edge of desperation, shame, anger, something in his voice.

I undid the zipper without looking and walked away. But I was willing to do this only when my mother wasn't near. When she was, I called her to do it. That was her territory.

The last time I visited Apá, he was weepy, agitated, and sad—all strange things for my father. He claimed that he wanted to die, claimed that God had kept him here long past his usefulness, to the point that he was sad and unhappy to still be on the planet. He felt totally useless and embarrassed to no longer have control of his body or its functions.

Two months later, I was writing at the kitchen table when Diamantina called me from Texas. "Apá is in the hospital to have the fluid cleared from his lungs. He seems fine. He should be out tomorrow."

Two hours later, she called again. "Apá is much worse; the doctor thought I should let everyone know."

In my gut, I knew this was it, even though not much had been said. I made a plane reservation for seven that evening, the soonest I could get to the airport. I would go alone, my husband would make arrangements for the dog, call in to work, and follow the next day with the kids. I packed my suitcase, including two sets of black funeral clothes. In my heart, I didn't want to be there at the moment of death. I spoke to Apá in my mind as I packed. "Apá, if this is your time to go, please don't wait for me."

I called Diamantina at the hospital at six-thirty from the airport. "He's gone, Elva," she said. They had all been there around the hospital bed, my five siblings and my mother.

"If he starts to fail, what do you think about life support equipment?" the doctor had asked.

"Do whatever you can," my sisters had said.

"Let him go," Rudy countered. "Don't keep him here by force."

They watched the blood pressure slowly drop on the monitor. At one point, it rose briefly when Delmira stroked his hair. Then he died.

Rudy stayed in the room long after everyone else left.

I got on the plane, not knowing when I would be able to give in to the grief. When I sat in my seat on the airplane, I saw his face clearly. It was full and healthy as it was when I was a child, and smiling joyfully. And he said,

> "Aquí estoy hija, fuerte y sano.
> No llores por mí.

Ustedes siempre me vieron bien mientras que yo viví.

Ahora no hay porqué llorar.

Quiéranse unos a los otros.

Ya no me duele nada,

y ya se acabaron las vergüenzas.

Dile a tu mamá que siempre fue la mejor esposa para mí."

(Here I am, my daughter, strong and healthy.

Don't cry for me.

You were all good to me while I lived.

Now there is no reason to cry.

Love one another.

I am no longer in pain, and all the shame is over.

Tell your mother that she was always the best wife to me.)

When he was healthy, Apá always laughed a lot and he would make us laugh with his jokes and his dichos. I like to remember him laughing.

When I saw him in the coffin, I knew it wasn't him. It was only the body that had carried him around, as his wheelchair had carried his body. But what made me cry were the people who had loved him and the ones he had loved. Older cousins came from all over the country. They told stories about how he had been kind to them, helped them, or saved them.

The funeral was only Apá's fourth time in church. The first was when he was baptized and the second was when he married Amá. But he always gave thanks to God, and he had a deep belief in the inherent goodness of life. He worked very hard for his living, and then he gave thanks to God for it.

I know that God took him in like a favorite son. He is safe and content.

I thank God that he was my father. I thank God, as my father used to say, "del mero corazón!" (from the very center of my heart!)

Chapter Twenty One

El que con lobos anda, a aullar se enseña.

He who walks with wolves learns to howl.

(Mexican dicho)

After that first two thousand dollars at my high school graduation, I never took money from Apá again. I figured out how to work the university's financial aid machine and got through four years with loans, scholarships, grants, and part-time jobs.

I went to the library every night until midnight, when it closed. Then I walked back to my room alone and happy, pinching myself to be sure it wasn't a dream. I was free. No responsibilities except reading and studying, both of which I loved—absolutely loved—to do. This was where I belonged. I was home at last.

My senior year in college, I was offered three jobs, but there was really no contest as to which one I would accept. Control Data Corporation made mainframes at the time. Their software was mostly written in Sunnyvale, California. After the initial on-campus interview, they offered to fly me out to California for a second interview.

This was big stuff for a barefoot migrant kid.

They had a long black limousine waiting for me at the San Francisco airport to take me to Sunnyvale. The voices in my head told me that I had finally arrived. My gut said that I was in way over my head. The two sides fought inside me all the way to Sunnyvale while I sat alone in the back of that long black limo.

It was my first taste of the seductions of corporate life. It went to my head. Two of my friends were going on to Harvard for

graduate school. The thought of two to four more years of counting the financial aid pennies to make sure I could get to the end
of the semester was suddenly abhorrent to me. I was hooked.

It took me two years to get out. Stanford University was just
down the road. I applied and they accepted me into the computer
science Ph.D. program with a full fellowship.

Two years later, tired again of being poor, I quit with a
Master's degree and went to work for IBM. I was a programmer
for awhile, then a sales support person. But it looked to me as
though the salespeople made all the money and had all the fun.
So I switched to sales. I worked for IBM in sales during the boom
years. The business came, and it came fast. Taking the customers
to briefings all over the country in the IBM corporate jet became
routine. Making multi-million-dollar sales became routine. It was
the six-figure income that made me dizzy.

When I went home to visit, Apá asked, "So how much do you
make now, hija?" There was no way to explain the sales plan to
my father, so I lied. "Fifteen dollars an hour, Apá." He was
thrilled for me.

I was awash in money and sales awards. I went shopping for
a Mercedes and joined the poshest health club I could find.
Located in Las Colinas, it had both an indoor and an outdoor running track. It had two golf courses and was expanding to four. The
Olympic-sized indoor swimming pool had thirty-foot-tall windows. We women had our own exercise machines, steam room,
sauna, and whirlpool. There were two huge, fluffy white towels
and a new pink razor waiting for me when I stepped into the
shower that had three dispensers for gel soap, shampoo, and con-
ditioner. When I came out of the shower, I wrapped my hair in one
towel and my body in the other. If I trailed a few drops of water
on my way to the mirrored make-up area, a female attendant
walked behind me cleaning it up.

When I sat down at the mirror, she offered to massage lotion
into my neck and shoulders. I let her—awash in guilt now—suddenly identifying with her and her station. I decided to leave her
a big tip.

I blow-dried my hair perfectly and dressed in silk and wool
crepe for work. The woman next to me talked on and on about

how well her sales were going. She sold chemicals that were injected into the soft, watery Las Colinas soil to make it solid enough to build on. Behind me, two women dressed in clothes that made it clear they were going back home to their Las Colinas mansions after this. They rarely spoke to us career women.

The next few years were a blur. First I had a three-state territory (Texas, Louisiana, and Oklahoma) helping other reps sell IBM Credit Corporation financing. Then I had a five-state territory. And finally I was helping other reps sell publishing systems all over the country.

Four years later I was in the window seat of a DC-10 hurtling toward New York. I got to sit in first class because I had half a million miles on my frequent flier number. I had packed in half an hour at four that morning. It was the fourth day that week that I'd been on an airplane.

My life was not my own. It belonged to IBM. I was no better off than my parents. In several days, I made what all my family together made in a migrant season. But, like them, I had no time.

I felt as though my life, like the plane, was hurtling forward. Soon I'd fall off a precipice into a dark abyss. I had too many responsibilities. I'd felt like that before. Perhaps I'd never felt any other way.

I sank farther into my leather airplane seat as the steward handed me coffee. The plane felt warm and was droning pleasantly. The tiredness and lack of sleep overtook me soon and I sank into sleepy oblivion the rest of the way into New York in spite of the coffee.

I had all the trappings of success. I was driving a Mercedes, flying all over the country on business, and vacationing in the Caribbean. As Gloria Steinem said, "We were becoming the men we had always wanted to marry." But the glamour of travel had long ago lost its appeal. Desperate for a change, I went back on sales quota, with a couple of local universities as my territory.

My IBM life didn't leave much time or energy for anything else. I gave my heart and soul to IBM. They gave me money in return.

But my soul was shriveling.

Then one night, I had a gangster dream. Those are always my worst ones.

The first role I play in this dream is a gangster who wants to pull out of the group. I am not really bad like the rest of them. So first, I conspire with my other friends and family to smuggle the money out of the gangster house. We smuggle it out under plants, in boxes, in the Volkswagen van and in a Volkswagen bug. This is successful and exciting, but scary.

Next I am the wife of the gangster. And I sit in the living room while he explains to the rest of the gangsters why we have decided to pull out. He and our daughter and I are allowed to leave. We all have blond hair and everyone else has dark hair. We feel very lucky to be allowed to leave.

Then I am the Mexican maid of a gangster who has opted to leave the group. And I have to leave after they do and on my own. I sneak out of the house at night. I go three houses down the block to another maid's house.

When I am walking around, I see tunnels going down into the earth. With long, long escalators that I imagine go straight down to Hell. There are two men on either side of the escalator urging me to "come on down." The roof of the tunnel is very hard and very thick. I know that if I go down there, I will be cut off from all that I have known. I keep passing these tunnels.

The whole block is small maids' houses. I happen to know that one particular maid is out of town. I go to her house and crawl under the back porch. A wolf comes by and begins to sniff at me. I try to cover myself up with dirt to hide myself. The wolf leaves and I go into the house. It is small and comfortable and empty.

I am afraid to leave because I know they will be on all the surrounding streets and they will be looking for me. If they catch me, they will cut off my breasts.

I examine the alternatives. I could go to a faraway village in Mexico where no one knows me. But it would be hard to start up with no money and no friends or relatives, but I could do it. This is what I do. I am the happiest I have ever been in my tiny, sunny adobe house. I then call up the gangster and ask him to send me money.

The dream was the blueprint for recovering my soul. As the dream spoke to me, my spiritual journey back to myself began. This is what the dream said to me:

At IBM I felt like a gangster, making so much money so easily, when my family had worked so hard.

If they caught me, they would cut off my breasts. At IBM I was cut off from my femaleness, even while I succeeded in a man's world. I don't believe this is true for everyone, but it was true for me.

The wolf meant that I was afraid of my wild, instinctual, intuitive nature. I only trusted my intellect.

The maid's house and the small house in Mexico meant that less is more for me.

Going down into the tunnels meant that the guardians on either side of the tunnels into the earth are paradox and confusion. If I can get past these two dragons, I can get to the rich inner world of my mind and soul.

So I began braving the dragons, going past them to that forgotten part of myself—my childhood and my Mexicanness. I started writing the stories I heard in my head. The more I wrote, the more stories came.

My childhood issues were abandonment, feeling less-than because I was Mexican, and shame that I was a "useless girl" in my father's eyes. Now I was no longer poor. Now I was succeeding in a man's world. I had proven that a Mexican migrant girl could do it all and have it all. But I was disconnected and distant from my culture, my family, and from my heart and soul.

The feeling of being constantly abandoned by my family, friends, and lovers would not go away. My earliest memory of abandonment was being left with the nuns. I could not tell the story of the nuns without feeling a lump in my throat. So I wrote it. I went to a party where the guests were to share their artistic side—sing, dance, read. I read the story. Afterwards the pain was less. I read it to my siblings. The pain diminished even further. More stories came and I wrote them.

Every time I wrote or read to someone aloud, the little barefoot girl woke up in my heart again. She took over my feelings and my body. I felt small, vulnerable, unprotected.

People liked my stories. I was invited to read them at a suburban women's group. I took my stories and went, wanting to gain experience. At IBM, I had spoken before hundreds of people. But there had been nothing of my own barefoot heart in that—only my intellect—and in that realm I was confident and safe.

The women started arriving. Perfect hair, perfect makeup, expensive clothes. Not one woman of color. If any of them had ever known deprivation, it hadn't been lately. As they settled into the room, I felt as if I was getting smaller and smaller. By the time I went to the chair at the front of the room, I was a five-year-old in a faded dress, with bare, dirty feet, from the Mexican side of the tracks.

I had brought my little girl and set her up to be judged by a roomful of white, well-dressed women.

At the end of the reading, they clapped, smiled, and said how much they liked my stories. They were perfectly nice. And my Barefoot Heart little girl was perfectly devastated. I felt her run away as I swallowed tears.

To protect myself, I put on my corporate persona. I told myself that I too was nicely dressed, and my feet were, in fact, perfectly clean and encased in expensive shoes. I became charming and detached, making facile conversation.

The source of the stories became silent for a long time. I decided writing and reading aloud (let alone publishing!) about deeply personal subjects were not for me. I looked into being a Merrill Lynch stockbroker. I took the entrance exam, passed, and went in for a two-hour interview.

I was ready to get off the writing boat and step ashore onto firmer, safer land. But the world wouldn't let me get off just yet. I was invited to speak to a women's group at church about my spiritual journey. What could be safer than speaking about spirit at church? I quickly typed five pages and went. This time I felt surrounded by love and affirmation afterwards. They crowded around me with hugs and shining, wet eyes. I was hooked again.

I pulled my heart and soul back from IBM. Then an amazing thing happened: my business/corporate life turned into a black-and-white movie and my childhood spoke to me in Technicolor. I left the corporate world altogether.

The pervasive aloneness I had felt in my life began to fall away as I connected with my siblings through writing about them. When I read the stories to them, they alternately cried, laughed, and were deadly silent. But always, as the stories had in Minnesota, our common history brought us together. The distance I had felt between myself and them started to melt away. We started calling each other for no reason—just to connect.

At a writing seminar, my teacher said, "If you want to be cool, get out of writing right now."

"The Storyteller" came to me in church. I got out my notebook and wrote half of it during the minister's talk. When the service was over, I went to the church basement to finish writing the story. Then I started crying.

As I wrote, the feelings I had that summer in Minnesota of being a motherless child came back full force. Marielena had been a spiritual mother to me when my own mother was too exhausted to care about me. Later, typing the story in my own basement, the feelings overwhelmed me and I had to stop typing because I could no longer see the screen or make my fingers work.

I had cut an emotional artery; I was bleeding profusely and I didn't know how to turn it off. I cried for hours, for all the times when I had felt alone and unloved.

In my low moments I wondered what I was doing. In the silence, pure and simple, the answer came: I needed to integrate my childhood Mexican side back into myself.

I used to think those years were all joy and comfort for me—that's all I remembered—but when I wrote, all I got was pain. When I wrote from the point of view of the little Mexican kid inside, it seemed I had nothing to contribute but sadness and hard stories. And that seemed wrong. My intellect and the strong critic in my head wanted to censor everything. My intellect had served me so well in the past; now it became a hindrance. I put it on the shelf and followed my heart. I wrote whatever came. I let myself write the unspeakable, the unwriteable, the inadmissible.

I wanted to take all the darkness and turn it into luminosity. I wanted to weave all the old, dark strands into the tapestry of my current life. I wanted to eat my experience and digest it until it became a part of me.

The joy I had thought was there was the joy of travel, newness, and excitement; the joy of being alone and free at the edge of the field; the joy of laughing with my family over jokes. The comfort I had thought was there was eating my mother's tortillas, warming our nalgas by the pot-bellied stove, me sleeping on the ledge by the rear windshield of the car on the way back to Texas in our '52 Chevy.

I constantly had to write past the question "Why am I doing this?" Would it matter if I wrote or not? Then I knew. If I didn't write, I would die inside while my body was still alive.

So I decided to embrace the ugliness of the migrant years. I took the ugliness into my lap as I would an unappealing child. I kissed it and held it until it quieted.

Clarissa Pinkola Estés, author of *Women Who Run with the Wolves,* quotes a poem by Charles Simic: "He who cannot howl, will not find his pack."

I howled on the page. I saw how much power there is in embracing exactly who you are. For me it is being a Mexican American woman writer.

I am no longer alone; I have found my pack.

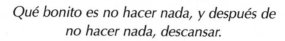

*Qué bonito es no hacer nada, y después de
no hacer nada, descansar.*

How beautiful it is to do nothing, and after
doing nothing, to rest.

(Mexican dicho)

Gratitude and Appreciation

Lou. You were with me every step of the way, saying yes, yes, yes! It was what I needed. You are an angel in every sense of the word and the greatest gift of my life.

Amá, Apá, Delia, Delmira, Luis, Diamantina, and Rudy. Sharing your lives has been a sacred privilege. I thank God that my life has been exactly as it was and that I shared it with you.

Juan, Roque, Bill, Lou, Lisa, Steve, Gina, Larry, Joan. You are my teachers and the joy in my life. You help me every day to know that love is all that matters.

Because of all my writing friends, readers, and teachers, my life is blessed and touched with magic. Belinda Acosta, Bill Brower, Ruth Cash-Smith, Sandra Cisneros, Jill Ker Conway, Bonnie Cote, Michael Ekizian, Barbara Freedman, Irene Garza, Natalie Goldberg, Kate Green, Pablo Guajardo, Sands Hall, Rob Hargraves, María Hilda Herrera, Harry Houston Hinkle, Barbara Janoff, Kathleen Kelly, Judy Lief, Bryce Milligan, Yolande Mistri, Shirley Norton, Gary Soto, Mary Lou Stevenson, Virginia Stuart, Virgil Suárez, Natalie Tobier, Margot Viesca: you taught me that I could write from my heart, with my body, getting my mind out of the way. Your deep love and naked courage are what drew me to you. They are the hallmarks I aspire to. You shared your life and your writing with me. It has enriched me beyond measure.

Note: The names of some persons in this book have been changed.